DOS

Covers through DOS 6.2

W9-AVL-435

Sue Plumley

Crystal Clear DOS

Library of Congress Catalog No.: 93-85251

ISBN: 1-56529-358-4

95 94 93   6 5 4 3 2 1

Interpretation of the printing code: the rightmost double-digit number is the year of the book's printing; the rightmost single-digit number, the number of the book's printing. For example, a printing code of 93-1 shows that the first printing of the book occurred in 1993.

Screen reproductions in this book were created with Collage Plus from Inner Media, Inc., Hollis, NH.

Publisher: David P. Ewing

Director of Publishing: Michael Miller

Managing Editor: Corinne Walls

Marketing Manager: Ray Robinson

Composed in Stone Serif and MCPdigital by Que Corporation

Credits

Series Director
Shelley O'Hara

Creative Consultant
Karen Bluestein

Acquisitions Editors
Sarah Browning
Nancy Stevenson

Product Director
Robin Drake

Production Editor
Anne Owen

Editors
Fran Blauw
Jodi Jensen

Technical Editor
Michael Watson

Book Designer
Amy Peppler-Adams

Graphic Image Specialists
Teresa Forrester
Tim Montgomery
Dennis Sheehan
Wilfred R. Thebodeau
Susan VandeWalle

Production Team
Angela Bannan
Claudia Bell
Danielle Bird
Ayrika Bryant
Charlotte Clapp
Anne Dickerson
Joelynn Gifford
Heather Kaufman
Bob LaRoche
Mary Beth Wakefield
Donna Winter
Lillian Yates

Indexer
Joy Dean Lee

Formatter
Jill Stanley

About the Author

Sue Plumley owns and operates Humble Opinions, an independent consulting firm in southern West Virginia. Sue has also written *Look Your Best with Word for Windows, Look Your Best with Ami Pro, Windows 3.1 Suresteps*, and *Quick and Dirty WordPerfect 6*. In addition, Sue has been a contributing author on several Que books including *Using WordPerfect 6 for DOS*, Special Edition, and *Using OS/2 2.1*, Special Edition.

Trademarks

Contents at a Glance

more ▶

Introduction

If DOS is something you use to get to your applications or something you try to get past in a hurry, then you need to know more about DOS. DOS is an operating system that's fundamental to your use of the computer. The more you know about how DOS works, the better you can use your computer.

Knowing how DOS works doesn't mean you have to be a software engineer or a programmer; it simply means knowing what DOS offers and how you can use it in your work every day. You can take advantage of DOS commands and programs that are easy to understand and use; plus you can work faster and more efficiently when you actually apply DOS's features.

Who Should Read This Book?

This book is not for the programmer; it does not describe the technical features of DOS or setting up your computer. What this book does is explain how you can use DOS in your everyday work. The articles are enjoyable to read and easy to understand. Each article provides instructions, illustrative figures, and examples that apply to everyday tasks. This book is for anyone who wants to apply DOS features to common, everyday tasks.

What's in This Book?

Crystal Clear DOS is comprised of short articles that explain how DOS works, beginning with basic information such as entering commands, starting programs, listing directories, using floppy disks, and using DOS Shell. Later articles cover more advanced subjects such as defragmenting your disk, configuring memory, performing backups, and checking your system for viruses.

Each article is from two to six pages in length and covers one topic or feature of DOS. Articles include a description of the feature, illustrations, shortcuts, and step-by-step instructions on how to use the command or program. This book is a comprehensive guide to using DOS to get the most from your computer.

more ▶

What's in This Book in Detail?

This book is divided into sections; each section contains articles relating to the section topic. Following is a brief overview of each section.

Section 1—DOS Basics

This section includes articles about common tasks and information you need to know to use DOS—such as naming files, changing drives, entering commands, and starting programs. Included is an article about getting on-line DOS Help.

Section 2—Directories

This section shows you how to use the directory structure on your hard and floppy disks. Included are articles about organizing directories and listing, changing, creating, removing, and renaming directories. Other articles describe how to display and control the directory structure of your disk.

Section 3—File Management

Section 3 discusses the most important aspect of your work on the computer—files. Articles explain how to list, view, name, and rename files; you learn to copy, combine, move, delete files, and more.

Section 4—Hard Disks

Section 4 demonstrates how DOS makes managing your hard disk easy. The section includes articles about copying files and directories, backing up and restoring data, creating a system disk, and checking the disk space. In addition, articles discuss ways to make your disk more efficient by way of defragmenting the hard disk, compressing the disk, and using the SMARTDrive disk-caching program.

Section 5—Floppy Disks

This section covers the processes you use to manage your floppy disks—such as formatting and unformatting disks, copying, comparing, and write-protecting your disks.

Section 6—Memory

Section 6 discusses ways you can optimize your system's memory by using DOS programs such as MemMaker—and devices such as HIMEM.SYS and EMM386.EXE. Included are articles on types of memory, checking memory, and adding memory to your computer.

Section 7—Configuring

Section 7 shows you how to fine-tune your system configuration to get the most from your computer. Articles discuss the components of configuration such as devices, and the AUTOEXEC.BAT and CONFIG.SYS files. In addition, this section covers how to edit configuration files to optimize your system for the type of work you do and how to create multiple configurations.

Section 8—Customizing

"Customizing" includes articles that show you how to change your system environment, the keyboard, your display, and even the date and time. Furthermore, articles describe more advanced features such as keeping track of your commands and creating your own commands.

Section 9—Batch Files

Batch files are one way of truly customizing your system to do your work for you. Section 9 explains the components of a batch file and how to use batch commands. The last article in this section even shows you how to use batch files to create a start-up menu on your computer.

Section 10—MS-DOS Shell

This section shows you the great potential of the DOS Shell. Not only can you display and view drive and directory contents with DOS Shell, you can create and remove directories and view, copy, move, rename, and sort files as well. Furthermore, DOS Shell enables you to open several programs at one time and switch back and forth between them.

Section 11—MS-DOS Editor

This section introduces MS-DOS Editor, which is terrific for editing text files and creating batch files. You learn about making changes in your CONFIG.SYS and AUTOEXEC.BAT files. This section takes you through the process of creating new files and editing existing ones with Editor.

Section 12 —Windows

If you're a die-hard Windows user, you'll be pleased to know that DOS can make running Windows easier and more efficient. This section shows you how to use such DOS features as Backup, Undelete, and Anti-Virus in Windows. And probably most important, this section includes an article that covers things you should and should not do when using Windows with DOS.

Section 13—Viruses

With so many computer viruses attacking systems every day, it's important to know how to protect your computer. Section 13 includes information about how your computer gets viruses and how the DOS program Anti-Virus can scan and remove viruses from your system.

Section 14—Troubleshooting

Section 14 covers common problems you may encounter when using DOS and what to do about them—including problems with DOS Setup, starting DOS, hardware problems, virus problems, problems with memory, and disk compression problems. The last article in this section includes problems and solutions you may encounter with Windows and application programs.

Appendix A—Error Messages

Appendix A includes many common error messages you may encounter when using DOS.

Appendix B—Command Reference

Appendix B presents DOS commands in a brief summary format. Commands include a description, syntax, notes on use, and examples of how to use the command.

What This Book Doesn't Cover

This book does not cover all commands and programs included with DOS 6; commands such as Debug, Mode, Interlink, and so on are beyond the scope of this book. In addition, this book does not discuss applications programming or computer-specific configuration.

Conventions Used in This Book

Crystal Clear DOS attempts to present the syntax of each DOS command in an easy-to-understand way; syntax is not presented the way it is in most DOS books. Instead, descriptive nouns are used to better describe what you type when using a command.

Any characters or words in **boldface** type are characters you actually type—commands, for example. Characters or words in *italic* are variables. Messages that appear on-screen are represented in a `special typeface`.

Many articles in this book describe how to enter commands or start programs. Following is an example and explanation of how a command might be represented:

> **DIR** *<filename>* */W* */P*

DIR is the name of the command; that which you actually type.

<filename> is a variable; you may or may not need to use the name of a file.

/W */P* are also variable switches; depending on the desired result, you may or may not want to use them.

Part One

Section 1—DOS Basics

DOS (which stands for *disk operating system*) controls the operations of your computer and the disks, printers, and other equipment you use with the computer. DOS takes input from the keyboard, mouse, and other devices, and interprets that information as language that the computer can understand and act on. Whether or not you are aware of it—even if your system is set up with a menu, or you use Windows—you interact with DOS *constantly* when using your computer. This section helps you to understand the basic information you need to know about working with DOS—how to start and turn off your computer, enter commands, get help when using DOS, and run programs.

DOS is an operating system, a set of computer programs that controls how the computer hardware—keyboard, display, hard disk, devices, and so on—communicates with the computer software and you.

An operating system provides many services—such as file management, memory management, and printer management—for the software you run on your computer. Each time you save a file in your word processor, for example, the operating system gives the hardware step-by-step instructions on how and where to save that file.

Most of the operating system's services run quickly, in the background, so it's invisible to you. But without an operating system, you or the application you're running would have to provide the system-management information to your computer. DOS acts as the interpreter between you and the hardware.

Things To Remember About DOS

Here are a few key things to remember about operating systems:

◆ You must have an operating system to use the computer. Every computer has an operating system.

◆ Many different operating systems are available: MS-DOS, PC DOS, DR DOS, IBM OS/2, and so on. DOS is the most popular operating system for IBM and IBM-compatible computers. DOS refers, in this book, to MS-DOS (Microsoft Disk Operating System).

◆ Most computers come with DOS already installed.

◆ DOS is stored in files on the hard disk of your computer, usually located in the DOS directory. Many of the files are programs that perform tasks, such as formatting floppy disks or creating a directory.

TIP

When you receive your computer, you should also receive a set of DOS floppy disks containing the DOS files that were installed on your computer. You should create a set of backup disks, or copies, of these original DOS disks and use only the set of copied disks when you need to restore information to your hard drive. For information about backing up floppy disks, see "Backing Up a Floppy Disk."

Functions of DOS

DOS performs many functions as an operating system; following are the common functions you'll use over and over again:

◆ *File Management.* When you create any type of document—a letter, a budget, or a report—you store the document in a file. Also, programs—such as DOS—are stored in files. DOS helps you manage the files on your computer. A later section in this book—"File Management"—covers file management.

◆ *Directory Management.* If you store all your files in the same spot, finding the one file you need would be impossible. DOS provides you with an efficient method of organization: directories and subdirectories. If you think of your computer as a file cabinet, each drawer in the file cabinet is like a directory. Within each drawer are file folders, or subdirectories, and within each file folder are your files. Directories are covered in the section "Directory Management."

◆ *Disk Management.* Two types of disks are available: floppy (removable) disks and hard (nonremovable) disks. Floppy disks enable you to exchange files with someone else, make backup copies or extra copies of documents, and install new programs. Hard disks enable you to store programs and files permanently. DOS enables you to manage both floppy and hard disks.

◆ *Memory Management.* Your computer's memory runs your programs and lets you create your files; without memory, your computer wouldn't work. Since memory is expensive, most of us can't add the memory we'd like to make our programs run faster and more efficiently. DOS has added some aids for our computer's memory problems—memory managers that can make the best possible use of the memory we have.

◆ *Running Software Programs.* DOS provides your computer with a great deal of services that enable you to run software applications easily. Among other services, DOS lets you organize your applications so they are easy to use, gives you an easy way to make copies of your programs as a backup in case you have problems, and lets you cure viruses that may damage your files and computer.

When you turn on your computer, it goes through a series of tests to ensure that your system is intact and will operate efficiently. This process is called booting the computer.

The term *booting* is borrowed from the phrase pulling yourself up by the bootstraps because DOS finds a place in your computer's memory to establish itself, tests for any problems your computer may have, and prepares the computer to run software applications.

You can boot your computer from the hard disk or a from a floppy disk, as long as the disk contains the DOS system files. The only difference between the two processes is that when booting from a floppy, you must insert a floppy system disk before turning on the computer. You probably will, at some point, need to use a floppy system disk to boot your computer.

TIP

Most computers come with the DOS operating system already loaded on the hard disk. If your computer does not have DOS installed, refer to the MS-DOS Reference Manual for information about installation.

Booting the Computer

During the boot, or start-up, several processes take place to prepare your computer for use:

◆ The computer checks the memory and then performs a power-on self test. The self test checks the system to make sure that it is functioning properly; this test may take a few seconds or a few minutes depending on the hardware and software installed on your computer. Information about the test may flash on your computer's display, and when the test is complete, you'll hear a beep.

◆ The computer checks drive A for a boot, or system, disk from which to load the DOS files. If the drive contains no boot disk, the system continues to search for the DOS system files.

◆ After your computer finds the system files, the computer loads DOS into the computer's *random access memory (RAM)*. RAM stores data and programs while the computer is on.

◆ DOS then searches for the CONFIG.SYS file, which contains information about hardware, configuration, applications, and so on. DOS follows the instructions within the CONFIG.SYS loading programs and commands that control parts of your computer. Additional messages may flash across the screen during this phase.

◆ DOS searches for a file called the AUTOEXEC.BAT and carries out any commands it contains. The AUTOEXEC.BAT is a batch file—a series of DOS commands—that customizes the screen, loads programs, and so on. More messages may appear on your screen and disappear.

At the end of the process, DOS displays the system prompt (c:\> or c:\DOS>), the DOS Shell, Windows, or a menu (depending on how your system is set up).

Start the Computer

1. Turn on the display, or monitor, first.

   (It's important that you turn on your display, or monitor, before you turn on the *central processing unit (CPU)* so you can see any messages that may appear as your system is being tested.)

2. Turn on the unit (CPU). As the system boots, watch your screen for error messages.

3. When the system prompt appears, your computer is ready for your commands.

If your system starts with MS-DOS 5.0 or 6.0 Shell, press F3 to exit the Shell and go to the system prompt.

Troubleshooting

◆ If you receive the message Non-System Disk or Disk Error when DOS starts, remove any floppy disks from the floppy drive and press Enter to resume the boot.

◆ If during the start-up of the system, you receive an error message on your display, refer to Appendix B or to your DOS Reference Manual.

C:\>

The DOS system prompt.

Choose File

Choose Exit Windows

To close Windows and display the DOS system prompt, choose File Exit Windows. A dialog box appears asking you to confirm that you want to exit Windows; press Enter.

If the system prompt is showing and no lights are flashing, you can safely turn off your computer.

It's obvious to say that to exit DOS you turn off your computer; and it's true. However, there are certain matters you should check into before exiting DOS so that you do not lose any data or damage your hard disk.

Before You Turn Off the Computer...

Before you turn off the computer, consider the following:

◆ If you're using an application program, save all files and exit the program by following the instructions for that program. You could lose data if you turn off the computer before properly exiting the program.

◆ If you're using Windows, exit Windows. Windows creates a temporary file that holds data until you correctly exit Windows; then the temporary file is cleared. If you turn off the computer or there's a power failure before you exit Windows, the temporary files can become lost data that takes up space on your hard drive. This lost data can build up over time and reduce the available disk space on your computer.

◆ If the hard disk drive light is flashing, wait until all activity has stopped before turning off the computer. You can damage your hard disk and the data stored on it if you interrupt the computer while it is working. The same is true for the floppy disk drive light.

◆ Check any devices—such as modems, printers, and so on—to see if there are special requirements or a sequence to shutting down their operation in conjunction with the computer shutdown.

TIP

Be sure to remove any floppy disks from the disk drives after you turn off your computer and store them in a safe place. You can remove floppy disks before you turn off your computer, as long as the drive lights are not flashing. If you leave a floppy disk in the drive, the next time you boot the computer, DOS displays the message Non-System disk or disk error. Replace and press any key when ready. If this happens, remove the disk from the drive and press Enter; DOS then boots normally.

Restarting DOS

If your computer locks up or does not respond to commands, you can restart the computer by performing a warm boot.

Restarting the computer when the power is on is known as a warm boot. A warm boot is easier on the electronic components than turning the power off and on again (cold boot).

When you perform a warm boot, the computer skips the preliminary test; it resets the system unit and loads DOS. A warm boot is not only easier on your computer than a cold boot, it's also faster.

Shutting DOS Down

1. Exit all programs.

2. Turn off the computer.

3. Turn off the monitor.

Restart Your Computer

1. Press and hold the Ctrl and Alt keys.

2. Press the Del key (also shown as Ctrl+Alt+Del). Release all three keys.

Troubleshooting

◆ Sometimes the computer's keyboard locks up and pressing Ctrl+Alt+Del has no effect. If this happens, press the Reset button to restart your computer; pressing Reset has the same effect as performing a cold boot.

◆ If your keyboard is locked up and your computer has no Reset button, you'll have to use the power switch to reboot the computer. Turn off the power, count to 10 to give the processor time to stop completely, and then turn the power back on.

◆ If you turned off your computer—or a power failure occurred—before all previously listed conditions were met, run the Check Disk command on your computer the next time you boot it. For more information about the CHKDSK (Check Disk) command, see "Checking the Hard Disk."

Note: As you would when shutting DOS down, you must make sure there are no disk lights flashing when you reboot your computer and remove all floppy disks from their drives. Reboot your computer only if it has locked up on you; rebooting your computer to just exit a software application is unnecessarily hard on your system hardware.

Why Reboot?

You may want to restart or reboot your computer for several reasons:

◆ If your computer stops responding to keyboard or mouse commands, or locks up, performing a warm boot most likely will correct the problem.

◆ If you change your system configuration, you must restart the computer in order for the changes to take effect. See "Editing CONFIG.SYS" and "Editing AUTOEXEC.BAT" for more information about changing the system configuration.

◆ If you have configuration problems, you may want to boot the computer from your system disk. See "Creating a System Disk" for more information.

◆ If you want to use a different DOS version that is stored on a floppy disk, you must restart the computer so that it boots from the floppy.

To perform a task in DOS, you type instructions at the system prompt to communicate your request to DOS.

You communicate with DOS by entering instructions— commands—that describe what you want DOS to do. Commands are made up of characters that often form words or abbreviations you can easily remember and understand.

Most often, commands are words representing the task— copy, move, format, and so on—so they are easy to remember and use. Other commands are abbreviations for the task—such as DIR for directory list or MD for make directory.

Entering a Command

Some commands stand alone—you type the command at the system prompt, press Enter, and DOS responds. Other commands require more information, such as a file or directory name. Still other commands offer options for completing the assigned task.

DOS requires additional information from you to carry out most commands. This information may include a file, drive, or directory name. In addition, you can add options to a command to tell DOS to perform a task in a particular way.

You must follow the correct format, or syntax, in order for DOS to recognize the command.

Common Commands

Here are just a few commands you will learn to use over and over again in DOS:

◆ COPY duplicates files. You can copy a file from one disk to another, from one directory to another, from one drive to another, and so on.

◆ REN enables you to change the name of a file.

◆ HELP opens a Help program within DOS that explains commands and how to use them in detail.

◆ DEL deletes files.

◆ CD changes to a different directory.

◆ MD creates a directory.

◆ RD removes a directory.

Command Syntax

The correct format for entering a command is called the syntax. Syntax is the proper order in which you type the elements of a command. If you do not use the correct syntax, DOS responds with the message Bad command or file name. Throughout this book, you are given the correct syntax and an example of the commands you use.

Many commands require more information—such as a drive, directory, or file name—to complete the command. This information, called parameters, supplies DOS with the object of the command and must follow the correct syntax. Suppose that you want to copy a text file. You must tell DOS the name of the file and the drive and directory in which the file is located. In addition, you must tell DOS where the file is to be copied. The file name, drive, directory, and location of the copied file are parameters. And, these parameters must be in a specific order or syntax in order for DOS to carry out the command. For example, the correct use of parameters and syntax to copy a file from drive A to drive B while at the C:\ prompt follows:

copy a:\sample.txt b:

When you add parameters to a command, you must separate the parameters so that DOS can understand the task. You separate a command from a parameter with a delimiter: a space or a backslash (\), depending on the command and the desired results. The backslash is used, for example, to separate a drive letter from a directory name, a directory from a subdirectory, and a file name from a directory.

TIP

Don't worry if all this sounds overwhelming; if it's all new to you now, remember, it gets a lot easier with practice. In addition, DOS has an excellent Help system that prompts you with syntax, parameters, and switches, so you don't have to memorize any of this information. For more information on the DOS Help feature, see "Getting Help."

Finally, many DOS commands include optional parameters, called switches. Switches modify a command's action. When you format a floppy disk, for example, you use a switch to tell DOS the size of the disk. When you use a switch, you separate the switch from the command, or parameter, with a space and a forward slash (/). The switch for formatting a 5 1/4-inch 360K floppy disk in a high density drive is /4, for example:

format b: /4

more ▶

DOS BASICS

Enter Commands

1. At the system prompt (C:\>), type the command.

2. Press Enter.

DOS responds with its version number when you enter the VERSION command.

Practice Commands

Here are some easy commands to try:

◆ To find out which version of DOS is on your computer, type the following at the system prompt and press Enter

ver

◆ To view the time, according to your computer, type the following at the system prompt and press Enter:

time

If the time is correct, press Enter to return to the system prompt. If the time is incorrect, type the time in the format hh:mm:ss and press Enter.

◆ To clear the screen and display only the system prompt, type the following at the system prompt and press Enter:

cls

The cleared screen.

◆ To list the files and directories in your root directory in a wide format, type the following at the system prompt and press Enter:

dir /w

◆ If you see the prompt Press any key to continue..., press any key on your keyboard until the listing is complete and the prompt is no longer displayed.

Troubleshooting

◆ If you type a command but change your mind before you press Enter, use the Backspace key to erase the command.

◆ If you change your mind about a command after you press Enter, press Ctrl+C to stop the command and return to the system prompt.

Command

Switch

```
C:\>dir /w

 Volume in drive C is WEP_0
 Volume Serial Number is 1BD5-2956
 Directory of C:\

[WINDOWS]        AUTOEXEC.BAK     [WP60]           CONFIG.BAK       [DOS]
[MOUSE1]         [SUREST]         [WPC60]          [BTFONTS]        [PSFONTS]
KTCCACHE.EXE     [LETTERS]        [COLLAGE]        [WEP]            [WPDOCS]
COMMAND.COM      SFINSTAL.DIR     CONFIG.NEW       CONFIG.TXT       CUFLOPPY.SYS
CUSS12.SYS       SPEED200.EXE     FILEINFO.FI      AUTOEXEC.QFX     WINA20.386
[OS2DISK]        [WINWORD]        AUTOEXEC.BAT     CONFIG.SYS
        29 file(s)      210241 bytes
                     18743296 bytes free

C:\>
```

DOS displays the directory in wide (/w switch) format.

Directories indicated by brackets

Files

Entering Commands 17

Where do the spaces go? What switches can you use? If you can't remember the correct format or switch for a command, use DOS on-line Help to display information about the command.

When using DOS, you'll find that you use some commands—such as DIR, CD, CLS, and COPY—over and over again. These are commands you're comfortable with, completely understand, and use with ease.

On the other hand, there are some commands you don't use as often. Perhaps you can't remember the syntax—the form of the command—or the right switches to use. Suppose that you want to search through your document directory for all files created on a certain date. You know there's a way to list the files in the directory by date, but you can't remember how. That's where DOS on-line Help enters the picture.

DOS 6 supplies extensive information about its commands, including the correct way to enter the command, switches you can use to specify certain results, examples, and related topics.

Getting Help

DOS includes a help command that's easy to use; just type HELP at the system prompt and press Enter. DOS displays a Help screen— called on-line help—that lists all DOS commands. Here's how you can take advantage of the DOS on-line Help feature:

◆ A Help table of contents gives you easy access to all DOS 6 commands. Choose a command by using the keyboard or mouse, and view detailed information about the command.

TIP
You can bypass the Help table of contents screen for faster access to a Help topic. At the system prompt, type the word **HELP**, a space, and the name of the command. To access help on DIR, for example, type the following at the system prompt and press Enter: **HELP DIR**.

◆ Help defines each command in three ways: syntax, notes, and examples. Syntax describes the correct format of the command including parameters and switches. Notes offers hints, tips, and related commands that help you understand and use the original command. Help also offers common examples of each command.

◆ Using the Help menu, you can print the information on any Help screen. From the File menu, choose Print.

◆ On-line Help also offers a search utility that enables you to find specific text such as commands, terms, topics, and so on. From the Search menu, choose Find.

TIP
Sometimes you may need help with only the syntax or switches of a command; for these times, you can use FASTHELP. FASTHELP displays a command, the proper syntax, and available switches and immediately returns you to the system prompt. To access FASTHELP, type the command at the system prompt, followed by a space, forward slash (/), and question mark. For FAST-HELP on the command CLS, for example, type the following at the system prompt and press Enter: **FORMAT /?**.

Get Help

1. At the system prompt (C:\>), type **HELP**.

2. Press Enter.

3. Select a command from the list and press Enter to display the Help screen.

4. To exit Help, choose Exit from the File menu.

Do this	To move
Press ↑ or ↓	Up one line or down one line
Press PgDn/PgUp	Up or down one screen at a time
Click the mouse on the scroll bar	Up or down the screen
Click the mouse on a <command>	View more information
Press Tab	From column to column in the table of contents
Esc	To view the preceding screen

more ▶

```
 File  Search                                              Help
┌──────────────────── MS-DOS Help: Command Reference ────────────────────┐
│Use the scroll bars to see more commands. Or, press the PAGE DOWN key. For│
│more information about using MS-DOS Help, choose How to Use MS-DOS Help   │
│from the Help menu, or press F1. To exit MS-DOS Help, press ALT, F, X.    │
│                                                                          │
│<ANSI.SYS>              <Erase>                  <Multi-config>           │
│<Append>                <Exit>                   <Nlsfunc>                │
│<Attrib>                <Expand>                 <Numlock>                │
│<Batch commands>        <Fasthelp>               <Path>                   │
│<Break>                 <Fastopen>               <Pause>                  │
│<Buffers>               <Fc>                     <Power>                  │
│<Call>                  <Fcbs>                   <POWER.EXE>              │
│<Cd>                    <Fdisk>                  <Print>                  │
│<Chcp>                  <Files>                  <Prompt>                 │
│<Chdir>                 <Find>                   <Qbasic>                 │
│<Chkdsk>                <For>                     <RAMDRIVE.SYS>          │
│<CHKSTATE.SYS>          <Format>                  <Rd>                    │
│<Choice>                <Goto>                    <Rem>                   │
│<Cls>                   <Graphics>                <Ren>                   │
│<Command>               <Help>                    <Rename>               │
│<CONFIG.SYS commands>   <HIMEM.SYS>               <Replace>              │
│<Copy>                  <If>                      <Restore>              │
│<Alt+C=Contents> <Alt+N=Next> <Alt+B=Back>              N 00006:002      │
└──────────────────────────────────────────────────────────────────────┘
```

The Help table of contents appears.

```
 File  Search                                              Help
┌──────────────────────── MS-DOS Help: DIR ────────────────────────┐
│◀Notes▶  ◀Examples▶                                               │
│──────────────────────────────────────────────────────────────── │
│                                                                   │
│                            DIR                                    │
│Displays a list of the files and subdirectories that are in the    │
│directory you specify.                                             │
│                                                                   │
│When you use DIR without parameters or switches, it displays the   │
│disk's volume label and serial number; one directory or filename   │
│per line, including the filename extension, the file size in bytes,│
│and the date and time the file was last modified; and the total    │
│number of files listed, their cumulative size, and the free space  │
│(in bytes) remaining on the disk.                                  │
│                                                                   │
│Syntax                                                             │
│                                                                   │
│    DIR [drive:][path][filename] [/P] [/W]                         │
│    [/A[[:]attributes]][/O[[:]sortorder]] [/S] [/B] [/L] [/C]      │
│                                                                   │
│Parameters                                                         │
│                                                                   │
│[drive:][path]                                                     │
│<Alt+C=Contents> <Alt+N=Next> <Alt+B=Back>         N 00001:002     │
└───────────────────────────────────────────────────────────────┘
```

Help on the DIR command.

Display Notes on the Command

Click on the Notes option if you have a mouse; alternatively, press the Tab key until the blinking cursor moves to Notes.

Getting around in the Help screen.

```
 File   Search                                                    Help
┌──────────────────────── MS-DOS Help: DIR--Notes ────────────────────────┐
 ◄Examples►  ◄Syntax►                                                    ▲

                              DIR—Notes

Using wildcards with DIR

You can use wildcards (* and ?) to display a listing of a subset of files
and subdirectories. For an example illustrating the use of a wildcard, see
the "Examples" screen.

Specifying file display attributes

If you specify the /A switch with more than one value in attributes, DIR
displays the names of only those files with all the specified attributes.
For example, if you specify the /A switch with the R and -H values for
attributes by using either /A:R-H or /AR-H, DIR displays only the names of
read-only files that are not hidden.

Specifying filename sorting

If you specify more than one sortorder value, DIR sorts the filenames by the  ▼
<Alt+C=Contents> <Alt+N=Next> <Alt+B=Back>                    N 00001:002
```

Display Examples of the Command

Click on the Examples option if you use a mouse; alternatively, press the Tab key until the blinking cursor moves to Examples.

```
 File   Search                                                    Help
┌──────────────────────── MS-DOS Help: DIR--Examples ─────────────────────┐
 ◄Syntax►  ◄Notes►                                                      ▲

                             DIR—Examples

Suppose you want to display all files and directories in a directory,
including hidden or system files. To specify this display, type the
following command:

    dir /a

Suppose you want DIR to display one directory listing after another, until
it has displayed the listing for every directory on the disk in the current
drive. Suppose also that you want DIR to alphabetize each directory listing,
display it in wide format, and pause after each screen. To specify such a
display, be sure the root directory is the current directory and then type
the following command:

    dir /s/w/o/p

DIR lists the name of the root directory, the names of the subdirectories of
the root directory, and the names of the files in the root directory        ▼
<Alt+C=Contents> <Alt+N=Next> <Alt+B=Back>                    N 00001:002
```

Shortcut Keys

Alt+C   Table of Contents screen

Alt+N   Next topic

Alt+B   Previous topic (back)

Troubleshooting

◆ To return to the original Help screen, Syntax, choose the Syntax option.

◆ If you can't find what you need in Help, press F1 for help on Help.

◆ To exit Help, choose the File menu and Exit by pressing Alt+F, x.

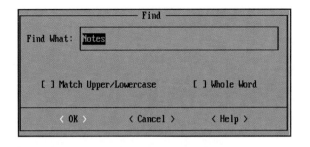

Search for a specific topic by choosing Search, Find; or by pressing Alt+S, F. Enter the topic in the Find What text box and press Enter.

```
┌──────────────────────────── Find ────────────────────────────┐
│                                                               │
│  Find What:  Notes                                            │
│                                                               │
│                                                               │
│   [ ] Match Upper/Lowercase         [ ] Whole Word            │
│                                                               │
│      < OK >          < Cancel >         < Help >              │
└───────────────────────────────────────────────────────────────┘
```

```
┌File  Search──────────────────────────────────────────Help─┐
│ File  Search                                          Help │
│┌─────────────┐ MS-DOS Help: APPEND ─────────────────────┐↑│
││ Print...  amples▶                                       │ │
││                ─────────────────────────────────────   │ │
││ Exit                                                    │ │
│└─────────────┘           APPEND                         │ │
│                                                         │ │
│ Enables programs to open data files in specified directories as if the files │
│ were in the current directory. Do not use this command when you are running  │
│ Windows.                                                │ │
│                                                         │ │
│ The specified directories are called appended directories because, for the   │
│ sake of opening data files, they can be found as if they were appended to     │
│ the current directory.                                  │ │
│                                                         │ │
│ Syntax                                                  │ │
│                                                         │ │
│   APPEND [[drive:]path[;...]] [/X[:ON¦:OFF]][/PATH:ON¦/PATH:OFF] [/E]          │
│                                                         │ │
│ To display the list of appended directories, use the following syntax:        │
│                                                         │ │
│   APPEND                                                │ │
│                                                         │ │
│ To cancel the existing list of appended directories, use the following        │
│ F1=Help │ Prints specified text              N 00001:002 │
└───────────────────────────────────────────────────────────┘
```

Choose File, Exit to exit Help and return to the DOS system prompt.

DOS BASICS

You have to deal with DOS to use a computer. But the good news is, you don't have to deal with it that often. Most of the time you spend using a computer will be while in a program or application.

Most people don't use the many features of DOS because they don't understand DOS or they think they don't have time to learn. DOS may just be a stepping stone to the word processor, database, or spreadsheet program they use day after day. That's what DOS is— a program that enables you to start the applications you need to complete your work.

DOS certainly has many more features than simply enabling you to start programs; but that is one of the most important. By typing a command at the system prompt, you can start any DOS-based application in your computer. But why must you use a specific set of characters, how does DOS know which program you want to start, and how does DOS find that program?

Starting Programs

Each software program on your computer has a specific file that starts that program. The file name usually ends with the COM or EXE extension. COM, short for command, and EXE, short for executable, identify files that can start a program in DOS.

When you type the program name, the program starts. The program file for Word-Perfect is WP.EXE, for example, the program file for MS Word 5 is WORD.EXE, and so on. If you type wp or word at the system prompt and press Enter, the program starts.

Note: Creating a file with an EXE or COM extension does not make it a program file. Actual executable files have internal differences that make them start a program.

Changing the Directory

Depending on how your computer is set up (or configured), you may or may not change directories to start your programs. Sometimes DOS knows where to look for the program because the directory name is included in the PATH. If not, you must first change to the directory, and then type the program name.

WordPerfect's program file is located in the WordPerfect directory, WP51 or WP60, for example. You may need to change directories before you can start the program.

If the program does not start after you enter the executable file name at the system prompt, type the Change Directory command (CD), followed by a space, and then the directory name, depending on which version of the software you are using. Then press Enter. To change to the WordPerfect 6 directory, for example, enter the following at the system prompt and press Enter:

cd wp60

The system prompt changes to C:\WP60>, signifying that you're in the correct directory. Type the executable file name again and press Enter to start the program. For more information about changing directories, see "Changing Directories."

Start a Program

1. If necessary, change to the directory that contains the program.

2. Type the program name.

Application	Command
WordPerfect	WP
Word	WORD
Windows	WIN
1-2-3	123
Quattro Pro	QP
Quicken	Q
dBASE	dbase
Q&A	QA
LetterPerfect	LP
Commander Keen	KEEN
Crystal Caves	CC1
Ventura Publisher	VP

Troubleshooting

◆ If you type the name of the program file at the system prompt and DOS does not recognize it, DOS displays the message

```
Bad command or file name
```

◆ Don't worry—you probably just made a typing mistake. Type the command again. If the program still does not open, consult the reference manual that came with the program for information on starting the program.

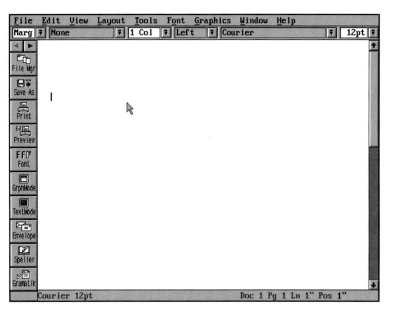

WordPerfect 6.0 for DOS.

Part Two

Section 2—Directories

If you think of a computer as a filing cabinet, *directories* are the drawers in the cabinet. Each directory can hold many *files*, which contain programs, word processing documents, spreadsheets, and other data. The directories help keep your data sorted into categories, so that all the information isn't jumbled together.

Section 3—Files

Files are the most important information in your computer. Some files run essential programs. Other files that you create—documents, databases, and so on—are equally valuable. Because so much computer work involves handling files, DOS has special commands for file-related tasks. DOS even provides special commands to help you find missing files. (Don't you wish your filing cabinet could do that?)

Section 4—Hard Disks

When you keep files on your computer's hard disk, they're much safer than they would be on floppy disks, which are easy to lose or damage. The *hard disk* is protected by the casing of the computer, and it can hold much more information than a floppy disk. This section is particularly important because it covers how to protect the hard disk and the information it holds.

Section 5—Floppy Disks

Floppy disks are like removable file drawers. You can use floppy disks to back up files from your computer's hard disk—in preparation for a "rainy day" when your computer breaks down or you accidentally delete an important file.

The small amount of time you spend up front organizing and planning your directories will save you an enormous amount of time when you're working later. Files will be easier to find, for example.

DOS enables you to organize your hard disk so that you can easily find your files. If you just started using the computer, you probably can't imagine the files being hard to keep track of. The longer you work on the computer, however, the more files you'll create. The more files you create, the harder it is to keep track of each file.

It's just like a filing cabinet. If you have a couple of papers, it's easy to find the paper you want. But imagine 100 or more papers stuffed into a filing cabinet with no organization. That's how your hard disk can end if you don't organize your directories.

DOS gives you the means to divide your disk into sections called *directories*. Each directory can hold other directories (sometimes referred to as *subdirectories*) and files—preferably groups of similar files (such as word processing, spreadsheet, or database files).

Your Hard Disk Is a Filing Cabinet

The best way to think of your computer's hard disk is to compare it to a filing cabinet. The cabinet is the same as the root directory of your disk. The root directory is the base from which all other directories are created. Everything is contained in the root.

Think of each directory in your disk as a drawer in the file cabinet. A drawer can hold many file folders; a directory, then, can hold many subdirectories. Just as you use file folders to hold similar files, you use subdirectories to the same end.

Planning Your Directories

DOS makes it easy to create directories and subdirectories; all you have to do is type a command and then name the directory. Before you sit down at the computer and start creating directory after directory, take a few minutes to plan the directory structure.

Consider the types of programs you use and the types of documents you produce. Most programs include a document directory for your use with their application; however, you may want to create your own directories to make finding files easier.

TIP If you plan your directories and subdirectories now, you can save yourself time and energy later when you can't find that file for an important meeting in five minutes.

Directory	Subdirectories	Store Files
DOCUMENT	ADVERTS (C:\DOCUMENT\ADVERTS)	Newspaper advertisements
	NEWSLETS (C:\DOCUMENT\NEWSLETS)	Company newsletters
	TEMPLATE (C:\DOCUMENT\TEMPLATE)	Document templates
GRAPHICS	ILLUSTR	Graphic images
	PRESENT	Slide presentations
REPORTS	ANNUAL	Yearly sales reports
	COSTGOOD	Cost of goods reports
	SALES	Monthly sales reports
WP60	GRAPHICS	Clip art images for WordPerfect
	DOCS	Your WordPerfect document files
	TEMPLATES	WordPerfect's style sheets and templates
CORELDRW!	DRAW	CorelDRAW!'s drawing program
	CHART	CorelDRAW!'s charting program
	SHOW	CorelDRAW!'s slide presentation program
	FONTS	TrueType fonts that come with CorelDRAW!
PROGRAMS	WP60	WordPerfect program files
	QUICKEN	Quicken program files
	LOTUS	Lotus 1-2-3 program files
DOCUMENT	LETTERS	Letters created in WordPerfect
	ACCOUNTS	Accounting documents from Quicken
	SPREADSH	Spreadsheets created in Lotus 1-2-3

Troubleshooting

◆ New users in particular, have trouble finding files after storing them in some obscure directory. If you take the time now to set up and use a directory structure that makes sense to you, you'll have a better chance of finding files when you need them.

◆ Don't be afraid to rename directories and reorganize your files when they seem too confusing. The time spent is well worth the time you save searching for a file.

You may want to list the files or directories on your hard disk or floppy disk so that you can see what you have or to see what a particular file or directory is named. Displaying directory listings is something you'll do often in DOS.

The most commonly used command is the DIR (Directory) command. The Directory command instructs DOS to list the files in the current directory. You can list the files of the root directory, subdirectories, and floppy disks using the same command. When DOS displays the directory's contents, it also displays certain information about the directory.

Suppose that you want to see when you last updated a particular file. You can find out by listing the directory's contents. If you want to find only those files created in your word processor, for example, you can list a directory of only those files containing a DOC extension.

What's in a Directory List?
When you list a directory by typing DIR and pressing Enter at the system prompt, DOS displays the following information:

◆ *Directory names.* DOS lists the names of any subdirectories within the current directory in the first column of the list, indicated by <DIR> in the second column.

◆ *File names.* File names consisting of up to eight characters and optional three character extensions are also listed in the first column.

◆ *File size.* The third column shows the size of the file in bytes.

◆ *Date/Time stamp.* The fourth and fifth columns show the date and time the file was created or last updated, according to your computer's internal clock.

◆ *Number of files.* At the end of the file list, the command displays the number of files contained in the list.

◆ *Amount of disk space used.* In addition to the number of files, DOS lists how much disk space is used by the files in the directory, measured in bytes.

◆ *Amount of available disk space.* The last line of the directory list shows the available disk space, measured in bytes.

Controlling How the Directories List
When you enter the DIR command, the list of files and directories scrolls by quickly and stops only at the end of the list. If you want to look more closely at the directory list, you can use switches to help you view the directory listing.

Some switches you can use to modify the way in which the directory lists follow:

/p	Pause	When followed by /p, the DIR command lists the files in the directory one screen at a time.
/w	Wide	When followed by /w, the DIR command lists the directory contents that so you can view all directory and file names simultaneously. You cannot, however, view the file size or date/time stamp with this directory listing.
*.	Directories only	When followed by *. (asterisk period), the DIR command lists only the directories or subdirectories with no extensions.

Listing Specific Types of Files

When listing files using the DIR command, you can specify certain types of files to display by using the wild-card characters, the question mark (?) and the asterisk (*). The question mark represents one character in the same position within the file name. The asterisk represents several characters.

Some examples of wild-card characters you can use with the DIR command follow:

?NEWSLET.TXT	All files ending with NEWSLET with an extension of TXT. For example, 1NEWSLET.TXT, 2NEWSLET.TXT, 3NEWSLET.TXT, and so on.
???	Three-letter file or directory names.
*.EXE	All files in a directory with the EXE extension.
LET*.DOC	All files in a directory beginning with LET and ending with the DOC extension. For example, LETJONES.DOC, LETSMITH.DOC, and so on.

Displaying the Directory Tree

DOS enables you to view your directory structure so that you can see a directory and all of its subdirectories. You can even show the files within the subdirectories. Using the TREE command displays the structure so that you can see the relationships between the directories and files on your hard disk or floppy disk.

Suppose that you are starting a new project and you want to find the most appropriate subdirectory for the files. Using the TREE command, you can view the entire directory structure of your hard disk.

By typing the TREE command at the system prompt, you display the directory and subdirectory structure of that drive.

Other Directory Tree Options

When you use just the TREE command, the tree scrolls by quickly and returns you to the system prompt. If your tree takes more than one screen, you either have to read fast or pause it as it scrolls by.

You can use another DOS command, MORE, to display the tree one screen at a time. To use the MORE command, separate it from the original command with a pipe or split vertical bar (|), type **MORE**, and press Enter. DOS displays the first screen with — more — at the bottom of the screen; press any key to continue the display.

If you want to display a list of files in each directory, use the /f switch with TREE.

You can print your directory tree for future reference by pressing Ctrl+Print Screen before entering the TREE command. When the display is finished, press Ctrl+Print Screen again to turn off the printing option. If you use a laser printer, or an IBM PS/2 keyboard, you may need to press Ctrl+P instead of Ctrl+Print Screen.

more ▶

DIRECTORIES

List a Directory

1. Change to the correct drive.

2. Change to the directory you want to view.

   For information on changing drives and directories, see the article "Changing Drives and Directories."

3. Type one of the following and press Enter:

Type	To list
DIR	The directory
DIR /p	The directory one screen at a time
DIR /w	Directories and file names in a wide format
DIR *.	Only the directories, no file names
DIR a:	The directory of drive A
DIR dos	The DOS directory

Troubleshooting

If you make a mistake while typing or enter the wrong command, use the following keys:

Backspace	Erases character to the left
Esc	Cancels the command you just typed; use before pressing Enter
Ctrl+C	Stops the directory listing and returns to the system prompt; use after entering the command and pressing Enter

File name   File size

```
Volume in drive C is WEP_0
Volume Serial Number is 1BD5-2956
Directory of C:\

WINDOWS      <DIR>     02-07-93  12:36p
AUTOEXEC BAK       221 03-16-93   8:31p
WP60         <DIR>     03-17-93   6:08a
CONFIG   BAK       238 01-30-93  10:52a
DOS          <DIR>     11-08-89   3:02p
MOUSE1       <DIR>     11-12-89   5:59p
SUREST       <DIR>     02-25-93  11:42a
WPC60        <DIR>     03-17-93   6:09a
BTFONTS      <DIR>     03-16-93   8:44p
PSFONTS      <DIR>     05-31-91   8:28a
KTCCACHE EXE      3338 07-17-91  11:37a
LETTERS      <DIR>     06-01-93   1:43p
COLLAGE      <DIR>     11-23-91   6:43p
WEP          <DIR>     03-27-93  10:39a
WPDOCS       <DIR>     04-05-93   7:59a
COMMAND  COM     52925 03-10-93   6:00a
SFINSTAL DIR       430 07-18-90  12:00p
CONFIG   NEW        77 12-23-89  10:25a
CONFIG   TXT       405 05-22-92   7:26p
Press any key to continue . . .
```

Directory   Date/Time stamp

Listing the root directory, one screen at a time.

```
C:\>dir /w

 Volume in drive C is WEP_0
 Volume Serial Number is 1BD5-2956
 Directory of C:\

[WINDOWS]       AUTOEXEC.BAK    [WP60]          CONFIG.BAK      [DOS]
[MOUSE1]        [SUREST]        [WPC60]         [BTFONTS]       [PSFONTS]
KTCCACHE.EXE    [LETTERS]       [COLLAGE]       [WEP]           [WPDOCS]
COMMAND.COM     SFINSTAL.DIR    CONFIG.NEW      CONFIG.TXT      CUFLOPPY.SYS
CUSS12.SYS      SPEED200.EXE    FILEINFO.FI     AUTOEXEC.QFX    WINA20.386
[OS2DISK]       [WINWORD]       AUTOEXEC.BAT    CONFIG.SYS
        29 file(s)      210241 bytes
                      18776064 bytes free

C:\>
```

Listing a directory in wide view enables you to see more entries on one screen.

— Amount of used space
— Amount of available space

— Total files in directory

Wide view of directory list

30   **Section 2—Directories**

Ctrl+S	Pauses a scrolling list; press any key to continue listing the directory
Pause	Pauses a scrolling list; press any key to continue listing the directory

Display a Tree

1. At the system prompt of your hard drive, type one of the following:

Type	To
TREE	Scroll the tree structure.
TREE|more	Display the tree one screen at a time. Press Enter when you're ready to see more.
TREE /f	Scroll the directories and all files.
TREE /f|more	Display the directories and files one screen at a time.

2. Press Enter.

Troubleshooting

If you change your mind after the tree begins to display and you decide to cancel the command, press Ctrl+C.

```
Directory PATH listing for Volume IBM_VP_638X
Volume Serial Number is 1ADB-5141
C:.
├──DOS
├──WINDOWS
│   └──SYSTEM
├──LL
├──LANTASTI
│   ├──LANTASTI.SHR
│   └──SOUNDS
├──LANTASTI.NET
│   ├──LANTASTI.SHR
│   ├──A-DRIVE
│   └──C-DRIVE
├──QA4
│   ├──QADATA
│   └──NRHA
├──123
│   ├──ADDINS
│   └──WYSIWYG
├──OLD_DOS.1
├──WP60
│   ├──MACROS
── More ──
```

A directory listing paused with the MORE command.

— Directories

```
Directory PATH listing for Volume WEP_0
Volume Serial Number is 1BD5-2956
C:.
│   AUTOEXEC.BAK
│   CONFIG.BAK
│   KTCCACHE.EXE
│   COMMAND.COM
│   SFINSTAL.DIR
│   CONFIG.NEW
│   CONFIG.TXT
│   CUFLOPPY.SYS
│   CUSS12.SYS
│   SPEED200.EXE
│   FILEINFO.FI
│   AUTOEXEC.QFX
│   WINA20.386
│   AUTOEXEC.BAT
│   CONFIG.SYS
│
├──WINDOWS
│   │   SETUP.EXE
│   │   SETUP.HLP
│   │   SETUP.TXT
-- More --
```

A directory listing with files displayed.

DIRECTORIES

When you want to access files in another place (on another disk or in another directory), you need to tell DOS which drive and which directory to use.

When you start your computer, DOS displays a system prompt representing the root directory (c:\>) or the DOS directory (c:\DOS>) as the current directory. The current directory is the one in which you are working.

In the same way that you change directories, you may also need to change drives. If you plan to use floppy disks for storing your data and for adding new applications to your system, you can easily change drives to access those disks.

Starting Programs

When you want to start a program, you need to change to the directory that contains the program file. Then type the program name. DOS starts the program.

Working with Files

You also may want to change directories so that you can copy, delete, or do something else to the files in that directory.

Suppose that you want to delete some files in your MS Word directory. You can include the path (the directory) to the file in the command. You can type **DEL c:\word5\letjones.doc** and press Enter; then type **DEL c:\word5\report05.aug** and press Enter, and so on, for example. On the other hand, you can change to the WORD5 directory and type less in the command line. You would be in the C:\WORD5 directory, so you wouldn't have to type the

path. You could just type **DEL letjones.doc**. You can also list, move, copy, and rename files quicker and easier if you first change to the directory that contains the files.

Use the DIR (Directory) command to view the contents of the directory. Type **DIR** at the system prompt.

Changing Directories

You change directories by entering the command (cd) at the command prompt, pressing the space bar once, typing the directory name, and pressing Enter. The command prompt changes to include the directory. For example, to change from the root directory to the DOS directory, enter the following at the command prompt: cd dos. The command prompt changes to: C:\DOS>.

If your system prompt does not display the current directory, you can change it for the current session by typing **prompt pg**. If you add the prompt statement to your AUTOEXEC.BAT file, you can change the prompt display for future sessions. See "Editing AUTOEXEC.BAT" for more information.

Directory Paths

A *path* is like a map to your files, listing all directories in their order from the root directory. Use a path to tell DOS how and where to find a file.

When you type a command that includes a file name, DOS looks for the file in the current directory. If the file does not exist in the current directory, DOS cannot complete the command. Therefore, you need to give DOS a path—a map to the file. Think of a path in relation to a filing cabinet: the file you want is in the second drawer and in the file folder labeled C-D. That's a path, too.

Suppose that you want to copy a file from one subdirectory to another. You must use a path to map out the subdirectories in order for DOS to be able to complete the command.

Typing a Path

When using a path, you separate directory names with a backslash (\). Each backslash in the path indicates that the directory to the left of the path is a parent directory. Consider the following example:

C:\LETTERS\BUSINESS\PARTNERS\

C: is the drive. The first backslash stands for the root directory, which is the parent of LETTERS. LETTERS is the parent of BUSINESS, and so on. All characters between the first and last backslash define the path.

TIP

DOS enables you to speed up your work; you can abbreviate the path by omitting the current drive letter or directory name from the path. If the current drive is C and the subdirectory is on drive C, for example, to list the DOC files in the BUSINESS subdirectory you enter the following command:

DIR \letters\business*.doc

Similarly, if you are already in the LETTERS directory, you can skip the current drive and current directory in the path as follows:

DIR \business*.doc

Paths and Programs

You've probably noticed that when you start some programs—Windows, WordPerfect, MS Word, and so on—you can enter the program name from any directory or subdirectory and the program starts. Other programs require you to change directories before you can start the program. The reason you can start some programs from any directory is because of the path.

DOS includes an AUTOEXEC.BAT file that contains a path statement. This path is a map; when you enter a command, DOS checks the current drive and directory, and then automatically checks this path statement to find the file you specify.

You can view the path by typing the command **PATH** at the system prompt and pressing Enter. In addition, you can change the path. See "Editing the AUTOEXEC.BAT File" for more information.

Changing Drives

If you want to work with files on another drive, you must change to that drive. In DOS, the drive represented by the system prompt is the current drive. For example, c:\> represents drive C, the hard disk. A:\>, on the other hand, represents a floppy drive. If your computer has both a hard drive and a floppy drive, or two floppy drives, you'll need to change drives when you want to access information on another drive.

more ▶

Change Directories

1. At the system prompt, type **cd** <*directory name*>:

cd letters

2. Press Enter.

Change to the Root Directory

1. At the system prompt, type **cd**.

2. Press Enter.

Troubleshooting

If you change your mind and want to return to the root directory, type the following at the system prompt:

cd

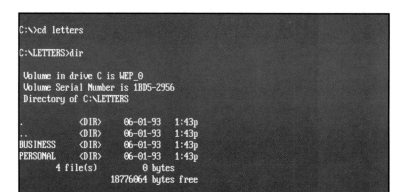

```
C:\>cd letters

C:\LETTERS>dir

 Volume in drive C is WEP_0
 Volume Serial Number is 1BD5-2956
 Directory of C:\LETTERS

.              <DIR>      06-01-93   1:43p
..             <DIR>      06-01-93   1:43p
BUSINESS       <DIR>      06-01-93   1:43p
PERSONAL       <DIR>      06-01-93   1:43p
       4 file(s)              0 bytes
                      18776064 bytes free
```

The system prompt shows the directory name.

```
C:\LETTERS>cd\

C:\>
```

Changing to the root directory.

Shortcuts

DOS offers an easy way to get from directory to directory:

> To return to the root directory, type **cd**. The backslash (\) is the name of the root directory. It is also used to separate directory names.

> You can also change from directory to directory. To change from the DOS directory to the WINDOWS directory, for example, at the C:\DOS> prompt, type **cd\windows**. The prompt changes to C:\WINDOWS>. To change from one directory to another, you must use a backslash after the cd command instead of a space, or DOS will not recognize the directory.

> The space separator between the cd command and the directory name signifies a subdirectory within a directory. When

you're in a directory and you want to change to a subdirectory within that directory—from C:\WINDOWS to C:\WINDOWS\SYSTEM, for example—use the change directory command followed by a space. At the system prompt C:\WINDOWS, type cd system.

DOS also offers a shortcut for moving from a subdirectory to its parent directory (the *parent* directory is the directory that holds the subdirectory). Suppose that you're in the WINDOWS\TEMP directory and want to move back to the WINDOWS (or parent) directory. If you type **cd**, you'll go back to the root. If, however, you type **cd..** (CD followed by two periods), you'll go back to the WINDOWS directory. The two periods represent the parent directory.

Change Drives

1. Place a floppy disk in the drive.

2. To change to drive A, type **a**:
To change to drive B, type **b**:

3. Press Enter.

Drive A is now the current drive.

Troubleshooting

◆ If you forgot to place a floppy disk in the drive before you tried to access the drive, or you forgot to close the drive latch, DOS checks the drive and gives you the following message:

```
Not ready reading drive A
Abort, Retry, Fail?
```

◆ Place a floppy disk in the drive and press R for Retry or F for Fail. If you press A for Abort, DOS tries over and over again to access the drive. To cancel the command and return to the C-prompt, choose F for Fail. DOS displays the following message:

```
Current drive is no longer valid>
```

◆ Type **c**: at the blinking cursor and press Enter. DOS returns you to the system prompt.

◆ To change back to the hard drive, type **c**: at the system prompt and press Enter.

DIRECTORIES

Organize your hard disk into directories so that you can find the files you want.

Using directories and subdirectories is an excellent way to organize your hard disk. All disks have a root directory—the base of the directory structure that can store other directories and files.

Keep the Root Directory Clean

Although the root directory can store files, it's best not to store too many files there for a couple of reasons:

◆ The root directory has a limited number of files and directories it can hold, depending on the size of the disk. If you divide the root directory with directories, you make more space available for holding files. The number of entries in a sub-directory is limited only by the disk space. For more information about disk space, see "Hard Disks."

◆ Many different file types—such as word processing files, program files, batch files, spreadsheet files, and so on—stored in the same directory are hard to view, sort, and locate. By creating directories, you organize your system and make files easier to find.

Store Like Documents Together

When you install software programs, the program sets up a directory to hold the program files. During installation of Microsoft Word, for example, Word's setup creates the directory WORD from the root directory.

Generally, the setup will also create a directory that holds your documents; the document directory is located within the program directory—for example, C:\WORD\DOCS.

You can take this structure a step further by creating more directories within the C:\WORD\DOCS directory—such as C:\WORD\DOCS\LETTERS, C:\WORD\DOCS\REPORTS, and so on. Using this method of organization, you store all Word documents in the Word directory.

Another way to organize your directories is to store like documents together. Suppose that you create your company's advertising documents—newsletters, forms, reports, and so on—and you would like to organize the files on your computer to make them easier to find. You can create directories to hold the various types of documents.

From the root directory, for example, say you create three directories: REPORTS, NEWSLETS, and FORMS. You can now save your documents in a directory that defines the type of document. What if you go a step further? In the REPORTS directory, say you create three subdirectories: ANNUAL, SALES, and PROSPECT. Now you can divide your reports into more specific categories—just like you would in a file cabinet.

Using this method of organization, you store program files in their respective directories—Microsoft Word in the C:\WORD directory, PageMaker in the C:\PM4 directory, and so on. You store the annual reports you create in Word in the C:\REPORTS\ANNUAL directory; and store newsletters created in PageMaker in the C:\NEWSLETS directory. Since each program uses a distinctive extension in the file name—PM4, DOC, and so on—you can easily discern the type of documents stored in each directory.

Adding Directories and Subdirectories

You use the MD (Make Directory) command to create a directory or subdirectory. The easiest way to create a directory is from within the parent directory. If you're in a directory called LETTERS (C:\LETTERS>), for example, and you use the MD command to create a subdirectory named BUSINESS—md business, the BUSINESS subdirectory is in the LETTERS directory (C:\LETTERS\BUSINESS>). If you want to create subdirectories in the BUSINESS subdirectory, you change to the business subdirectory before issuing the MD command (C:\LETTERS\BUSINESS\AUGUST>). At the C:\LETTERS\BUSINESS prompt, type md august and press Enter.

You must follow a few guidelines when creating directories in DOS:

◆ When choosing a name for the directory, you must keep that name to eight characters or less. You can add a three-letter extension to any directory name—such as DATABASE.OO1.

◆ The new directory name must be unique—no other directories in the parent directory can have the same name.

◆ You can only make one directory at a time; the parent directory must exist before you can create a subdirectory.

◆ Making a directory does not change the current directory; you must use CD (Change Directory) to change to the new directory you created.

TIP

You can always change the name of a directory if you need to by using the MOVE command. To change the directory LETTERS to BUSLETT, for example, enter the following at the system prompt: **MOVE c:\letters buslett.**

Renaming Directories

No matter how much you plan and organize your directories, you will, at some point, need to change the name of one or more directories.

You can rename a directory without affecting the contents of that directory; all files and subdirectories remain intact. Suppose that you want to change the name of the REPORTS directory to REPSALES. You can rename the directory in just seconds by using DOS.

To rename a directory or subdirectory, you use the MOVE command. Naming a new directory requires the same guidelines as creating a directory—the name can contain no more than eight characters and the characters must follow file-naming conventions.

more ▶

Create a Directory within the Root

1. In the root directory, type **MD** *<directory name>*. For example, type **MD letters**.

2. Press Enter.

   DOS creates the directory and returns you to the command prompt at the root directory level.

3. Change to the new directory by typing **CD** *<directory name>*. To change to the LETTERS directory, for example, type **CD letters.**

4. Press Enter.

```
C:\>md letters    1
C:\>cd letters    2
C:\LETTERS>    3
```

The prompt includes the directory name (C:\LETTERS>).

```
1  C:\>cd letters
C:\LETTERS>md business    3
5  C:\LETTERS>cd business
C:\LETTERS\BUSINESS>
```

The prompt includes both directory names.

Create a Directory within another Directory

1. Type **CD** *<directory name>* to change to the directory you want. To change to the C:\LETTERS directory, for example, type **cd letters**.

2. Press Enter.

3. Type **MD** *<directory name>* at the system prompt. For example, type **MD business**.

4. Press Enter.

5. To change to the directory, type **CD** *<directory name>*. For example, type **CD business.**

6. Press Enter.

Troubleshooting

If you create a directory and decide that you don't want it, you can delete the directory by using the RD (Remove Directory) command. See "Removing Directories" for more information.

Rename the Directory

1. Change directories so that you are in the parent directory of the subdirectory to be renamed. If the directory to be renamed is REPORTS and it is a subdirectory of DOCS, for example, type **CD\DOCS** to go to the DOCS directory.

2. Press Enter.

3. At the system prompt, type **MOVE** <oldname> <newname>. At the prompt C:\DOCS>, for example, type:

   MOVE reports repsales

4. Press Enter.

Troubleshooting

You can't rename a directory that you are moving to a different disk. Move the directory first, then rename it.

```
C:\>cd docs

C:\DOCS>move reports repsales
c:\docs\reports => c:\docs\repsales [ok]

C:\DOCS>
```

DOS renames the REPORTS directory as REPSALES.

If you have one or more directories you no longer use, you can easily delete them using the RD (Remove Directory) command.

As you work with directories and subdirectories, you'll eventually find the need to delete one. You may no longer need the directory, or you may want to combine files from two or more directories and delete the leftover directories. You can use the RD command to accomplish this task.

Removing a Directory

There are two requirements for deleting—removing—a directory. One is that you cannot remove a directory while you are in it. (If you think of a directory structure like a tree and each directory as a branch, deleting the current directory would be like trying to saw the branch you were standing on.) You must move to the parent directory.

The other requirement is that the directory must be empty of all files and subdirectories. If the directory has subdirectories in it, you must delete the subdirectories. If the subdirectories have files in them, you must delete or move the files. See "Files" for more information.

TIP

To quickly delete the files in a subdirectory, you can type the command DEL and the name of the subdirectory. This method does not delete the directory name, any directories within the directory, or hidden files within the directory. Any time you delete files using this method, make sure you don't accidently delete any files you may need later.

Deleting a Directory Tree

If you have several directories to delete, and they contain several subdirectories and files, deleting all those files can be tedious and time consuming.

DOS 6 provides you with a command that can delete an entire tree, or branch, of your directory structure. Suppose that you've just finished an annual report for your company. You've backed up your files and you're ready to delete all files and directories you used to store the annual report. You could delete the files in each subdirectory, remove the subdirectory, move to the next subdirectory, and repeat the process. On the other hand, you could delete the entire directory, including its subdirectories and files, with one command.

Be Careful When Deleting a Tree!

Be careful, however, when using the DEL-TREE command. If you type the wrong path or wrong directory, you could delete more files and directories than you planned.

In addition, DELTREE deletes all files, including system files, hidden files, and read-only files. See "Assigning File Attributes" for more information.

Because of the DELTREE command's potential for disaster, DOS prompts you before deleting; but if you aren't paying attention, you could lose everything.

Remove a Directory

1. Remove all files and subdirectories from the directory to be deleted.

2. Change directories to the parent directory. To remove the subdirectory BUSINESS from the LETTERS directory, for example, you must be in the LETTERS directory. Type **CD letters**.

3. At the system prompt, type **RD** <*directory name*>. At the system prompt C:\LETTERS>, for example, type **RD business.**

4. Press Enter.

5. To confirm that the directory is deleted, type **DIR** and press Enter.

Delete a Tree

1. From the root directory of the hard or floppy disk, type the following at the system prompt:

DELTREE <*drive*><*path*>

To delete the directory WORDPROC and all its files and subdirectories, for example, type the following at the system prompt:

DELTREE c:\wordproc

2. Press Enter.

3. Respond to the confirmation message by pressing Y to continue the deletion or N to cancel the deletion.

```
                                    2
C:\>cd letters
                                         3
C:\LETTERS>rd business
                                5
C:\LETTERS>dir

 Volume in drive C is IBM_VP_638X
 Volume Serial Number is 1ADB-5141
 Directory of C:\LETTERS

.              <DIR>        08-22-93    9:43a
..             <DIR>        08-22-93    9:43a
PERSONAL       <DIR>        08-22-93   10:48a
SALES          <DIR>        08-22-93   10:48a
ADVERTIS       <DIR>        08-22-93   10:48a
        5 file(s)              0 bytes
                       58097664 bytes free

C:\LETTERS>
```

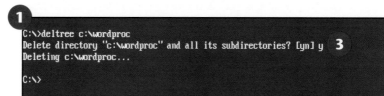

```
C:\>deltree c:\wordproc
Delete directory "c:\wordproc" and all its subdirectories? [yn] y    3
Deleting c:\wordproc...

C:\>
```

DOS displays a message confirming the directory to be deleted and asks you to confirm. Press Enter to confirm; DOS deletes the directory and its subdirectories.

DIRECTORIES

At times, you may have wanted to hide a directory and its contents so that no one else could view it. You'll be glad to know that you can accomplish that task with attributes.

*A*ttributes are conditions you can apply to files or directories—such as hiding a directory from casual view. Suppose that you keep employee records on your computer and you don't want anyone to view those records. You can assign an attribute to the directory containing those records; the attribute prevents the directory from listing under normal circumstances. (If someone is a DOS whiz, he or she can figure out how to display the hidden directory, however.)

Note: This article discusses directory attributes; for more information about using file attributes, see "Assigning File Attributes."

Hiding a Directory

Use the Attribute command to apply the hidden attribute to a directory. The hidden directory does not list when you use the TREE command or the DIR command.

Attributes are represented by one character; the hidden attribute is represented by an h. To turn on an attribute, you specify the command, a plus sign, the attribute, and the name of the directory. To turn off an attribute, you use a minus sign in place of the plus sign.

If you type DIR or TREE at the system prompt, the directory list will not include the hidden directory. To show the hidden directory and its attribute, you must type the Attribute command and the name of the directory. You change directories to the hidden directory as you would a normal directory, with the CD (Change Directory) command.

Hide a Directory

1. In the parent directory at the system prompt, type the following command:

   ATTRIB +h *<directory name>*

   To hide the subdirectory EMPLOYEE in the DOCUMENT directory, for example, type the following at the C:\DOCU-MENT> prompt and press Enter:

   ATTRIB +h employee

Unhide a Directory

To remove the attribute, type the following command and press enter:

   ATTRIB –h *<directory name>*

View Attributes of a Directory

1. To view the attributes of a directory, type the following and press enter:

   ATTRIB *<directory name>*

Troubleshooting

◆ If you don't provide a directory name when you apply the hidden attribute, DOS assumes you want to hide all directories.

◆ If you misspell the directory name, DOS returns the error message: File not found.

```
C:\DOCUMENT>dir

 Volume in drive C is WEP_0
 Volume Serial Number is 1BD5-2956
 Directory of C:\DOCUMENT

.              <DIR>      06-05-93  11:08a
..             <DIR>      06-05-93  11:08a
LETTERS        <DIR>      06-05-93  11:09a
MEMOS          <DIR>      06-05-93  11:09a
FORMS          <DIR>      06-05-93  11:09a
COSTS          <DIR>      06-05-93  11:09a
        6 file(s)             0 bytes
                     17735680 bytes free

C:\DOCUMENT>attrib employee
        H      C:\DOCUMENT\EMPLOYEE

C:\DOCUMENT>cd employee

C:\DOCUMENT\EMPLOYEE>
```

Hide a directory.

```
C:\DOCUMENT>attrib +h employee

C:\DOCUMENT>dir

 Volume in drive C is IBM_VP_638X
 Volume Serial Number is 1ADB-5141
 Directory of C:\DOCUMENT

.              <DIR>      08-22-93  11:01a
..             <DIR>      08-22-93  11:01a
MANAGER        <DIR>      08-22-93  11:02a
INVOICE        <DIR>      08-22-93  11:02a
        4 file(s)             0 bytes
                     58064896 bytes free

C:\DOCUMENT>cd employee

C:\DOCUMENT\EMPLOYEE>
```

Enter the attribute command and list the directory; the hidden directory does not list, yet you can change to the directory.

Hiding Directories   43

File Names and Types

Your computer's memory is temporary, lasting only during the time the computer is turned on. To permanently save data so that you can work with it again, the information must be stored in a file. DOS imposes certain rules on file names.

DOS and software programs store information in files; that information can be a *program* (a set of instructions or commands created by the software manufacturer) or *data* (text, documents, and so on created by you). When data is stored in a file, DOS and software programs can read the data, load it into the computer's memory, and then use the data.

When you load a program onto your computer, installation or setup copies the files from the floppy disk to your hard disk. The files it copies include programs and data needed to run the application—such as a dictionary, a grammar checker, graphic images, fonts, and so on in a word processor. These are program files.

When you create documents, spreadsheets, databases, and so on with a program, you save them in files called data files.

Program Files

Program files, or command files, contain instructions DOS needs to carry out commands. When you type a command in DOS, for example, DOS uses a command file to complete the command. Similarly, when you start a word processing program, command files carry out the tasks you perform while in the program. Command files differ from data files in that they contain encoded commands instead of characters.

TIP Command files, also know as executable files, use the extensions COM and EXE.

Data Files

You use the program files to create data files (a memo, a list of addresses, or a budget, for example). You can store, read, retrieve, and alter data files.

File-Naming Basics

The more you use your computer, the more files you'll create and save. Each time you add a new application, you add more files. Likewise, each time you use the application and save a document, you add more files. The files you add by loading a new application are already named by the software vendor; however, you must name the files you save to disk.

TIP Text files have many extensions. Most programs add their own extensions—such as DOC, TXT, WK3, and so on; these default program extensions are helpful in enabling you to identify the type of document—DOC is an MS Word document, WK3 is a Lotus document, and so on. Or, you can use any extension that helps you organize your files—REP, AUG, SUE, and so on. Using your own extensions can be helpful if, for example, you use MS Word as your only word processor—so DOC is always the default extension—but you change extensions to help you better identify your documents.

When you create files in your application, name your files so that you can easily recognize them in a list of files. Suppose that you do the publications—newsletters, brochures, reports, and so on—for your company. If you use names such as NEWSLET, BROCHURE, and REPORT, you'll know the type of publication each file contains.

File-Naming Guidelines

Most applications use certain extensions to help differentiate their files from other files. WordPerfect 5.1, for example, suggests that you use the WP5 extension, Microsoft Word uses the DOC extension, and so on. You can also use file names and extensions to differentiate your files from other files. Here are some suggestions you can use to name your files:

◆ Create file names that are as descriptive as possible when naming your files. Use names such as BROCHURE, INVOICE1, COSTGOOD, and so on so that you can easily recognize the file contents by the name you use.

◆ Use numbers within the eight-character file name to differentiate between files or documents in a series, such as newsletters—for example, NEWS01.DOC, NEWS02.DOC, and so on.

more ▶

DOS Rules on File Names

Most software programs follow DOS conventions for naming files. DOS restricts the file name length and characters you can use. Following is a list of guidelines for naming files in DOS:

◆ You can use no more than eight characters for the file name, although you can use less than eight characters. SAMPLE01 and FORM are valid file names.

◆ DOS allows an optional extension of one to three characters separated from the eight-character name with a period. SAMPLE01.TXT and FORM.123 are valid file names. The extension is usually used to indicate the type of file.

◆ You can type a file name in uppercase or lowercase letters; DOS stores all file names as uppercase.

◆ You can use the letters a through z, numbers 0 through 9, and many punctuation characters, including the following:

~	tilde
!	exclamation mark
@	at symbol
#	number symbol
$	dollar sign
^	caret
&	ampersand
(	left parenthesis
)	right parenthesis
–	hyphen
_	underline
{	left bracket
}	right bracket
`	single left quote
'	apostrophe

◆ You can't use the following characters in a file name:

	space
+	plus sign
=	equal sign
/	forward slash
\	backslash
"	quote mark
:	colon
;	semicolon
,	comma
?	question mark
*	asterisk
>	more than
<	less than
		pipe
[	left bracket
]	right bracket

◆ Each file name must be unique within its directory.

- Use the same extension for like files. Use DOC for all Microsoft Word files, LET for all business letters, REP for all reports, and so on. Like extensions make it easier to find like files in directories.

- Use numbers representing the date, or other sequence, in the file name. If you create a cash sales report every morning, for example, use file names such as 08-19-93.REP, 08-20-93.REP, and so on to identify those reports.

- Be careful when using symbols within a file name. You want to recognize the file's contents by the name. If you name a file !!#$&&@@.DOC, later, you'll have no idea of what the file contains.

Don't Use These Extensions!

Following are extensions you should not use when naming your files:

BAK	Represents a backup file
BAS	Contains a program written in the BASIC programming language
BAT	Represents a batch file—a file containing DOS commands that perform a set of tasks
DRV	Program device driver file
INI	Windows initialization files
SYS	System file or device driver

Renaming Files

Often you find that a file name doesn't adequately represent the file's contents. You can change the file name using the REN (Rename) command.

You will often find reasons for changing the names of your files; perhaps the file contents have changed or you want to use the file name for a different file. Another likely reason to rename a file is to enable you to use a backup file. Many software programs use a BAK or similar extension for automatically backed-up files. If you find that the original file is damaged or unusable, you can rename the backup file and use it in the original file's place.

Guidelines for Renaming a File

These are the file-renaming conventions:

- You must follow file-naming conventions. See "File Naming" for more information.

- You can rename a file by changing from one character to eleven, including the extension.

- When you rename a file in DOS, the file's location and contents remain the same.

- You can't use a new file name already in use in the same directory.

- You can use wild-card characters to rename a set of files. (See the next article for information on wild cards.)

- You can rename a file from the parent directory or use a path to the file.

Rename a File

1. Change to the directory that contains the file you want to rename.

2. At the system prompt of the parent directory, type the following:

   REN <oldname> <newname>

   To rename the file DATAREP.DOC to DATA01.DOC, for example, you type the following command:

   REN datarep.doc data01.doc

3. Press Enter.

4. Type **DIR**.

5. Press Enter. Check to make sure that the file was renamed.

Troubleshooting

If you don't like the new name, simply rename the file again.

Original name

```
Volume in drive C is IBM_VP_638X
Volume Serial Number is 1ADB-5141
Directory of C:\DOCUMENT

.             <DIR>      08-22-93  11:01a
..            <DIR>      08-22-93  11:01a
DATAREP  DOC        655 08-21-93  12:00p
       3 file(s)         655 bytes
                    58011648 bytes free

C:\DOCUMENT>ren datarep.doc data01.doc    (2)

C:\DOCUMENT>dir  (4)

Volume in drive C is IBM_VP_638X
Volume Serial Number is 1ADB-5141
Directory of C:\DOCUMENT

.             <DIR>      08-22-93  11:01a
..            <DIR>      08-22-93  11:01a
DATA01   DOC        655 08-21-93  12:00p
       3 file(s)         655 bytes
                    58011648 bytes free

C:\DOCUMENT>
```

New name

The first directory listing shows the original file name. After using the REN command, the file name is changed, as shown by the second directory listing.

When you want to work with a group of files, use wild cards (certain characters) to select the files you want.

Suppose that you want to list all files that have the TXT extension in a directory. Or suppose that you want to delete all files in a directory. You can use wild-card characters to list files with the DIR command, copy files, rename files, delete files, and so on.

DOS uses two wild-card characters to help speed your work: the question mark (?) and the asterisk (*).

The Asterisk

The asterisk is the most commonly used wild card. It can represent any group of characters in a file name.

The most common use of the asterisk is *.*. This is usually referred to as *star dot star* and means all files. The first * matches any file name. The second * matches any extension.

You can also use the asterisk to include only certain files. Suppose that you want to list a directory of files such as NEWSLETT.DOC, NEWSLETT.IMG, NEWSLETT.PCX, and so on. Replace the extension with the asterisk to list the files: NEWSLETT.*.

Or suppose that you want to list all DOC files (CHAP01.DOC, CHAP02.DOC, and CHAP03.DOC). Replace the file name with an asterisk: *.DOC. All DOC files will be listed.

The asterisk represents all characters following it in the file name. Using MYDOC*A.TXT is the same as MYDOC*.TXT, for example, and using MYDOC.*XT is the same as MYDOC.*. DOS does not recognize any character except the period after an asterisk.

The Question Mark

The question mark is a pickier wild card. The question mark (?) represents any one character in a file name. When you need to be more precise about which files to include, use the question mark.

Use the question mark to represent one character in a file name, in the same position. Suppose that you want to list a directory of files such as 01FORM.DOC, 02FORM.DOC, and so on. You can use the question mark to represent the first two characters in the file name: ??FORM.DOC. Used with the DIR command, you would see all files ending with FORM.DOC. Since you're specifying several files when you use wild cards, a *file spec* is a file name with wild cards.

Most directories don't have extensions; most files do. If you want to list only directories, type **DIR *.** This lists files and directories without extensions.

Commands You Can Use with Wild Cards

Here are the commands you can use wild cards with:

Command	Example	Result
DIR	DIR *.exe	Lists all files with EXE extension
COPY	COPY rep* .pcx a:	Copies all files that begin with rep and end in a PCX extension to drive A
DEL	DEL *.*	Deletes all files
DISKCOPY	DISKCOPY *. a:	Copies all files with no extension to drive A
PRINT	PRINT ???.txt	Prints all files with three characters in the name and a TXT extension
XCOPY	XCOPY ??? a:	Copies all files with three-letter names to drive A
MOVE	MOVE mydata .?ak c:\database	Moves all files named my-data having an extension ending in ak to the DATABASE directory

Example Wild Cards

Wild Card	Specifies
.	All files
*.EXE	All files with an EXE extension
*.	All files with no extension, also lists directories
REP*.PCX	All files beginning with REP and having a PCX extension
REP*.*	All files beginning with REP
???	All three-letter files with no extension
???.TXT	All three-letter files with a TXT extension
??DATA.123	All six-letter files ending in DATA and having a 123 extension
MYDATA.?AK	All files beginning with MYDATA and with an extension ending in AK

Troubleshooting

◆ Be careful when using wild cards to delete files. You may delete more than you intended. Check out the command first with the DIR command.

◆ If you accidently delete files by using the DEL command and wild-card characters, you may be able to recover them by using the UNDELETE command. See "Deleting and Undeleting Files" for more information.

When you want to see a list of the files, use the DIR command.

The DIR command doesn't deal just with directories, although the name of the command would lead you to think so. The DIR command displays a list of the directory contents. When you want to see what files you have in a directory, use the DIR command.

TIP

You can use the MORE command to view only one screen of the directory at a time. Type |**MORE** (pipe more) at the end of the command; you don't need a space to separate the pipe and the last character of the command; for example, to list one screen of the directory at a time, type **DIR|MORE** and press Enter.

Sorting Files

Normally, when you list a directory, you display the files in no particular order. If you're looking for particular files, your search can be tedious. By using certain switches with the DIR command, you can sort the order in which your files list.

TIP

You can combine the sort switches to list files alphabetically by name and numerically by file size, for example.

Suppose that you want to look at the document files you created in late July and early August. Searching through a large list could take quite a bit of time, and you still may miss some of the files you're searching for. By using a sort order switch, you can list the files chronologically by date and find the exact files you need.

Sort Options

By using the appropriate switch, here's what you can do:

◆ Sort files alphabetically by name. Use this option when you know the name of the file.

◆ Sort files alphabetically by file extension. Use this option when you know the type of file—but may not remember the exact name.

◆ Sort files chronologically by date and time. Use this option when you know when you saved a file but may not be sure of the name.

◆ Sort files numerically by file size. Good for when you're cleaning off your hard disk and trying to see whether you have any really big files you can delete.

◆ View just the file names—no dates, file sizes, and so on—in a directory.

List Files

1. Change to the directory that contains the files you want to list.

2. Type **DIR**. Use wild cards to list only certain files.

   To display only BAK files, for example, type **DIR *.bak**.

   To display all files with the file name CONFIG, type **DIR config.***.

3. Press Enter.

Sort Files

1. Change to the directory that contains the files you want to sort.

2. Type **DIR** <*order:switch*>.

3. Press Enter.

Here are some examples:

Type	To Sort
DIR /O:N	Alphabetically by name
DIR /O:D	Chronologically by date and time

```
C:\>dir *.bak

 Volume in drive C is WEP_0
 Volume Serial Number is 1BD5-2956
 Directory of C:\

AUTOEXEC BAK        221 03-16-93   8:31p
CONFIG   BAK        238 01-30-93  10:52a
        2 file(s)          459 bytes
                     17604608 bytes free

C:\>dir config.*

 Volume in drive C is WEP_0
```

Specify the files you want to list using switches and/or wild cards with the directory command.

```
 Volume in drive C is WEP_0
 Volume Serial Number is 1BD5-2956
 Directory of C:\DOS

.              <DIR>       11-08-89   3:02p
..             <DIR>       11-08-89   3:02p
4201     CPI       6404 04-09-91   5:00a
4208     CPI        720 04-09-91   5:00a
5202     CPI        395 04-09-91   5:00a
ANSI     SYS       9065 03-10-93   6:00a
APPEND   EXE      10774 03-10-93   6:00a
ASSIGN   COM       6399 04-09-91   5:00a
```

Using DIR /O:N to sort alphabetically by name.

```
 Volume in drive C is WEP_0
 Volume Serial Number is 1BD5-2956
 Directory of C:\DOS

REBOOT   COM         16 03-15-87   2:29p
.              <DIR>       11-08-89   3:02p
..             <DIR>       11-08-89   3:02p
EDLIN    EXE      12642 04-09-91   5:00a
MIRROR   COM      18169 04-09-91   5:00a
SMARTDRV SYS       8335 04-09-91   5:00a
PACKING  LST       2650 04-09-91   5:00a
RECOVER  EXE       9146 04-09-91   5:00a
```

Using DIR /O:D to sort chronologically by date and time.

Copying and Moving Files

If you want to make a copy of your files—to give the files to someone else or keep an extra copy—use the COPY command. To move files from one directory to another—to help you organize files, or if a file somehow ended up in the wrong directory—use the MOVE command.

You may want to copy a file for many reasons. You may want to give a copy of your file to a co-worker, or you may want to take a copy of your file home to work on. Sometimes you make a copy of a file so that you can change the data and create a new, yet similar file. If you want a spare copy of files, you can also make copies. Whatever your reason for wanting to copy a file, you can easily accomplish this task at the DOS command line. If a COPY operation will overwrite an existing file, DOS asks you if you want to continue.

MOVE is similar to COPY. First, the original files are copied to the new directory, and then DOS deletes the originals. Use the MOVE command when you put the files in the wrong directory or when you create a new directory and want to keep files in the new directory. If a MOVE operation will overwrite an existing file, DOS asks you if you want to continue.

Copying Files

You can type and use the COPY command in several ways. Here are the most common:

◆ You can copy a file to a new location (a different directory or drive) using the same name.

◆ You can copy a file to the same location, using a new file name.

◆ You can use wild cards to copy sets of files. Sometimes you may want to copy all files in a directory to a floppy disk or another directory. This also works with copying files from one floppy disk to another. Use the wild cards (*.*) to accomplish the copy.

Other Copy Options

You can use other copy options in special circumstances:

◆ The COPY command includes an optional switch (/v), which verifies that the copied file was transferred correctly. Use this switch when you want to be extra cautious about the copied file.

◆ You can copy a file to a device—printer, modem, and so on—using the device name after the command. To print a file, for example, you can copy it to the print device by typing **COPY** *mydoc.txt prn*, where prn is the print device.

◆ You can use the COPY command to combine several similar files—such as combining word processing files to other word processing files—into one new file, without altering the original files. Although this technique works best with ASCII files, you can use it on other text files as well. Avoid using the COPY command to combine files that have a lot of text formatting—such as various font sizes, graphics boxes, screens, footers, and so on. Formatted pages may not combine into a readable document.

To combine two or more files by using the COPY command, you enter the command, the file names to be combined (the *source* files) joined with a plus (+) sign, and the new name of a file that will hold the combined files (the *target*). If you don't specify a target, DOS combines the source files and saves them in the first document you specify. To combine NEWS01.DOC and NEWS02.DOC into a new file named NEWS93.DOC, for example, type the following command:

**COPY news01.doc+news02.doc
    news93.doc**

Moving Files

When you have a file that is out of place in its current directory, you can move it to a new directory by using the MOVE command.

Moving a file, unlike using COPY, means that the file transfers from one directory to another, and a copy is not left behind. Moving files enables you to keep your directory structure organized and similar files together. Suppose that you saved a database file in your document directory by mistake. You can easily move the file to your database directory so that all like files remain together.

Guidelines for Moving Files

Here are some guidelines to consider when moving files:

◆ You can use the MOVE command to move files from one directory to another.

◆ If you want to, you can also use MOVE to rename files as you move them.

◆ DOS enables you to use wild-card characters with the MOVE command. You can move a set of files with the same extension or similar names, for example.

◆ The MOVE command requires a *source* (the file to be moved) and a *target* (the new location). You can alternatively specify a new file name with the target location if the source is only one file.

◆ You must specify a path for the source or the target, or both. If you don't specify a path in the source or the target, you'll copy the source file over the target file.

more ▶

FILE MANAGEMENT

Copy a File

1. Change to the directory that contains the files you want to copy.

2. Type **COPY** *<filename> <destination>*.

   For the file name, you can type the name of one file or use wild cards to specify a group of files.

   For the destination, you can type a new file name, a directory name, a directory name and a file name, or a drive letter.

3. Press Enter.

Here are some examples:

◆ To copy a file from one directory to another using the same name, type the following at the system prompt, and then press Enter.

   COPY *<filename> <directory name>*

◆ To copy NEWS01.DOC to the directory REPORT05.DOC, for example, type the following at the system prompt and press Enter:

   COPY data01.doc c:\repsales

◆ To copy files from one disk to another using the same name, type the following at the system prompt and press Enter:

   COPY *<filename> <drive>*

```
C:\>cd document

C:\DOCUMENT>copy data01.doc c:\repsales
        1 file(s) copied

C:\DOCUMENT>
```

Copying the file means the original file is located in the C:\DOCUMENT directory and a duplicate of the original file is located in the C:\REPSALES directory.

```
C:\DOCUMENT>copy *.* a:
DATA01.DOC
        1 file(s) copied

C:\DOCUMENT>a:

A:\>dir

 Volume in drive A has no label
 Volume Serial Number is 1458-14FE
 Directory of A:\

SUBDIR   1   <DIR>     08-20-93  12:00a
SALESMEN DOC       655 08-21-93  12:00p
SALEFORM DOC       209 08-21-93  12:04p
DATA01   DOC       655 08-21-93  12:00p
        4 file(s)       1519 bytes
                     689152 bytes free

A:\>
```

Copy all files in the C:\DOCUMENT directory to drive A; list the directory of drive A to see the copied file.

◆ To copy all DOC files from drive C to drive A, type the following at the C:\> prompt:

COPY *.DOC a:

◆ To copy a file to a new file name, type the following at the system prompt and press Enter:

COPY _\<oldname\> \<newname\>_

◆ To make a copy of the file NEWS01.DOC and call it NEWS02.DOC, for example, type the following and press Enter:

COPY NEWS01.DOC NEWS02.DOC

Troubleshooting

If you get the error message File cannot be copied onto itself, you tried to copy a file to the same disk and directory. Check your spelling of the file name and command, check to see that you didn't omit part of the path, then try the command again.

more ▶

```
A:\>copy news01.doc news02.doc
        1 file(s) copied

A:\>dir

 Volume in drive A has no label
 Volume Serial Number is 1458-14FE
 Directory of A:\

SUBDIR   1   <DIR>      08-20-93  12:00a
SALESMEN DOC         655 08-21-93  12:00p
SALEFORM DOC         209 08-21-93  12:04p
DATA01   DOC         655 08-21-93  12:00p
NEWS01   DOC         655 08-21-93  12:00p
NEWS02   DOC         655 08-21-93  12:00p
        6 file(s)         2829 bytes
                      687104 bytes free

A:\>
```

NEWS01.DOC and NEWS02.DOC are the same file but with different names.

Move a File

1. Change to the directory that contains the file(s) you want to move.

```
C:\BUSINESS>move news93.doc a:
c:\business\news93.doc => a:\news93.doc [ok]
```

DOS moves the file to drive A; therefore, DATA01.DOC no longer exists in the C:\BUSINESS directory.

2. Type **MOVE** *<filename>* *<path>*. For the file name, you can type the name of a single file or use wild cards to specify a group of files. For the path, you can type a directory name or drive. You can also specify a new name as part of the path.

3. Press Enter.

Here are some examples:

◆ To move a file from the current directory to another drive, keeping the same file name, type the following and press Enter:

MOVE *<filename>* *<drivepath>*

◆ To move the file DATA01.DOC from C:\DOCUMENT to the root directory of the A drive, for example, type the following at the C:\DOCUMENT> prompt and press Enter:

MOVE data01.doc a:

◆ To move a file and rename it, type the following and press Enter:

MOVE *<filename>* *<drivepath>*
   <newname>

◆ To move NEWS02.DOC from C:\BUSINESS to C:\REPORT05 and rename it NEWS.DOC, type the following at the C:\BUSINESS> prompt and press Enter:

**MOVE news02.doc
   c:\report05\news.doc**

◆ To move a group of files to another directory without changing to the directory, type the following and press Enter:

MOVE *<filename>* *<path>*

◆ For the file name, type the path to the files. To move all REP files from the BUSINESS directory to the REPORT05 directory, for example, type the following at the system prompt and press Enter:

**MOVE C:\BUSINESS *.REP
   C:\REPORT05**

```
C:\BUSINESS>move news93.doc a:
c:\business\news93.doc => a:\news93.doc [ok]

C:\BUSINESS>move news02.doc c:\report05\news.doc
c:\business\news02.doc => c:\report05\news.doc [ok]

C:\BUSINESS>
```

Move documents from one directory to another.

```
C:\>move c:\business\*.rep c:\report05
c:\business\08-19-93.rep => c:\report05\08-19-93.rep [ok]
c:\business\08-20-93.rep => c:\report05\08-20-93.rep [ok]

C:\>
```

All files with an REP extension no longer exist in the C:\BUSINESS directory.

Troubleshooting

If you move a file to a directory that already contains a file of the same name, DOS overwrites that file with the moved file.

If you want to copy files and directories, even empty directories, the COPY command won't work; but the XCOPY command will.

XCOPY copies files, directories, and subdirectories, making a perfect copy of your directory structure; you don't have to stop what you're doing to create directories before copying files. In addition, XCOPY enables you to copy selected files, directories, subdirectories, and their files; to update specific files; and more. You can use XCOPY to back up files to a floppy disk or to transfer files to another computer. Finally, you can use the XCOPY command to copy files to a disk and when the disk is full, insert a new disk and resume copying.

Suppose that you and a co-worker need the same files to complete your work. The files are in your word processing directories C:\WORD5\DOCS and C:\WORD5\REPORTS. You can copy both subdirectories and the files within them to a floppy disk with XCOPY and hand them to your co-worker in a matter of minutes. Your co-worker can then quickly transfer the files to another computer with the XCOPY command. You can even XCOPY those files again once they're updated and use XCOPY to replace only the files that changed on your co-worker's computer.

XCOPY not only gives you many options for copying files and directories, it also copies them faster than the standard COPY command. XCOPY first reads a group of the files to be copied into memory and then copies them to the target. The result is faster copying and less work for you.

Effectively Using XCOPY

Here's how you can use XCOPY:

◆ Use XCOPY to move an entire directory structure from one disk to another.

◆ Copy only files that are marked with an Archive attribute.

◆ Copy only files that have been changed since the date you specify.

◆ Copy subdirectories to the target, even if they are empty on the source.

◆ Verify the copy.

TIP The XCOPY command is limited in that it can't copy hidden files and it won't overwrite read-only files.

Using XCOPY

XCOPY is a versatile command that can copy files and directories to another directory or disk. As with the COPY command, you must specify a source and target with the XCOPY command. In addition, there are many switches you can use with XCOPY that enable you to specify which files or directories to copy, and how they will be copied.

You can use paths and wild cards with the XCOPY command.

Use XCOPY

1. At the system prompt, type the following:

XCOPY *<source>* *<target>*

For the source, you can type the name of a file, a file spec (using wild cards), or a directory name.

2. Press Enter.

XCOPY Command Switches

Here's a list of useful switches you can use with XCOPY:

◆ **/a** copies only files that are marked with the Archive attribute, leaving the attribute of the source unchanged.

◆ **/d:<date>** copies only files created or altered on or after the date you specify.

◆ **/e** copies subdirectories even if they are empty in the source. You must use the /e switch with the /s switch.

◆ **/m** copies only files that are marked with the Archive attribute, turning off the attribute of the source files.

◆ **/p** prompts for confirmation before each file is copied. Press Y to continue copying; press N to skip the file in question.

◆ **/s** copies all subdirectories in the source that are not empty, plus the files within the subdirectories.

◆ **/v** verifies that the source files were copied correctly.

```
A:\>xcopy *.doc c:\report05
Reading source file(s)...
7EWS01.DOC
BROCHURE.DOC
INVOICE1.DOC
COSTGOOD.DOC
7EWS02.DOC
DATA01.DOC
        6 File(s) copied

A:\>
```

Copying a set of files using wild-card characters.

```
A:\>xcopy a:\business c:\business
Does BUSINESS specify a file name
or directory name on the target
(F = file, D = directory)?d
Reading source file(s)...
A:\BUSINESS\BROCHURE.DOC
A:\BUSINESS\INVOICE1.DOC
A:\BUSINESS\COSTGOOD.DOC
A:\BUSINESS\DATA01.REP
A:\BUSINESS\DATA02.REP
A:\BUSINESS\SALEMARK.123
A:\BUSINESS\SALEDELL.123
A:\BUSINESS\DATA03.REP
A:\BUSINESS\08-19-93.REP
A:\BUSINESS\!!#$&&@@.DOC
A:\BUSINESS\!@!@!@##.DOC
A:\BUSINESS\DATA01.DOC
A:\BUSINESS\SALESREP.123
A:\BUSINESS\REPORT.DOC
A:\BUSINESS\08-20-93.REP
        15 File(s) copied

A:\>
```

Copying an entire directory.

When you're ready to clean up your disk, use the DELETE command to erase files you no longer need or want. If you make a mistake, use the UNDELETE command to undelete the files.

Because storage space is not unlimited on either a hard disk or a floppy disk, you will most likely need to delete files at some point. You may also want to delete files you have a back up for; or you may have obsolete files on your disk you no longer need. If you delete files you need or files you didn't really want to delete, you can use the UNDELETE command to undelete them.

Deleting Files

You can delete files to free up disk space with the DELETE command; when you delete a file, DOS can no longer access that file. You may, however, be able to recover all or part of the deleted file by using the UNDELETE command.

Suppose that you just completed a large annual report for your company. You backed up your files to tape, printed out hard copy, and have no further reason to keep the file on your hard disk. If you delete the files on your hard disk, you free up disk space for your next project.

TIP

If there's even the slightest chance you will someday refer to the files you are about to delete, copy those files to a floppy disk or make a backup. For more information on making backups, see "Configuring for a Backup."

*Caution: Be very careful when using the DEL command with wildcard characters; it's easy to type **DEL *.*** —meaning delete all files in this directory—and press Enter before you realize what you did. Luckily, DOS always prompts you for confirmation before deleting all files; but if you aren't paying attention, you may respond with Yes before you realize it.*

Ways To Delete Files
Here are the ways to delete files:

◆ You can first change to the directory that contains the files, and then type the DELETE command. Or you can use a path to specify the location of the file if you're not in the directory that contains the file.

◆ You can use wild cards to delete more than one file at a time. If you want to delete all files, use the wild card *.*.

◆ If you are deleting a number of files at one time, consider using the /p switch with the DELETE command. The /p switch prompts you for confirmation before DOS deletes each file. Press Y to delete or N to skip the file without deleting it.

◆ Although the DELETE command does not delete or remove a directory, you can use it to delete all the files in a directory. From the parent directory, enter the command and the name of the subdirectory. To delete the files in the subdirectory REPORTS, for example, from the parent directory of REPORTS, type **DEL reports**. The REPORTS directory will still display, but it will contain no files.

Note: The DELETE command does not erase files with attributes. Attributes are special conditions you can place on a file—such as read-only, hidden, or system. For more information about file attributes, see "Assigning File Attributes."

What Happens When a File Is Deleted?

When you delete a file from a disk, DOS does not really erase the file. Instead, it locates the file in the directory and marks it as deleted. The space the deleted file takes up becomes available and is used when you save a new file or add to a file. If you use UNDELETE before you save another file to the disk, you can recover most of, if not all of, the deleted file.

Undeleting Files

If you accidentally delete some files, you may be able to get them back—if you act quickly. Use the UNDELETE command immediately by entering it at the system prompt. You can specify a file or use wild cards to specify a set of files; however, if no files are specified, DOS attempts to undelete all deleted files in the directory.

If you do not undelete a file before other data has been stored over it, you may not be able to undelete the file. UNDELETE prompts you if only part of the file is available; and asks if you want to continue. If the file is unrecoverable, UNDELETE notifies you that the file cannot be undeleted.

TIP

When you are using wild cards to delete files, it is a good idea to first test the file spec (the combination of file name and wild cards) with the DIR command. Before you delete all files that start with D with the command DEL D*.*, for example, test the command by typing **DIR d*.***. Be sure that you want to delete all the files that match the specified wild cards.

more ▶

Delete a File

1. Change to the directory that contains the file(s) you want to delete.

2. Type **DEL** *<filename>*. For the file name, you can type the name of one file or use wild cards to delete several.

3. Press Enter.

Here are some examples:

◆ To delete the file NEWS.TXT in the REPORT05 directory, type the following at the current directory system prompt:

DEL news.txt

Troubleshooting

If you accidentally delete files, try using the UNDELETE command to restore them. If you use the UNDELETE command as soon after the accidental deletion as possible, you'll be more likely to get back all, or at least part of, your files.

```
C:\>cd report05

C:\REPORT05>del news.txt

C:\REPORT05>
```

Deleting a file in a directory.

```
C:\REPORT05>del *.*
All files in directory will be deleted!
Are you sure (Y/N)?
```

Are you really sure you want to delete all of the files in this directory? Press N for No if you're not sure.

Undelete a File

1. Change to the directory of the undeleted files.

2. Enter the command **UNDELETE**.

3. Press Enter.

   The UNDELETE screen appears, notifying you of how many files are deleted and how many can be recovered.

4. At the Undelete (Y/N) prompt, press Y to undelete the file or N to skip the file.

   If you press Y, UNDELETE asks that you type the first character for the file.

5. Enter the character.

   UNDELETE notifies you that it has successfully undeleted the file.

6. Continue to undelete or skip files. If you want to cancel the UNDELETE program, press Ctrl+C.

```
C:\BUDGET>undelete

UNDELETE - A delete protection facility
Copyright (C) 1987-1993 Central Point Software, Inc.
All rights reserved.

Directory: C:\BUDGET
File Specifications: *.*

     Delete Sentry control file not found.

     Deletion-tracking file not found.

     MS-DOS directory contains      5 deleted files.
     Of those,     5 files may be recovered.

Using the MS-DOS directory method.

     ?ALES01  REP        114  6-07-93  1:44p  ....  Undelete (Y/N)?y
     Please type the first character for ?ALES01 .REP: s

File successfully undeleted.

     ?ALES    REP        110  6-07-93  1:45p  ....  Undelete (Y/N)?
```

The UNDELETE screen.

FILE MANAGEMENT

If you aren't sure what a file contains, you may be able to display its contents with DOS. You can also use DOS to print text files.

Sometimes you're not sure what your files contain. Certain types of files, in particular README files, can be displayed. Other types, like program files, can't be displayed.

Also, you can use DOS to print some types of files.

ASCII Files

For the most part, DOS can display only *ASCII* files. ASCII, which stands for *American Standard Code for Information Interchange*, is a standardized file format used for text files; the extension is normally TXT. ASCII files are the most common file format, used with most word processors, many spreadsheet programs, and in all configuration and batch files.

DOS can print ASCII files as well as some other file types—those files you save within a word processing or spreadsheet program, for example, with a PRN extension.

Viewing Files

Many programs include text files that contain information that does not appear in the reference manual or updates for products or special tasks. You can read text files by using the TYPE command, if the text file is in ASCII.

If you use the TYPE command on a file that is not an ASCII file, DOS will try to display

it anyway. An executable file would display as unreadable graphical characters, for example, and you would probably hear a series of beeps. Viewing an executable file may also lock up your computer.

 TIP
You can also print a copy of the file by typing **>Prn** after the command to view the file.

Printing Files

You can send one file or several files to the printer and continue working; DOS will print the file(s) while you continue your work. This process is called *printing in the background.*

The PRINT command sends data to the printer as the print queue empties. The print queue contains a list of files to be printed. You can print almost any file with the Print command; however, text (ASCII) files present the most readable output.

Suppose that you want to print the README.TXT file that is located in the DOS directory. You can print the file to your printer from the system prompt by using the PRINT command.

When you enter the PRINT command followed by a file name, DOS places the file in the Print queue and prints the file.

Files are printed in the order you enter them at the system prompt. When printing multiple files, those files must all be on the same disk drive.

The Print Queue

If you enter the PRINT command by itself, a list of all files in the print queue appears. The queue lists the files in the order they will print, beginning with the file currently being printed. If there are any errors or problems with the printing process, an error message appears.

You can also use switches to control the PRINT command. You can use the following common switches with the PRINT command:

◆ You can cancel the printing of particular files with the /c switch. Enter the file name and then the switch.

◆ The Print command's default is to place all files in the Print queue. If, however, you cancel the printing of a file, you must use the /p, or Print Queue, switch to add subsequent files to the queue.

◆ You can also terminate printing with the /t switch. The /t switch removes files from the queue, including the file being printed.

The Printer Port

When you enter the PRINT command followed by a file name, DOS asks for the name of the port to which your printer is connected. That port can be a parallel port, in which case the DOS device value is LPT1, LPT2, or LPT3. If the port is a serial port, the device value is COM1, COM2, COM3, and so on. The default port is LPT1; if LPT1 is your printer port, press Enter to continue.

You can only specify the parameters for printing—the port, for example—the first time you enter the PRINT command. Thereafter, you only enter the files to be printed.

Printing the Screen

To print the contents of the screen, you can press Shift+Print Screen. Shift+Print Screen prints the screen shown at the time you press the key combination. Another method of printing what's on-screen is to press Ctrl+Print Screen. DOS prints everything that displays on-screen from that point on until you press Ctrl+Print Screen again.

Printing a Directory List or other Output

To print the output from a command—such as the DIR, TREE, or CHKDSK (Check Disk) command—type the following at the system prompt and press Enter:

<COMMAND> > prn

To print the directory, for example, type **DIR > prn**.

You can also use the COPY command to print a text file, by "copying" it to the printer. Use the following syntax:

COPY <drivepath><filename> prn

To print a file called REPORT.DOC on drive A, for example, type the following at the system prompt and press Enter:

COPY a:report.doc prn

more ▶

View a File

1. Change to the directory that contains the file you want to view.

2. Type the following at the command prompt:

   TYPE *<filename.extension>*

3. Press Enter.

To view the README.TXT file in the DOS directory, for example, type the following at the command prompt and press enter:

TYPE readme.txt

To read the text one screen at a time, type the following and press Enter:

TYPE readme.txt|more

Troubleshooting

If you want to stop the text file in the middle of scrolling to view a particular screen or at a —more— prompt, press Ctrl+C.

```
README.TXT

NOTES ON MS-DOS 6
=================

This file provides important information not included in the
MICROSOFT MS-DOS 6 USER'S GUIDE or in MS-DOS Help.

This file is divided into the following major sections:

1. Setup
2. MemMaker and Memory Management
3. Windows
4. Hardware Compatibility with MS-DOS 6
5. Microsoft Programs
6. Third-Party Programs
7. DoubleSpace

If the subject you need information about doesn't appear in
this file, you might find it in one of the following text
files included with MS-DOS:

* OS2.TXT, which describes how to remove and save data on your
-- More --
```

\README.TXT viewed with the TYPE|MORE command.

Shortcut Keys	
Ctrl+S	Pauses scrolling
Pause	Pauses scrolling

Print a File

1. Change to the directory that contains the file you want to print.

2. At the system prompt, type the following:

   PRINT *<filename>*

   For the file name, you can type the name of a single file or use wild cards to print several files.

3. Press Enter.

   DOS displays a prompt:

   ```
   Name of list device [PRN]:
   ```

4. Press Enter to accept the default, LPT1, or enter the correct port assignment.

View the Print Queue

1. Type **PRINT**.

2. Press Enter.

Troubleshooting

◆ If you want to stop printing, enter the following command:

   print /t

◆ If DOS displays an error message, refer to Appendix B for more information.

```
C:\>cd document

C:\DOCUMENT>print news01.doc
Name of list device [PRN]:
Resident part of PRINT installed


  C:\DOCUMENT\NEWS01.DOC is currently being printed

C:\DOCUMENT>
```

Enter the print command and press Enter to accept the default. DOS prints in the background as you continue your work.

```
C:\DOCUMENT>print *.doc


  C:\DOCUMENT\SALESMEN.DOC is currently being printed
  C:\DOCUMENT\SALEFORM.DOC is in queue
  C:\DOCUMENT\NEWS01.DOC is in queue
  C:\DOCUMENT\NEWS02.DOC is in queue

C:\DOCUMENT>
```

Use wildcards to print a set of files.

```
C:\COLLAGE>print *.pcx
PRINT queue is full


  C:\COLLAGE\21FIG02.PCX is currently being printed
  C:\COLLAGE\21FIG03.PCX is in queue
  C:\COLLAGE\21FIG04.PCX is in queue
  C:\COLLAGE\21FIG05.PCX is in queue
  C:\COLLAGE\21FIG06.PCX is in queue
  C:\COLLAGE\21FIG07.PCX is in queue
  C:\COLLAGE\21FIG08.PCX is in queue
  C:\COLLAGE\21FIG09.PCX is in queue
  C:\COLLAGE\21FIG10.PCX is in queue
  C:\COLLAGE\21FIG11.PCX is in queue

C:\COLLAGE>print
PRINT queue is empty
```

Viewing the print queue. If the queue is empty, DOS prints the message PRINT queue is empty.

FILE MANAGEMENT

Finding one file you created two months ago in a sea of various file types can be near to impossible. With DOS, however, you can find files in this "sea," even if you only know part of the file name.

DOS enables you to search your hard disk or floppy disk for files you need. As long as you know a character or two contained in the file name, you can find the file. If you know the file name, you may want to search for the directory that holds the file. You can search one directory or all directories on the disk.

Suppose that you saved a memo to your boss four months ago and now you can't find it. A common problem is lost files. You know you saved that file, but where? Surely it was in a directory you just knew you would remember. What about those expense forms you print once every six months? Didn't you copy those files to the FORMS directory? Now you can't find them. Don't panic. If you know the name of the file, or any part of the file name, you can search for the file.

Finding a File

To find a file on your disk, you use the DIR command. After the command, you type the search criterion and the search switch (/s). The search criterion can be a specific file name or you can use wild-card characters (* and ?) to fill in the part of the name you are unsure of.

Remember that memo you were looking for? You know there are hundreds of memos stored on your hard disk; but your memo has the initials JL included in the extension. Use that information to search for the memo by entering the following command at the system prompt in the root directory: dir *.JL?. DOS searches the entire disk and issues a report of every file it finds meeting the search criterion you specified. Entering the command at the root directory instructs DOS to search the entire disk for your file.

To conduct a partial search, you enter the command in the directory you want to search. Suppose you're looking for expense forms that have EXP at the beginning of the file name. You're sure those expense forms are in the FORMS directory, you just can't find the file name when scrolling through the directory list. Change to the FORMS directory and enter the following command: **DIR exp?????.* /s**. DOS searches for the file names and lists any entries it finds.

Find a File

To search the entire disk for a file, enter the following at the system prompt of the root directory and press Enter:

DIR *<filename>* /S

To find a file that starts with cost, for example, type the following and press Enter:

DIR cost*.* /S

```
C:\>dir cost*.* /s

 Volume in drive C is WEP_0
 Volume Serial Number is 1BD5-2956

Directory of C:\BUSINESS

COSTGOOD DOC         7 06-04-93    2:28p
        1 file(s)          7 bytes

Directory of C:\DOCUMENT

COSTS        <DIR>        06-05-93  11:09a
        1 file(s)          0 bytes

Directory of C:\REPORT05

COSTGOOD DOC         7 06-04-93    2:28p
        1 file(s)          7 bytes

Total files listed:
        3 file(s)         14 bytes
                  17522688 bytes free

C:\>
```

DOS searches the disk and displays a report telling you where each matching file is found.

Directory found

Directory and file found

Total report

FILE MANAGEMENT

Finding Files 69

If you have two files the same length and you wonder if they are the same file, you can find out with FILE COMPARE. If you want to be doubly sure that a command is carried out without errors, use the VERIFY command.

FILE COMPARE can save you the time and effort of printing and reviewing similar files to see if they are exactly the same. FILE COMPARE checks each text file, line by line, and reports any differences on-screen.

Verifying files isn't the same as comparing, but it may be important to you if you are working with critical information.

Comparing Files

Suppose that you find several floppy disks with files you believe to be the same, but you aren't sure. If the files are the same, you can delete some of them so that you have more disk space on the floppy. Use FILE COMPARE to find out.

To compare two files, you enter the command and the two file names; you can use FILE COMPARE in the current directory or use a path. You can use wild-card characters with the FILE COMPARE command; however, FILE COMPARE compares the files in sets, as is the case with any command using wild-card characters.

Compare Switches

There are two switches you'll find particularly useful with the FILE COMPARE command:

/c	Ignores case in alphabetic characters
/n	Lists a line number beside lines in the report

When using the switches with FILE COMPARE, place the switches between the command and the first file name.

If FILE COMPARE checks 100 lines without finding a match, it displays a message that the files are too different to continue the comparison.

Verifying Files

When you work with critically important data, you can turn on the Verify feature in DOS to ensure that your data is written without error to your disk.

The VERIFY command either turns on or off the Verify setting. When you turn on Verify, DOS checks to make sure that data is not written to a bad sector of your disk; this command is particularly effective with commands such as COPY, BACKUP, RESTORE, XCOPY, DISKCOPY, and REPLACE. Using VERIFY slows the execution of these commands; you may want to use VERIFY only when working with critical files.

The COPY command offers a Verify switch (/v) to verify that the files were copied correctly. If you have turned on VERIFY with the Verify command, you do not need to use the /v switch with the COPY command.

It's a good idea to turn on Verify so you're sure each sector of the backup is written without error to the backup disk.

Compare Files

To compare two files, ignoring case, type the following at the system prompt and press Enter:

FC /C *<filename1> <filename2>*

To compare the files SALESREP.TXT and SALES01.REP, for example, type the following and press Enter:

FC /C salesrep.txt sales01.rep

Troubleshooting

If you want to stop the file comparison, press Ctrl+C.

Use Verify

To turn on Verify, type the following at the system prompt and press Enter:

verify on

To turn off Verify, type the following at the system prompt and press Enter:

verify off

To check the status of Verify, type the following at the system prompt and press Enter:

verify

```
C:\BUDGET>fc /c salesrep.txt sales01.rep
Comparing files SALESREP.TXT and SALES01.REP
FC: no differences encountered


C:\BUDGET>
```

DOS finds no differences between the files.

```
C:\>fc c:\budget\sales.rep c:\budget\sales01.rep
Comparing files C:\BUDGET\SALES.REP and C:\BUDGET\SALES01.REP
***** C:\BUDGET\SALES.REP
Sales Report--1992
1992 is a record year for Humble Opinions.
January
February 3, 1992
March
***** C:\BUDGET\SALES01.REP
Sales Report--1993
1993 is a record year for Humble Opinions.
January
February
March
*****
```

DOS reports the differences between the files.

Check status of Verify

Turn on Verify

Turn off Verify

FILE MANAGEMENT

Use REPLACE as a way to update existing files and to copy new files to a disk or directory.

The REPLACE command is similar to the COPY command, but more selective. Use REPLACE to copy files from one disk to another or from one directory to another. You can use the REPLACE command to replace existing files, add files, or update files to a disk or directory. You must be careful with the REPLACE command, however; REPLACE removes the files you're replacing and overwrites them with the new files. You can never get the replaced files back.

Suppose that you do the same report for your company every six months; there are some files from the old report you use, but most files are updated. Rather than saving your new files to another floppy disk, you can use the REPLACE command on the old floppy disk. You replace some of the old files with new files of the same name, update some of the old files, and you add some new files to the disk. All of this is accomplished quickly and easily with the REPLACE command.

With the REPLACE command, you can selectively copy files to directories and floppy disks. You can use wild cards to replace sets of files; you can use paths, as well.

Replace Switches

The REPLACE command has several switches you can use; the switches enable you to designate which files are copied to the target.

Switch	Name	Description
/A	Adds	Copies only source files that do not already exist on the target drive or directory. You cannot use /A with /U or /S.
/P	Prompts	Prompts for confirmation before replacing.
/S	Replaces	Replaces each file on the target directory with a file in the source when the file names match. You cannot use /S with /A.
/U	Updates	Copies source files with a more recent date and time than target files with the same name. You cannot use /U with /A.

Caution: REPLACE can be dangerous to your filing system if you don't use it carefully. DOS rapidly replaces files when you enter the command; you could lose valuable files you don't want to overwrite. You can use the REPLACE command successfully, however, if you exercise caution.

First, limit the destination path when replacing files. Don't search the entire disk if you know the files you want to replace are contained in one or two specific directories. Second, use the /P switch if you have any doubts. REPLACE searches and then asks your permission before it replaces. This process takes a little longer, but at least you know your data is safe. Third, you can use the /U switch to compare the files' date and time stamps. That way, only the files older than the source files are replaced. Finally, you can use all of these precautionary measures and feel safe using the REPLACE command.

Replace a File

To replace files on the target with new versions of the same name, type the following at the system prompt of the current drive and directory and press Enter:

REPLACE <source> <target>

For example, to replace your backup of the BUDGET directory on drive A with the revised documents on drive C, enter the following:

REPLACE c:\budget*.* a:\budget

Troubleshooting

Before you use the REPLACE command, make backups of the files on your target disk or in the target directory. You can't undo any actions taken by the REPLACE command.

```
A:\BUDGET>replace c:\budget\*.*

Replacing A:\BUDGET\SALES01.REP

Replacing A:\BUDGET\SALES.REP

Replacing A:\BUDGET\SALES.TXT

Replacing A:\BUDGET\SALES01.TXT

4 file(s) replaced

A:\BUDGET>
```

Replacing files.

```
A:\>replace a:\budget\*.* c:\budget /a

Adding C:\BUDGET\SALES01.REP

1 file(s) added

A:\>
```

To add any files in the source that don't exist on the target, use the /A switch.

```
C:\>replace c:\budget\*.* a:\budget /u

Replacing A:\BUDGET\SALE22.DOC

1 file(s) replaced

C:\>
```

Use the /U switch to replace only those files on the target that are older than the files of the same name on the source.

Have you ever wished that you could make a file invisible or unalterable? You can with file attributes.

You can control your files by using attributes. File attributes are conditions, or qualifiers, you place on a file that restricts others from using it. You can place a read-only attribute on a file to protect it from others' changes, for example. A file with a read-only attribute can be opened and viewed but not altered by DOS commands such as DEL.

Another attribute that protects files is the Hidden attribute. A file that is hidden does not display with other files when you use the DIR command. The Archive attribute is used for backup purposes; it tells DOS whether a file has been changed since the last time it was backed up.

Suppose that you are the person responsible for keeping track of the account representative's commission. It's easier to keep it on computer, but other employees have access to the computer as well. To keep others from seeing your files, you can assign the Hidden attribute to them. You can also assign the Hidden attribute to a directory.

Assigning Attributes

You use the Attribute command to view, assign, and remove attributes. Here's a description of the three most commonly used attributes:

◆ *Hidden*. Any file or directory with the Hidden attribute is concealed from view with most commands—DIR, TREE,

COPY, and so on. You can view hidden files and directories by using the Attribute command.

◆ *Read-only*. A read-only file does list with the DIR command and can be copied. You cannot delete or change the file, however, without first removing the attribute. Note that you can delete a read-only file in DOS Shell; see "MS-DOS Shell" for more information.

◆ *Archive*. The Archive attribute signals certain DOS commands—such as XCOPY and BACKUP—that the file has changed or been modified. When the Archive attribute signals that the file has changed, BACKUP, for example, "knows" to include it in the new backup, which saves disk space and time. See "Configuring for Backup" for more information about backing up your files; see "Copying Files and Directories" for more information about the XCOPY command.

When assigning an attribute, you use a plus (+) sign to turn it on and a minus (–) sign to turn it off. You can assign more than one attribute to a file, and you can use wild cards to assign attributes to a set of files.

TIP

If it is not already a read-only file, assign the attribute to your COMMAND.COM file. If this file is accidentally deleted from the hard disk, your computer won't start.

Assign Attributes

To assign the read-only attribute to a file, type the following and press Enter:

ATTRIB +r *<drivepath>* **** *<filename>*

To assign the read-only attribute to the COMMAND.COM, for example, at the system prompt in the root directory of the hard drive, type the following and press Enter:

ATTRIB +r command.com

To assign the Archive attribute to all files in a directory, type the following and press Enter:

ATTRIB +a *.*

To remove an attribute, type the following and press Enter:

attrib -r *<drivepath>* **** *<filename>*

To view attributes on files, type the following and press Enter:

attrib

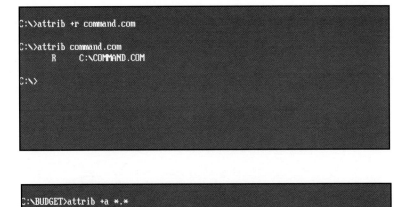

```
C:\>attrib +r command.com

C:\>attrib command.com
      R       C:\COMMAND.COM

C:\>
```

Assign a read-only attribute to your COMMAND.COM file; new users often delete this file by mistake. Without this, your computer won't boot.

```
C:\BUDGET>attrib +a *.*

C:\BUDGET>attrib
  A           C:\BUDGET\SALE22.DOC
  A           C:\BUDGET\SALES01.REP
  A           C:\BUDGET\SALES.REP
  A           C:\BUDGET\SALES.TXT
  A           C:\BUDGET\SALES01.TXT
```

Assign the Archive attribute to all files.

```
C:\BUDGET>attrib
              C:\BUDGET\SALE22.DOC
              C:\BUDGET\SALES01.REP
              C:\BUDGET\SALES.REP
              C:\BUDGET\SALES.TXT
              C:\BUDGET\SALES01.TXT

C:\BUDGET>attrib +a *.*
```

View file attributes.

As ugly a truth as it is, your computer, at some point, will not start.

All computers *lock up*—stop responding to input—at times. The reasons are many and varied: a glitch in a program, altered configuration, corrupted memory or data, mistyped commands, and many causes you'll never know. Sometimes when the computer locks up, DOS doesn't start up again. This is when you need a system disk.

Why Won't DOS Start?

Sometimes new, and even experienced, users accidently delete the COMMAND.COM from their root directory; the COMMAND.COM file loads instructions to run DOS. Without the COMMAND.COM file, DOS will not start. Problems may also occur when you change the configuration of your system or if a virus infects your system. If DOS does not start (you don't see a system prompt), you can't use your computer.

Your Information is Probably Safe

Even though the system prompt is not visible, all of your information is most likely safe. It's sort of like being locked out of your house. You can't get any of your possessions, but they are still all there. You just need a way to get into the house. That way is a system disk.

A system disk contains the COMMAND.COM. In addition, a system disk is *bootable*, meaning that it contains system files necessary to start, or boot, your system.

Creating a System Disk

You can transfer system files to a floppy disk by formatting the disk with the system (/s) switch or by using the SYS command. See "Formatting a Floppy Disk" for more information about using the /s switch.

To create a system disk with the SYS command, start with an empty, formatted floppy disk. You should use a high-density disk so that you can add files to the system disk as you learn more about DOS and its features. Enter the SYS command to transfer the system files and the COMMAND.COM to the floppy disk. Label the disk as a system disk and keep it in a safe place. It's important to test your system disk by placing it in the floppy drive and rebooting your computer. If the prompt displays from the floppy drive, your system disk works; if the prompt doesn't display, you need to redo the system disk. If your system disk does not work during the test, you have the opportunity to correct any problems; if it doesn't work when you really need it, you're up the creek without a paddle.

TIP

For the safety and protection of your system, use the COPY command to copy your CONFIG.SYS and AUTOEXEC.BAT files to your system disk. Other files you may want to put on this disk are listed in the table on the last page of this article. Be sure to include DBLSPACE.SYS if you need to access disks compressed with DoubleSpace.

Using a System Disk

If your computer boots and does not display a system prompt, you have to reboot—warm boot—your system with the system disk. Insert the system disk into the floppy drive and press Ctrl+Alt+Del. The system performs a normal warm boot, except that when it checks the floppy drive for a disk, it finds your system disk and boots from it instead of the hard disk. (That's why the computer always looks to drive A first—so that you can always boot from a floppy if needed.)

The system prompt appears as an A:\> or B:\> to represent the floppy drive. You can now access your hard disk by typing c: at the system prompt. You can check your directories and files and perform any DOS commands from the hard disk. Your first step is to transfer the system files back to your hard disk by using the same SYS command you use to create a system disk. Do not format your hard drive with the /s switch; you'll lose all your data.

After transferring the system files, remove the floppy disk from the drive and perform a warm boot on your computer to see if it can now boot and supply you with a system prompt. If it does, you may have solved your problem.

If your system does not boot up on its own, try booting with the system disk again and copying the CONFIG.SYS and AUTOEXEC.BAT files to your hard disk along with the system files. If your computer still does not boot on its own, you may need to have a technician check it for you.

more ▶

Create a System Disk

1. Place a clean, formatted floppy disk in the drive (preferably a high-density disk).

2. At the system prompt on the root directory, type the following:

   sys *<source> <target>*

   To transfer the system files from drive C to drive A, for example, type

   sys c: a:

3. Press Enter.

4. Copy your AUTOEXEC.BAT file to the system disk in the floppy drive by typing the following at the system prompt in the root directory of your hard drive:

   copy autoexec.bat a:

5. Press Enter.

6. Copy your CONFIG.SYS file to the system disk in the floppy drive by typing the following at the system prompt in the root directory of your hard drive:

   copy config.sys a:

7. Press Enter.

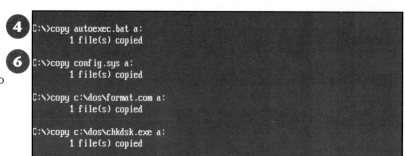

```
C:\>sys c: a:
System transferred
```

*Transferring files
from one drive to
another.*

```
4  C:\>copy autoexec.bat a:
           1 file(s) copied
6  C:\>copy config.sys a:
           1 file(s) copied

   C:\>copy c:\dos\format.com a:
           1 file(s) copied

   C:\>copy c:\dos\chkdsk.exe a:
           1 file(s) copied
```

Other Files To Put on a System Disk

File	For more information, see article in section	
C:\CONFIG.SYS	"What is a CONFIG.SYS?"	"Configuring your System"
C:\AUTOEXEC.BAT	"What is an AUTOEXEC.BAT?"	"Configuring your System"
C:\DOS\FORMAT.COM	"Formatting Your Hard Disk"	"Hard Disk Management"
C:\DOS\UNFORMAT.COM	"Unformatting Your Hard Disk"	"Hard Disk Management"
C:\DOS\CHKDSK.EXE	"Checking the Hard Disk"	"Hard Disk Management"
C:\DOS\MSAV.EXE, C:\MSAV.HLP C:\MSAVHELP.OVL, C:\MSAVIRUS.LST	"Scanning for Viruses"	"Checking for Viruses"

Troubleshooting

If you receive an error message when your system starts, refer to Appendix A, "Error Messages," for more information.

Computers, like any other type of electronic or mechanical equipment, can fail. It's not usually a question of *if*, but of *when*. To safeguard the information on your computer, make copies of the data, called *backups*.

If a hard disk fails, you can lose all of the data on that disk. Other disasters can happen, too. You could accidentally wipe off the data on your disk, or a virus could infect your system. The list is endless and the results can be catastrophic.

Don't panic. If you have a backup of your files, you can restore the data you've worked so hard to compile; all you've lost is a little time.

Using the Backup Program

Although the COPY and XCOPY commands are perfect for copying small amounts of data, DOS includes a complete backup program that can serve your needs by backing up your entire hard disk. DOS supplies two backup programs: Backup for MS-DOS and Backup for Windows, both unique to MS-DOS 6.0. For more information on Backup for Windows, see "Using DOS with Windows."

Before you can back up your data for the first time, DOS automatically runs a program—part of Backup for MS-DOS—that tests for compatibility. This compatibility, or configuring, program tests your floppy disk drives, your hard drive, the speed of your processor, and so on. DOS must run the test before you can use backup; after the compatibility test, you can safely back up the data on your hard disk.

Configuring for Backup

DOS will run the configuring program only the first time you run Backup for MS-DOS. The test checks your system and runs a test backup and compare. During the configuration process, you insert one or two floppy disks into the test drive. Use formatted disks that do not contain any information you want to keep; all information on the disk will be overwritten.

As the program tests your system, it displays various messages on your screen; it communicates with you. These messages are in the form of dialog boxes; dialog boxes require a response from you before the program can continue. A dialog box may ask your permission to continue the configuration, ask you to make choices, display information and ask if it is correct, or request that you insert a floppy disk.

Dialog boxes contain *buttons*—small boxes with choices written in them. You can press Tab to move to the button and press Enter to accept it. If you use a mouse, click on the correct choice in a dialog box and click the OK button.

What the Configuration Tests

The configuration test checks compatiblity between your computer hardware and the Backup program. It tests your floppy drive, the speed of your processor, and your hard disk. The test also runs a sample backup and compare so it can verify that the program is working correctly. The test is important for several reasons: you want the Backup program to work properly when you back up those valuable files; Backup creates a file in which it saves settings such as which disk drive you want to back up to; and if there are any problems with the Backup program, it's better to find out during a test than during a backup of your entire disk.

The process of the configuration follows:

◆ Tests video and mouse configurations

◆ Tests the floppy drives

◆ Tests processor speed

◆ Tests backup menus and compatibility with the floppy drives

◆ Runs a test of backup using one or two floppy disks

◆ Displays a report of the backup test

◆ Runs a check of the data on the floppy disk, comparing it to the data on the hard disk

Options Offered During the Test

During the compatibility test, Backup displays two screens in which you can change options for the default setup. To change an option, move the cursor to the option and press enter or click the mouse on the option. Choose a new option from the list and choose OK when you are done. The two screens that offer options are as follows:

◆ *Video and Mouse Configuration*. You have the choice of changing screen color, display lines, and mouse sensitivity and acceleration.

◆ *Backup Devices*. Choose which drive or device you want to use for primary backups.

Troubleshooting

If you receive a message titled "DMA Buffer size too small," you must cancel the test. Before you can continue the test, refer to Appendix B, "Error Messages" for a possible solution to the problem.

more ▶

Configure Backup

1. Format two floppy disks and keep them handy.

2. At the system prompt, type the following command:

   msbackup

3. Press Enter.

4. Choose Start Configuration by pressing Enter.

5. Make changes to the selections or choose OK to accept the defaults. The defaults are most likely correct but you can make changes if you want. It's probably best to leave the Screen Options as they are; however, you may want to change the Mouse Options—for example, choose a left-handed mouse, or change the speed of the mouse's double-click. Choose OK when you are finished.

6. As Backup checks your system configuration, it displays a dialog box informing you that it is testing the floppy drives. Backup prompts you to select a drive to test. Choose the drive you want to use for your backups and choose OK.

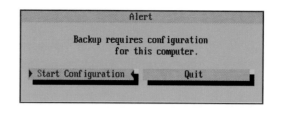

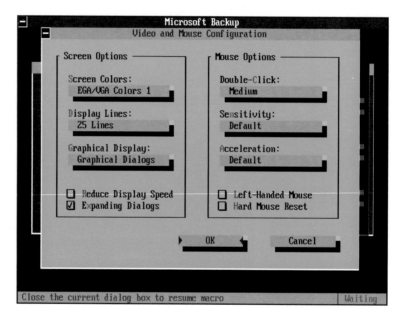

Before you can perform an actual backup, you must first run the compatiblity test; choose Start Configuration to continue.

The first options screen.

7. When the drive test is complete, Backup begins a mock backup. An Alert dialog box appears telling you the test pauses and asks you to select a drive for the test. Choose Continue.

8. Backup automatically runs through several dialog boxes choosing the files it will back up during the test. When Backup is ready to start the backup, it displays the Backup To dialog box. Choose the drive you want to use for the backup test by clicking the option buttons or by pressing the down arrow to highlight the button; choose OK.

more ▶

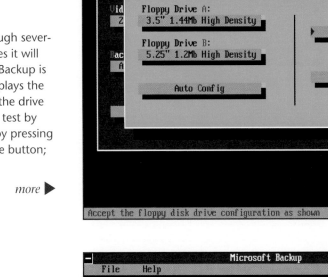

Backup reports the size and type of backup devices available on your computer; choose the backup device you want to use.

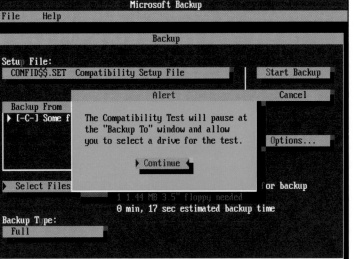

Backup is ready to begin a test backup of a few DOS files.

9. Backup requests that you insert a disk into the floppy drive. It then performs a test backup showing you the progress on-screen. Backup may or may not request another disk. At the end of the backup test, a report is displayed.

10. Choose OK when you've finished viewing the report.

    Backup next compares the backup copies to the original files.

11. Follow the directions when Backup asks for the floppy disks.

    Backup displays the Configure dialog box with the Save option highlighted.

12. Press Enter to save the configuration.

    Backup displays the Microsoft Backup screen.

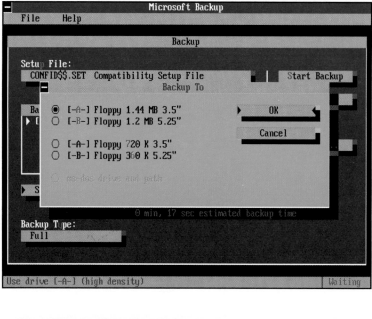

Choose the drive and capacity disk you want to use during the backup test.

A report of a successful backup test; if the test is unsuccessful, Backup instructs you to quit and run the test again.

13. Choose Backup to create a backup (see the following pages). Or choose Quit to return to the system prompt.

Troubleshooting

If the configuration program displays a message stating DMA Buffer size too small or a message stating that your computer failed the compatibility test, see Appendix B, "Error Messages," for information.

more ▶

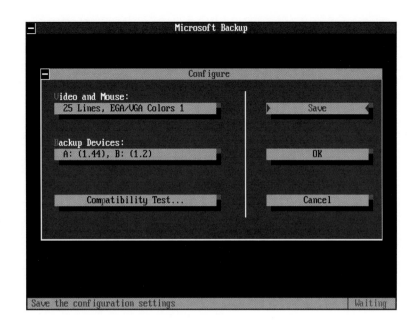

The option to Save the default settings is highlighted, press Enter to save.

HARD DISKS

Planning Your Backup

You need to plan the number of disks you need and the time you need to do a backup. You also need to create a backup plan of what to back up and when.

Depending on the size of your hard disk and the files you back up, you could use anywhere from a couple of floppy disks to 35, 40, or more disks. That's one reason you need to plan your backup. Another reason is time. How much time will it take to make a backup filling 40 disks? Planning your backup will eliminate needless time and effort spent.

What Should You Back Up?

You can back up the files that are important to you and leave others that can easily be duplicated. Consider, for example, the following:

◆ Back up all of your programs—Windows, WordPerfect, Lotus, and so on—one time and keep the backup in a safe place. This way, if your hard disk fails, you can restore your programs easier than loading them all on individually. In addition, the backup of your programs contains all of those customized settings of how you like to work within a program.

◆ Don't back up the program files again, unless you have major changes in the programs and their setups. Not only do you have your one full backup, you have the original program disks you can reinstall at any time.

◆ Do back up the document directories of your program files regularly—the directories in which you store data, documents, spreadsheets, and so on, are invaluable to your work.

◆ As for your data files, consider how often these files change. If you add and delete files from a customer database every day, for example, back that file up daily. On the other hand, some word processing documents may only be used once a month; back up these only when they have changed.

◆ Don't back up the DOS directory of your hard disk after the first full program backup. You also have the original DOS disks and you can reinstall those at any time.

◆ Do back up the files on your root directory regularly—CONFIG.SYS, AUTOEXEC.BAT, special device drivers, and so on. These files are configured especially for your system and often change when you add a command or a new program; backing them up can save you a lot of time.

After deciding which files to back up, you need to schedule the backup. Perform a full backup of your data files every week, for example. Back up files that change often, every day or two. Just be sure that you always back up at the time you schedule; as sure as you miss one backup, your system will fail.

Choosing the Type of Backup

Microsoft Backup enables you to back up your files by offering two choices of partial backups. You perform a full backup first, and then supplement the full backup with other backups that update changed and added data files.

With the full backup, you can back up all files or selected files on your hard disk. If you back up all files—program and data— you can restore your entire system if the occasion arises, and it will at some point in time. You can back up selected files, as well, leaving out program files and so on.

It's a good idea to make two full backups of your system. First, make a full backup of all program files and data files, as an insurance policy. Update this full backup every couple of months. Then perform a full backup every week of data files plus any other files that regularly change. The extra copy is in case one copy fails or the data becomes damaged on one backup.

After you have a full backup, you must update the backups with a partial backup. Usually, these partial backups are performed daily. You have a choice of two partial backups; choose the one that best suits your working situation.

Partial backups are created on a separate set of disks and take less time than full backups. Use partial backups to copy the files you work on every day. You can choose from two types of partial backups. Regardless of the backup you choose, perform the backups regularly and faithfully. That one day you want to go home early and skip the backup is the day your computer will rebel.

TIP

Perform a full backup every week or every two weeks; perform a partial backup every day. If this seems like a lot of backing up, consider how much time it would take to re-create the data if you lose it.

Performing a Full Backup

First, make sure that you have plenty of floppy disks; it wouldn't hurt to buy four to six boxes of disks; you can always use the leftovers. Use high-density disks if your floppy drives takes them because high-density disks hold more information.

Backup will estimate the number of disks for you, as well as the amount of time to perform the backup. Make sure to correctly label each floppy disk with the date, the type of backup—full, and the number of the disk in the series.

When you configured your backup, the first time you started Microsoft Backup, the configuration program created default setup files that work with your system. Use the DEFAULT.SET file for your backup.

more ▶

HARD DISKS

Backing Up 87

Backup Options

Within the Backup program are options you can choose to control your backups:

◆ **Verify Backup Data**. Reads the data on the backup disk and compares it to the original. Using Verify takes twice as long to back up your files, however.

◆ **Compress Backup Data (default)**. With this option, you can store more information on a floppy disk without the data being changed in any way.

◆ **Password Protect Backup Sets**. Enables you to use a password to access the backed-up files.

◆ **Prompt Before Overwriting Used Diskettes (default)**. The Backup program checks the floppy disk you use for the backups and if it detects data on the disk, it prompts you before overwriting the data.

◆ **Always Format Diskettes**. Formats the backup floppies before backing up the data; this requires more time.

◆ **Use Error Correction on Diskettes (default)**. Makes restoring the backup easier if the backup disks become damaged.

◆ **Keep Old Backup Catalogs (default)**. Catalogs help locate the files on the backup disks and make them easier to restore.

◆ **Audible Prompts (Beep) (default)**. Beeps when a dialog box or prompt appears.

◆ **Quit After Backup**. Quits the program after backing up.

Because you can select the files you want to back up, you can also create backup sets for special data—like that 30-page catalog you spent weeks compiling or the database with more than 10,000 names and addresses. For special backups, you can select the files individually, by directories, with wild-card characters, by date, or by attribute using the full backup option.

Performing Partial Backups

A partial backup is one that copies just the files that are new or have changed since the last full backup. DOS enables you to perform two types of partial backups—incremental or differential. The type of backup you choose depends on how many files you work with each day and how you work.

If you work on many different files each day, use the incremental backup; if you work on the same small number of files day after day, use a differential backup.

The difference between an incremental and differential backup lies primarily with the treatment of the Archive attribute. An incremental backup turns off the Archive attribute after copying it, meaning that if the file does not change before the next backup, it will be skipped. On the other hand, a differential backup does not reset—or turn off—the Archive attribute. That file therefore will be copied during the next differential backup whether or not it has changed.

Performing an Incremental Backup

As with any backup, have your floppy disks ready. Label each disk with the date, number of the disk in the series, and the type of backup—incremental. Because the incremental backup only backs up those files that are new or have changed and the backup process overwrites the floppy disk, use new disks each time you perform an incremental backup between full backups. After the next full backup, you can recycle the incremental disks.

When you perform an incremental backup, you choose the backup type from the Backup dialog box. Microsoft Backup takes over from there.

Performing a Differential Backup

You only need one set of floppy disks for a differential backup because this backup copies the same files over and over again. Be sure to label each disk with the date, number of the disk in the series, and the type of backup.

When performing a differential backup, choose the backup type from the Backup dialog box and continue as you would with a full backup.

TIP When you use disks over and over again, they can become worn out or damaged. Replace the disks every few months to guarantee the safety of your data.

Comparing the Backup

Use Compare to make sure your backups are usable. Compare not only checks for errors in the backups, but it can also correct most errors it finds, thus guaranteeing that your backups will be useful if you need to restore them. If by chance, Compare finds errors that cannot be corrected, it's better that you find out now and repeat the backup than to wait until you restore. The time it takes to run the Compare program is well worth the effort.

Always use Compare when you create a full backup; you don't want to go to all the time and trouble of backing up just to find out, when it's too late, that your copies are not accurate. It's also a good idea to use Compare on incremental backups, because each disk builds on the next. One bad set of incremental backups can ruin all your data.

Comparing the Backup

Start Compare in the Microsoft Backup welcome screen. A dialog box similar to the Backup dialog box appears. Choose your files and directories as you did in Backup and start the comparison.

Compare issues a report at the end summarizing the results. If there were errors found, Compare tries to correct them. If Compare notifies you that it could not correct the errors, redo your backup and use Compare again.

more ▶

Perform a Full Backup

1. At the system prompt of your hard disk, type the following command:

   msbackup

2. Press Enter.

3. Choose Backup.

4. Choose Select Files.

5. Choose to back up the entire disk by selecting Include or use the arrow keys and Tab to select directories and files. Press the space bar to select a file or directory.

Hard drive is the source   Use the default setup file

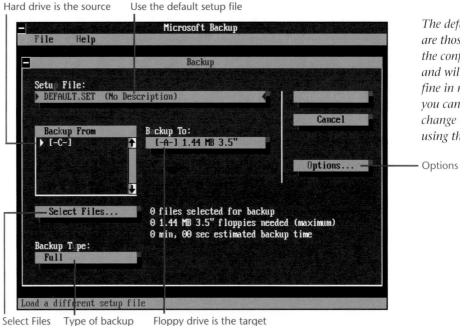

Select Files   Type of backup   Floppy drive is the target

The default settings are those set during the configuration test and will probably be fine in most cases; you can, however, change the options by using this screen.

Options

Select entire directories or individual files.

6. Choose OK to return to the Backup Screen.

7. Choose Start Backup.

Backup prompts you for a floppy disk and backs up the files. When Backup is finished, it displays a report of the backup.

8. Choose OK to return to the Backup welcome screen.

9. Choose Quit to exit to DOS.

Troubleshooting

If you want to cancel the process or any dialog box, press Esc or choose the Cancel button.

more ▶

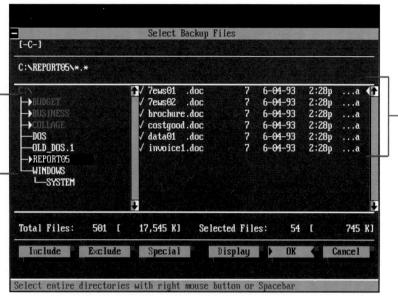

Selected directories

Selected files are marked with a check-mark; selected directories are highlighted and marked with an arrow.

Selected files

Backup summarizes your choices in the lower right corner. You can accept the changes by choosing Start Backup.

Number of files for backup
Eight disks needed
Time backup will take

Perform a Partial Backup

1. At the system prompt, type the following:

   msbackup

2. Press Enter.

3. At the Microsoft Backup welcome screen, choose Backup.

4. Choose Backup Type.

5. Choose Incremental or Differential and choose OK.

6. Continue with the backup as you would a full backup.

Troubleshooting

◆ When you quit the Backup program, DOS may inform you that the default settings—disk drive, selected files, and so on—have not been saved. Choose the File menu, Save As to save the settings to make it easier the next time you run a backup.

◆ Remember that the backup program erases target disks as it backs up your data. Do not use a disk containing information you want to keep; and use new disks whenever you perform an incremental backup, since one incremental backup builds on the last incremental backup.

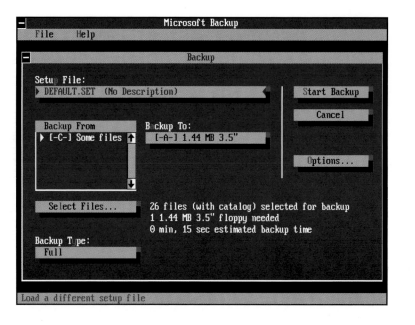

The Backup dialog box appears.

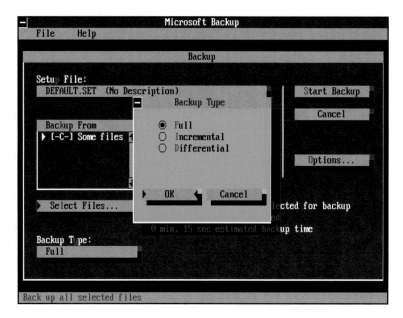

The Backup Type dialog box appears.

Compare the Backup

1. At the system prompt, type the following and press Enter.

   msbackup

2. At the Microsoft Backup welcome screen, choose Compare.

3. Choose the Backup Set Catalog to compare. The catalog—your backup file—listed when the screen first appears is the last backup you completed. If you choose Backup Set Catalog, a list of backup file names appears and you can choose the one you want to compare.

4. You can compare all files (default) that were previously backed up by selecting Start Compare now. Or you can select files to compare in the Compare Files list box. Choose this option if you only want to compare a few files instead of all backed up files. Choose Start Compare.

   When Compare is done, it displays a report of the comparison.

5. Choose OK to return to the welcome screen or choose Quit to return to the system prompt.

Troubleshooting

If the Compare report shows the data did not match or that files were skipped during the backup, perform the backup again. This may take you extra time; but the previous backup is useless if it doesn't pass the compare test.

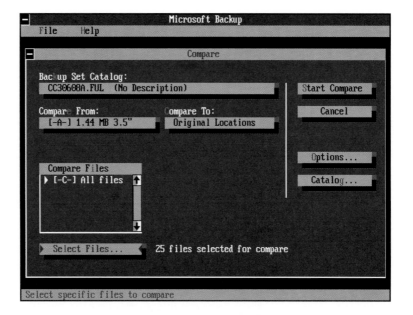

The Compare screen lists the backup file you last created plus the options you chose when you backed up that file. You can accept the choices or change them.

A successful Compare report; if the compare is unsuccessful, perform the backup and compare again.

If you lose some or all of the data on your hard disk, you can use your backups to restore the data. If you didn't create backups, now is the time you'll wish you had!

The data on your hard disk may be deleted or become corrupted, or your hard disk may fail and you could lose everything. Unfortunately, the possibilities of using your backup are more likely than you might think. If a catastrophe strikes and you have backups, you can restore the data to your hard drive and continue working as if nothing happened.

If all of your data is lost (as happens with a hard disk failure), you must first reformat your drive, or perhaps even purchase a new hard drive. When the hard drive is ready, you can begin to restore your data.

It is recommended that you have an extra system disk containing the MSBACKUP program files and data files. This will allow you to make a full backup without reinstalling MS-DOS.

If your hard disk fails and you must restore the entire disk, keep all of your backup disks intact until you are sure that your hard disk is working properly. If you overwrite your backups with a new, full backup, for example, you may be copying the hard disk problem as well as your files—as is the case with a virus.

Restoring Backups

With Restore, you can reclaim one file, selected files, or your entire hard disk.

Start with the last full backup of your hard disk. From there, restore the incremental or differential backups. If you use incremental backups, you must restore all sets of disks since the last full backup, in chronological order, because each backup set builds on the last. If you use differential backups, you'll only have one set of disks to restore.

After choosing Restore from the Microsoft Backup welcome screen, a dialog box similar to the Backup dialog box appears. Choose the Backup Set Catalog, select the files to restore, and start the restore.

Restore copies the files to their original locations; if the original directory no longer exists, Restore creates it. In addition, you can restore to other directories or drives by selecting Restore To in the Restore dialog box. At the end of the process, Restore displays a report about the restoration.

When you restore files, the Restore program automatically overwrites files of the same name on the target.

Restore your Backups

1. At the system prompt, type the following:

   msbackup

2. Press Enter.

3. At the Microsoft Backup welcome screen, choose Restore.

4. Choose the files and directories to restore by selecting Restore Files. Choose directories and files from the list and choose Start Restore.

5. Insert the requested disk into the floppy drive.

6. Choose OK to return to the welcome screen.

7. Choose Quit to return to the system prompt.

Troubleshooting

Since the DOS 6.0 Backup program can only restore files backed up in Backup for MS-DOS or with one of the Norton backup programs, make sure that your backup was created by one of these programs.

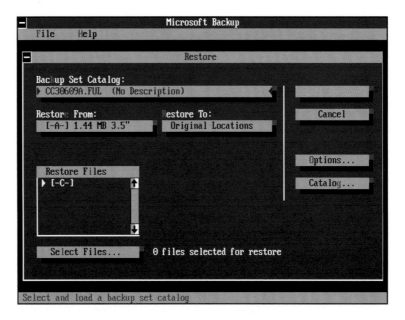

The Restore dialog box appears.

Restore copies the backed up files to your hard disk and displays a report about the restore.

A disk must be formatted before you can use it; however, if your computer has DOS on it, your hard disk has already been formatted. Do not format it again unless you have a good reason.

Formatting a disk that has been formatted once is called *reformatting*; doing so completely erases all data from the disk. **Do not reformat your hard disk unless you fully understand why you are doing so.**

What Happens During Formatting

When you format a disk (hard or floppy), DOS's Format command prepares the disk to receive data by analyzing the disk, checking for defects on the disk, creating a root directory, and setting up a storage table. In the process, the Format command completely erases all data, program files, directories, and even the root directory from your disk. You cannot use the system after formatting until you install an operating system—DOS, for example—and reinstall all of your program files.

TIP
You can restore a full backup to a formatted hard disk to recover your programs and data files after installing DOS.

Formatting Your Hard Disk

When formatting your hard disk, you must use the /s switch to install system files. Without system files, your hard drive is not bootable. Format your hard disk from a floppy drive using the first DOS program disk or a system disk you created.

When you issue the Format command, your system responds with a message warning you that all data will be lost; this message always brings on a tinge of foreboding, whether you're a new or experienced user. The message gives you two choices: proceed with format or cancel the format. Check the message carefully to make sure that the drive you want to format is the drive listed in the message. If you proceed, Format displays reports on the formatting. Formatting your hard drive may take a few minutes or a half an hour, depending on the size of your hard disk.

Format displays a message when formatting is completed telling you the format is done and the system files were transferred. Format then asks if you want to enter a *volume label*—a name for the disk. When Format is finished, it displays a report of disk space used for the system files, defective sectors, and available disk space. For more information about volume labels, see "Adding a Volume Label."

After you format your hard disk, you must load DOS or another operating system back on your computer before you can load program or data files. If you choose to install DOS, insert disk one of the DOS program in your floppy drive and type: a:setup or b:setup. Press Enter. Follow the instructions on the screen. Have a blank, formatted disk handy for the Uninstall disk Setup requests at the beginning of Setup.

Format Your Hard Disk

1. Insert a system disk or the first DOS program disk into your floppy drive and type a: and press Enter.

2. At the system prompt, type the following:

   format <drive>

   For example, if your drive is C, type

   format c:

3. Press Enter.

4. Press Y when prompted to proceed with format.

5. When formatting is complete, load DOS or another operating system onto your hard disk. Running DOS Setup automatically installs the system files you need.

Troubleshooting

If you accidentally format your hard disk, see the next article, "Unformatting Your Hard Disk."

```
C:\>a:

A:\>format c:

WARNING: ALL DATA ON NON-REMOVABLE DISK
DRIVE C: WILL BE LOST!
Proceed with Format (Y/N)?
```

Format the drive by entering the command. When prompted, answer Y(es) to the question. Proceed with Format.

Why Reformat?

You may need to reformat your hard disk if you have a lot of problems with program and data files, if your hard disk fails, if you want to change your operating system, and so on. Suppose that your system constantly displays errors and corrupted files and data; the operation of the system is slow and not at all reliable. You try all of DOS's programs for checking memory, tracking viruses, optimizing your hard drive, and so on, and nothing seems to help. You may want to reformat your hard drive and start from scratch

Before you format your hard disk, consult with an experienced computer user to see if there is another option and to make sure you have proper backups.

Sometime when you're busy and not concentrating on the task at hand, you may accidentally format your hard disk.

DOS follows your commands; if you tell it to format your hard disk, it will format your hard disk. Luckily, DOS does issue a warning message and asks for confirmation before it continues: `WARNING: ALL DATA ON NON-REMOVABLE DISK DRIVE C: WILL BE LOST! Proceed with Format (Y/N)?` If you enter N, the format is canceled. If, however, you enter Y, DOS formats your hard disk.

If you accidentally format your hard disk, you may be able to recover some or all of the data with the UNFORMAT command. The amount of data you can recover depends on what you have done to the disk since you reformatted it. If you reinstalled DOS after formatting the hard disk, for example, you've overwritten many of the files you want to recover. You should still try to unformat the drive, however; any data you can recover is better than none.

TIP

You can reboot your computer using a system disk instead of installing DOS on the hard disk you want to unformat. When you create a system disk, copy the UNFORMAT.COM file to it for extra protection.

Unformatting a Disk

If you have the UNFORMAT command on your system disk, you can use it to issue the command at the floppy drive system prompt. Or you can use the first DOS program disk.

When you enter the UNFORMAT command, the system displays a message saying that UNFORMAT searches the drive first and will prompt you before writing changes to the disk. You can proceed or cancel the operation. As UNFORMAT searches the disk, it displays the progress report.

The last step of UNFORMAT is to write the changes to the disk—to recover the files. If you press Y, UNFORMAT continues; if you press any other key, UNFORMAT cancels the operation. If you proceed with unformatting your hard disk, UNFORMAT may find parts, or fragments, of files that can be recovered. UNFORMAT prompts you to delete the file or to recover the part. See "Defragmenting the Hard Disk" for information about fragments.

At the end of the process, UNFORMAT displays a message stating that the operation is complete. Some of your files may be complete, some may be missing, and others may contain parts of other files. The only way to find out how much damage was done is to open program files and test them, and to view the data files.

Unformat the Hard Disk

1. At the system prompt, type the following:

unformat <drive> /l /p /test

To unformat your drive C, for example, type the following:

unformat c:

To test the drive to see how successful an unformat would be, for example, type

unformat c: /test

2. Press Enter.

3. Answer all prompts displayed by the Unformat screen.

Troubleshooting

To unformat your hard disk, you must boot from drive A using the system disk and the UNFORMAT command must be located on that system disk.

Unformatting Command Switches

You can use several switches with the UNFOR-MAT command. Some helpful switches to use with UNFORMAT follow:

/l displays a list of files and directories that may be recovered from the formatted disk.

/test runs a test to indicate the possibility of success for unformat.

/p sends output, such as the list of recoverable files, to the printer.

```
CAUTION !!

This attempts to recover all files lost after a FORMAT, assuming
you've NOT been using MIRROR. This method cannot guarantee com-
plete recovery of your files.

The search-phase is safe: nothing is altered on the disk. You will
be prompted again before changes are written to the disk.

Using drive c:

Are you SURE you want to do this?

If so, type Y; to cancel the operation, press any other key.
```

UNFORMAT's first screen. You have nothing to lose; choose Y to continue.

```
Files found: 47

Warning!  The next step writes changes to disk.

Are you sure you want to do this?

If so, type Y; to cancel the operation, press any other key.
```

At the end of the search, UNFORMAT notifies you of found files. Enter Y to continue.

If you want to assign a name to a hard or floppy disk, you can do so. The name will be displayed in all directory listings.

Adding a volume label to a disk is optional; but it's a good idea to add a label in some cases. Suppose that you're making backup disks for your program files. Each program disk usually has a volume label; and often you cannot use the backup without labeling it the same as the original. You can add the volume label to your backup disks with the LABEL command.

You might label disks with your name, your company's name, the version of DOS, your department, and so on.

How To Add a Label

When you format a disk, DOS prompts you to enter a volume label. You can also use the LABEL command to add a volume label to a disk with no label. Furthermore, you can delete and view the volume label of a disk.

Some commands—such as DIR (Directory), TREE, and CHKDSK (Check Disk)—display the volume label of the disk they check.

You can view any disk's volume label by typing the command **vol** at the system prompt of the disk.

Labeling a Disk

You can name a disk using up to 11 characters. You can use the same characters for a volume label as you use to name files and directories.

To change the volume label of a disk (either a floppy or a hard disk), you enter the command at the system prompt. DOS displays the current label and prompts you for the new label. If you press Enter at the prompt, DOS displays a prompt asking if you want to delete the current volume label. If you delete the current label, you leave the disk nameless.

Label a Disk

1. Type the following:

   label

2. Press Enter.

3. Type the label name and press Enter. To delete the label, just press Enter.

Troubleshooting

If when you display the label you decide you don't want to change it, don't press Enter. Enter deletes the current label. Instead, press Ctrl+C to cancel the LABEL command.

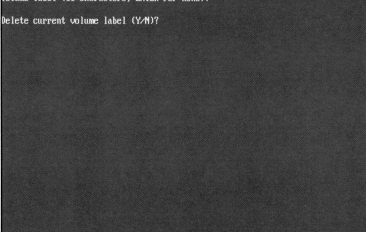

```
C:\>label
Volume in drive C is MS_DOS_6
Volume Serial Number is 1AC8-425D
Volume label (11 characters, ENTER for none)?

Delete current volume label (Y/N)?
```

Add or change a volume label using the LABEL command; you can change the label of both hard and floppy disks.

Defragmenting the Hard Disk

If your computer is running slow, it may mean that your disk is fragmented. You can make your computer run faster and more efficiently by defragmenting it.

Your hard disk is broken up into different segments. When DOS stores a file, it cannot always store the file within one location. It breaks the files into sections and stores them—if possible—all together. It keeps track of where the file is stored.

How Fragmentation Happens

When you save a file, DOS stores it in a specific spot on your disk—either hard or floppy. Say you open that file again and make some changes, delete half of the file, then save the changed file. You've freed some space on the disk surrounding the file because you deleted some of the file.

Now say you save a new file to disk. DOS finds just the right amount of space around the first file to save the new file. You go back to the first file and add several pages of data, making the file bigger, and save it. DOS cannot save the entire file in the same spot because the second file is now wedged in there; so DOS saves part of the first file in its old place, and finds a new spot for the rest of the file. This is fragmentation.

As you work each day, you add a file, delete a file, add data to a file, and then add another file, the data becomes disseminated over your disk. The more you work, the more scattered the data becomes. A single file may be stored in bits here and pieces there. Scattered files and bits of data over a disk is called *fragmentation*.

The more your disk is fragmented, the slower your computer runs. When the computer reads a fragmented file, the disk head has to move first to one spot, then to another, thus slowing the speed at which it can read and write.

MS-DOS supplies a program that can defragment your disk; Defrag moves the data to the beginning of your disk and moves fragmented files together. When you defragment your hard disk, you make it run faster more efficiently.

If your disk is not badly fragmented, the recommendation may be to optimize the disk. To optimize, Defrag repositions and rearranges the files and places all file bits and pieces together, thus freeing disk space and making it faster and easier for DOS to find files. Optimizing the disk may leave a few fragmented areas—not enough, however, to cause any problems. During the defragmentation, the program reads the data, moves blocks around on-screen, and writes the data to a new area of the disk—it looks somewhat like a video game.

Defragmenting your Disk

To run the Defrag program, you enter the DEFRAG command at the system prompt and choose the drive you want to defragment. Defrag analyzes your hard disk, displays a map of the disk, and issues a recommendation. If you're new to the Defrag program, take the recommendation; DOS usually knows the best way to handle your disk and files.

To move around in the dialog boxes of the Defrag program, use Tab or the arrow keys. Make a selection by highlighting it and pressing Enter. Alternatively, you can click on the selection with the mouse.

Your first selection is to choose the drive to defragment; choose your hard drive, or insert a disk in a floppy drive and choose it. Defrag then analyzes your disk and makes a recommendation.

If your disk is not badly fragmented, the recommendation is to optimize the disk. If you choose this option, Defrag optimizes your disk. During the defragmentation, the program reads the data, moves blocks around on-screen, and writes the data to a new area of the disk—it looks somewhat like a video game.

If the disk is badly fragmented, Defrag recommends a full optimization. Press Enter to accept. Defrag may take a few seconds or several minutes, depending on how badly fragmented the disk is.

If the disk is not fragmented, Defrag issues a message stating that the disk is OK.

TIP

Don't use DEFRAG on a drive that has been compressed with the MS-DOS 6.0 doublespace utility. Instead, run DBSSPACE and choose the **Defrag** option from the Tools menu.

After Defrag finishes, it displays a dialog box. Choose to exit or run the program on another disk.

TIP

Even though Defrag offers a recommendation, it also offers an Optimize menu from which you can choose to fully optimize your disk or unfragment files.

Decoding the Map

The map of your disk shows how the disk space is used. A legend in the bottom right corner shows you what the blocks on the map mean. Areas of gray are unused portions of the disk; areas of white are used portions. Gray areas appearing within white areas show that your disk is fragmented.

more ▶

Defragment your Hard Disk

1. At the system prompt, type the following:

   defrag

2. Press Enter.

3. Choose the drive you want to defragment.

4. Choose an option, as described in the preceeding section "Defragmenting your Disk."

   When Defrag is done, you see a message stating that Defrag is done.

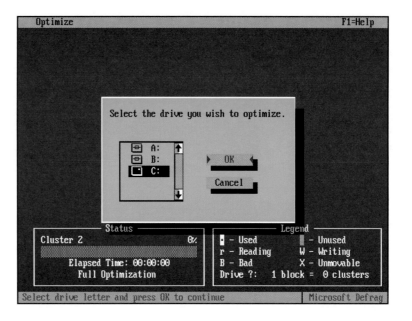

Choose the drive you want to defragment.

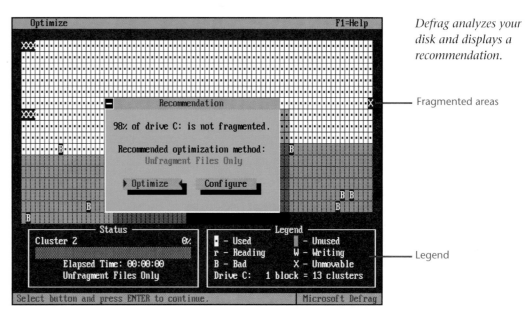

Defrag analyzes your disk and displays a recommendation.

—— Fragmented areas

—— Legend

5. Choose OK.

6. Defrag displays the Optimize menu. Choose to e**X**it Defrag.

Troubleshooting

♦ If Defrag displays an Allocation error, exit the program and run the CHKDSK/F command. MS-DOS 6.2 users can use the SCANDISK/AUTOFIX command. Then run Defrag again.

♦ If Defrag displays an Insufficient memory to defragment the target disk error, exit the program. Free some disk space by moving some files to another disk, then run Defrag again.

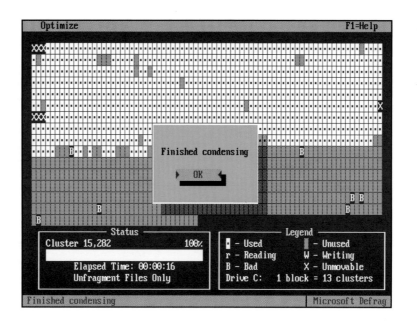

Defrag notifies you it has finished defragmenting the disk.

Check your hard disk for problems periodically.

Check Disk and SCANDISK are commands that examine the specified disk to see whether all your data is in its proper place. Check Disk and SCANDISK check for various problems within your hard disk, and if you specify, will fix the problems.

Sometimes data can get lost on your hard disk; lost data takes up space and is not useful to you. This lost data doesn't hurt anything, but it does take up valuable disk space. Another problem with data files is the possibility of fragmentation. If a disk is especially fragmented, two files could be taking up the same spot on the disk. This causes a real problem when you try to save new data to either file. By running Check Disk periodically, you can solve problems such as these before they get out of control.

Checking for Lost Clusters

Check Disk and SCANDISK run to find lost clusters, or allocation units. A *cluster* is the smallest unit of storage DOS uses. Normally a cluster is chained, or linked, to other clusters to form a saved file. Lost clusters are unlinked bits of information floating around on your disk that just take up space.

Suppose that you are working in a word processor when the power goes off. Your computer shuts down and reboots on its own when the power comes back on. The data in the word processor was not saved when the power went off so you've lost it, right? Not quite. That data is now floating around on your disk in lost clusters or

allocation units, taking up valuable disk space. Because you can no longer use the data, get rid of it. Most of us need all of the disk space we can get; why waste it on useless floating data? If you run the Check Disk or SCANDISK command on your computer, you can gather those clusters and delete them so they no longer take up space.

Another problem Check Disk and SCANDISK can fix is cross-linked files. A cross-linked file occurs when two or more files occupy the same space on the disk. The reason files become cross-linked is generally because of a badly fragmented disk. When two files are cross-linked and you open one of the files, data becomes jumbled and neither file is usable. Cross-linking is bad enough when it occurs to data files; it's disastrous when it happens to program or system files. Cross-linking could prevent a program from opening or operating properly or worse, keep DOS from operating correctly. Running Check Disk or SCANDISK periodically helps prevent cross-linked files.

Lost allocation units and cross-linked files are the most common problems that Check Disk and SCANDISK fix. In addition, Check Disk and SCANDISK can fix the following problems with a disk: invalid cluster numbers, defective sectors where the FAT is stored, file attributes that DOS does not recognize, and damage to directory's or subdirectory's entries. If you make a habit of running Check Disk or SCANDISK every month or every two weeks, your disk will operate more efficiently and your files will retain their integrity.

MS-DOS users should use SCANDISK, a new and more powerful utility that replaces CHKDSK. Unlike CHKDSK, SCANDISK can diagnose and repair drives compressed with DoubleSpace.

Checking for Defragmentation

The Check Disk command can also check to see if the files on your disk are in contiguous (adjoining) sectors. Files that are not contiguous (are fragmented) slow down your computer and may even cause problems within the disk later. If you find the files on a disk to be noncontiguous, run the Defrag program to clean up the disk. See "Defragmenting the Hard Disk" for information.

To check for noncontiguous files on drive A, for example, type the following at the system prompt: **chkdsk a:*.***. Then press Enter.

TIP

Lost cluster chains are converted to files with names like FILE0000.CHK, FILE0001.CHK, and so on. These files are placed in your root directory. To view the files, type **type file0000.chk|more** and press Enter. To delete the files, type **del *.chk** at the system prompt and press Enter.

Running Check Disk and SCANDISK

To run Check Disk or SCANDISK, you enter the command at the system prompt. You can check drives other than your hard disk drive, as well. If you run the command by itself, DOS performs the test and reports its findings.

more ▶

HARD DISKS

Checking the Hard Disk 107

Check the Hard Disk

1. Type **chkdsk**. To check a floppy disk, type **chkdsk a**: or **chkdsk b:**.

2. Press Enter.

Correct Errors

1. Type the following:

   chkdsk /f

2. Press Enter.

3. When prompted to save lost allocation units to a file, press Y.

Troubleshooting

If you already have cross-linked files and you run Check Disk, it will show which files are cross-linked in the report. Before allowing Check Disk to fix the problem, you may be able to save the data in the files. Write the file names down and exit Check Disk without fixing the problem. Copy one file onto a floppy disk; then copy the second file to a second floppy disk. Run Check Disk again and let it fix the problem. Now copy the two files back to your hard disk.

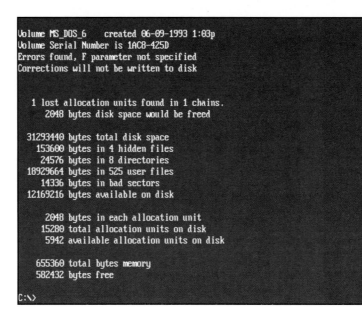

Check Disk found no errors.

Check Disk with errors. Errors not corrected.

Check Disk Results

Check Disk displays information about the disk including the following:

- The volume name and creation date

- Volume number

- Number of allocation units found (if any) and the disk space they take

- Total disk space

- Available disk space

- Total memory

- Available memory

- And information about hidden files, directories, and user files

If Check Disk finds errors, it reports the errors but does not correct them unless you specify the /f (fix) switch. To specify that Check Disk fix errors, run the command again with the switch. When Check Disk finds errors this time, it displays the message Convert lost chains to files (Y/N)? Answer yes by pressing Y. The lost cluster chains are converted to files and you can now delete them from your disk.

SCANDISK Results

Unlike CHKDSK, SCANDISK displays its progress as it operates. SCANDISK checks the following disk characteristics:

- Media descriptor

- File allocation tables

- Directory structure

- File system

- Surface scan (optional)

When checking a drive compressed with DoubleSpace, SCANDISK checks these additional characteristics:

- DoubleSpace file header

- DoubleSpace file allocation table

- Compression structure

- Volume signatures

- Boot sector

Want to speed up your computer? If so, use SMARTDrive.

Suppose that you're working in a word processing program. You open files, save files, and print files several times during each work session. The data the program uses to open, save, and print is stored and read from disk over and over. With a disk-caching program, you can keep that information available. DOS offers its own disk-caching program—SMARTDrive.

What's a Disk Cache

A *disk cache* is a section of the memory allocated for temporary data storage. The data stored in the cache is information a software program uses over and over again in a normal work session. When those common commands are in a disk cache, your computer can access them fast. The program can read and access the data—*read-caching*—faster from the cache than the hard disk.

DOS's disk-caching program is SMARTDrive; SMARTDrive takes disk-caching one step further. SMARTDrive performs read-caching and write-caching. In addition to storing often-used commands and data in the cache for fast access, SMARTDrive stores the data you're working on to the cache. This data is then written to the disk when a certain amount is gathered and when it's convenient, speeding up your work.

TIP
Because write-cache temporarily stores data, you must tell SMARTDrive when you're about to turn off your computer, or you'll lose the data in the cache.

TIP
You can add a command to your AUTOEXEC.BAT that tells your computer to use SMARTDrive every time you start your computer.

Using SMARTDrive Disk-Caching

To use the SMARTDrive disk-caching program, enter the command at the system prompt. The program loads into memory and applies itself whenever needed. When you load SMARTDrive from the system prompt, the program remains loaded only until you turn off your computer.

When you load SMARTDrive, it uses both read- and write-caching on your hard drive and only read-caching on your floppy drives, unless you specify otherwise. To specify write-caching in addition to read-caching on drive A, for example, you enter **a+** after the command.

To view the statistics of the SMARTDrive cache, use the /s switch after the command. The statistics include the name and version of the program, space available and number of items that fill the space, cache size in bytes, and the disk-caching status of each drive.

Turning Off SMARTDrive

When you finish your session for the day, you *must* tell SMARTDrive that no more data will be written to the disk; SMARTDrive finishes writing all data stored in temporary memory to the disk. Enter the command with the /c switch before you turn off your computer.

Use SMARTDrive

1. At the system prompt, type the following:

smartdrv

To apply both read- and write-caching to a floppy drive (A, for example), type the following at the system prompt:

smartdrv a+

To view SMARTDrive statistics, type the following:

smartdrv /s

2. Press Enter.

Troubleshooting

To notify SMARTDrive that you're about to turn off the computer, type the following and press Enter:

smartdrv /c

If you use DoubleSpace or some other disk compression program, use SMARTDrive on the uncompressed drive only.

Beginning with MS-DOS 6.2, SMARTDrive is able to cache CD-ROM drives. This produces a noticeable speed improvement in a typically slow device.

```
C:\>smartdrv /s
Microsoft SMARTDrive Disk Cache version 4.1
Copyright 1991,1993 Microsoft Corp.

Room for    108 elements of    8,192 bytes each
There have been     65 cache hits
     and     27 cache misses

Cache size:   884,736 bytes
Cache size while running Windows:    0 bytes

              Disk Caching Status
drive   read cache   write cache   buffering
─────────────────────────────────────────────
  A:        yes          no           no
  B:        yes          no           no
  C:        yes          yes          no

For help, type "Smartdrv /?".

C:\>
```

SMARTDrive statistics.

No matter what size hard disk you have, it's never enough. You can double the space on your hard disk with a program that comes with DOS.

DOS includes a disk compression program—DoubleSpace—that you can load onto your computer. A disk compression program, using mathematical techniques, reduces the number of bytes in a file, compressing the data into a smaller space without changing the data in any way. DoubleSpace compresses not only your data, but program files as well.

You can also use DoubleSpace on floppy disks.

How Disk Compression Works

DoubleSpace divides a disk (either hard or floppy) into two drives when it compresses the data. One drive, the larger section, stores the compressed data and program files. The compressed drive is assigned to your normal drive—C, for example. The other drive is used to store files that have not been compressed. DoubleSpace assigns another letter to this drive, E or H, for example. Certain DOS system files reside on the drive that is not compressed, as do other files that should not be compressed— such as the Windows swap file. The DOS system files and Windows swap file will not work if compressed. You can also save other data and program files to the uncompressed drive.

To compress your disk with DoubleSpace, enter the command at the system prompt. Make sure that you exit all programs—such as DOS Shell and Windows—before you install DoubleSpace.

> **TIP**
> Make a full backup of your hard disk before you use DoubleSpace, as you would before doing anything that changes your system or system configuration.

DoubleSpace checks your disk, analyzes your system, reboots your computer, and begins the disk compression. This could take from several minutes to half an hour or more, depending on the size of your hard disk and the type of data stored there.

As DoubleSpace compresses the data, it displays a screen updating you of its progress. When DoubleSpace is finished compressing your disk, it displays a screen giving you the amount of free space you had before compression, the amount of free space after compression, and the compression ratio. In addition, DoubleSpace tells you the letter representing the uncompressed drive and how much space is allotted to that drive.

Disadvantages of DoubleSpace

After DoubleSpace compresses the data on your drive, it must decompress the data each time you use it; it therefore may take a little longer to access your data. If you have at least a 386 or 486 processor, the difference in negligible.

The DoubleSpace utility in MS-DOS 6.0 isn't able to uncompress drives that it has previously compressed. To uncompress these drives, you must back up all files that you wish to keep, and then reformat. The DoubleSpace utility in MS-DOS 6.2 is able to uncompress a drive that was previously compressed if the drive has enough free space to hold all files after uncompressing.

Another disadvantage to using DoubleSpace is that once you compress your hard disk, you cannot uncompress it; the data remains compressed unless you reformat your disk and reinstall your programs.

You can use the DOS Defrag or the Check Disk command on the compressed drive, but neither command performs properly with a compressed drive. DOS, therefore supplies you with special Defragment and Check Disk commands to use with DoubleSpace. To access the special commands, enter the DoubleSpace command at the system prompt. Choose the Tools menu, and then choose Defragment or CHKDSK.

more ▶

If you use MS-DOS 6.2, you can check DoubleSpace drives with the SCANDISK command. SCANDISK will diagnose and repair both compressed and uncompressed drives. You can even access DoubleSpace drives which haven't been mounted.

TIP

You can display information about your compressed disk at any time by typing the DBLSPACE command at the system prompt and pressing Enter. Press Alt+D, select Info, and press Enter to list how much space is used, how much space is available, and the compression ratios of each.

HARD DISKS

Compress Your Disk

1. At the system prompt, type the following:

dblspace

2. Press Enter.

3. Press Enter to continue.

4. Choose Express Setup.

5. The third setup screen gives you more information about how DoubleSpace works. After reading the screen, press C to continue.

6. DoubleSpace compresses your disk and issues a report about the compressed drive.

```
Microsoft DoubleSpace Setup
─────────────────────────────

     Welcome to DoubleSpace Setup.

     The Setup program for DoubleSpace frees space on your hard
     disk by compressing the existing files on the disk. Setup
     also loads DBLSPACE.BIN, the portion of MS-DOS that provides
     access to DoubleSpace compressed drives. DBLSPACE.BIN
     requires about 40K of memory.

     If you use a network, then before installing DoubleSpace,
     start the network and connect to any drives you normally use.

       o To set up DoubleSpace now, press ENTER.

       o To learn more about DoubleSpace Setup, press F1.

       o To quit Setup without installing DoubleSpace, press F3.



 ENTER=Continue   F1=Help   F3=Exit
```

The Microsoft DoubleSpace Setup screen.

```
Microsoft DoubleSpace Setup
─────────────────────────────

     There are two ways to run Setup:

     Use Express Setup if you want DoubleSpace Setup to compress
     drive C and determine the compression settings for you. This
     is the easiest way to install DoubleSpace.

     Use Custom Setup if you are an experienced user and want to
     specify the compression settings and drive configuration
     yourself.

       ┌──────────────────────────────────────────────────────┐
       │ Express Setup (recommended)                           │
       │ Custom Setup                                          │
       └──────────────────────────────────────────────────────┘

     To accept the selection, press ENTER.

     To change the selection, press the UP or DOWN ARROW key
     until the item you want is selected, and then press ENTER.

 ENTER=Continue   F1=Help   F3=Exit
```

The DoubleSpace Setup screen.

Troubleshooting

◆ If you format a compressed disk, you cannot unformat it; the data is lost.

◆ You can't uncompress a disk compressed with MS-DOS 6.0 DoubleSpace; you must reformat the disk and reload DOS, if necessary. The MS-DOS 6.2 DoubleSpace utility can uncompress a disk that it has previously compressed.

```
 Drive  Compress  Tools  Help

                                              Free        Total
          Drive  Description               Space (MB)   Space (MB)
              ┌──────── Compressed Drive Information ────────┐
              │                                              │
              │ Compressed drive C is stored on uncompressed drive H │
              │ in the file H:\DBLSPACE.000.                 │
              │                                              │
              │      Space used:            20.21 MB         │
              │      Compression ratio:     1.7 to 1         │
              │                                              │
              │      Space free:            14.13 MB         │
              │      Est. compression ratio: 2.0 to 1        │
              │                                              │
              │      Total space:           34.34 MB         │
              │                                              │
              │  < OK >   < Size >   < Ratio >   < Help >    │
              │                                              │
              └──────────────────────────────────────────────┘

 DoubleSpace    F1=Help  ALT=Menu Bar  ↓=Next Item  ↑=Previous Item
```

View information about the compressed drive.

HARD DISKS

If you think of your hard disk as a filing cabinet, you can think of a floppy disk as an extra filing cabinet for file storage.

If you use a computer, you use floppy disks. Floppy disks supplement the hard disk; you use them for data storage and to hold backup copies of program and data files. But to use a floppy disk, you first must know how to put it in the computer, how to format it, how to read files from it, and how to write files to it.

Handling Floppy Disks

If you take care of your disks, the data is less likely to be damaged and the disks will last longer. Many of the following guidelines are good safety precautions for hard and floppy disks:

◆ Keep food, drinks, smoke, and dust away from disks.

◆ Keep disks away from magnets and magnetic sources such as telephones, answering machines, electric pencil sharpeners, vacuum cleaners, and so on.

◆ Store disks in a paper or cardboard pocket or a box, protected from extreme heat or cold.

◆ Don't touch the exposed plastic disk.

◆ Don't write on 5 1/4-inch disks with a ball-point pen or pencil; write on the label first, and then attach the label to the disk.

◆ Don't place other objects—such as a cup of coffee, heavy books, and so on—on top of floppy disks.

◆ Never remove a floppy disk from the disk drive while the drive light is flashing. Use care when inserting and removing disks from the drive.

Floppy Disk Commands

Many of the DOS programs and commands you use with a hard disk work the same with floppy disks. The following list provides some commands and programs that work with both kinds of disks.

◆ **XCOPY**. Quickly copy files and directories from one disk or directory to another.

◆ **Volume Label**. Add, delete, or change the label, or name, of a disk.

◆ **Defragmenting**. Optimize a disk by running the DEFRAG program, which checks a disk for scattered data and can correct some disk errors.

◆ **Check Disk**. Check a disk for lost allocation units and correct errors.

◆ **DoubleSpace**. Compresses the data on a disk so that more data fits in the same amount of space.

◆ **SCANFIX**. Diagnoses and repairs errors on disks. Recognizes, diagnoses, and repairs errors on floppy disks compressed with DoubleSpace.

Insert a Disk

1. Hold a 5 1/4-inch disk so that the exposed magnetic material is facing away from you and the write-protect notch is on the left. The label should face up.

   Hold a 3 1/2-inch disk so that the protected magnetic material is away from you, label up.

2. Gently guide the disk into the floppy drive door; do not force the disk. You hear a click or a whirr when the disk is completely in the disk drive. If the disk drive has a latch, close it.

3. To remove the disk, press the eject button on the floppy disk drive or open the latch. The disk pops out a short way.

Troubleshooting

◆ If the disk does not easily glide into the disk drive, check that the label is not loose and catching as you are inserting the disk. Also check for a warped disk or damaged disk casing. If the disk is damaged or warped, use another disk to avoid damaging your disk drive.

◆ If the computer cannot read the disk, eject it and insert it again. Check to see that the disk is the right size for the drive, make sure it is not upside down, and, finally, check to see that the disk is not damaged.

◆ Only one disk fits into a drive at one time; always remove the disk before inserting another one.

◆ If your computer cannot read a disk, make sure the disk is the proper capacity for the disk drive. A double-density drive, for example, cannot read a high-density disk. Use the correct capacity disks for your floppy disk drive.

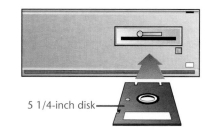

5 1/4-inch disk

Disk is inserted

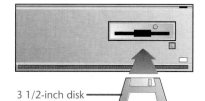

3 1/2-inch disk

Disk is inserted

Formatting a Floppy Disk

Formatting a floppy disk is very important. The computer won't recognize an unformatted disk. On the other hand, if you use a disk that's formatted incorrectly, you could lose all data on that disk.

Before you can use a floppy disk with your computer, you have to format it so that the computer can read and write to the disk. For a little more money you can buy preformatted disks, or you can choose to format them yourself. Remember, if you buy unformatted floppy disks, you *must* format them before you can use them. In addition, you may want to reformat used disks to completely erase the old data before you reuse them.

Formatting is a procedure that prepares a disk for use. When DOS formats a disk, it sets up a "filing system" on the disk and checks the disk for bad sectors. DOS then marks those bad sectors as unusable.

Caution: *Don't format a disk that contains files you may still need. Formatting the disk erases all files on the disk.*

Formatting and Disk Capacity

Although DOS knows what type of floppy drives you use, DOS doesn't know how much data a particular disk can hold unless you tell it. Without specifications, DOS formats the disk to the highest capacity that your floppy drive can use.

Suppose that you have a 5 1/4-inch *double-density* (also called *low-density*) disk, which has space for 360 kilobytes (abbreviated *K*) of data. If you format the disk in a high-density drive without telling DOS that the disk only holds 360K, DOS formats it to hold 720K. This may sound like a bargain—two for the price of one—however, the disk

can't actually hold 720K. Eventually, the data on the disk may become *corrupted* (damaged), and you could lose everything on the disk.

When you format a double-density disk as a high-density disk, you may save files on the disk and everything seems to be working fine. You may be able to save files to fill one quarter, one half, or even three quarters of the disk. You might even save two or three files to the disk and open the files once a year and all is well.

The data on the improperly formatted disk, however, is not stable and will, at some point, become corrupted. Sometime you may try to open a file saved to the disk and find that the data is corrupted. You might be able to open the file, but the data is jumbled or missing; or, the file might disappear completely from the disk. After that, you will begin noticing the same problems with other files on the disk.

To save yourself from these kinds of data headaches, DOS offers a switch you can use to tell the FORMAT command the capacity of the floppy disk you are formatting. To use the switch, you must know the capacity of the disk. The following table shows the disk capacities of various disk sizes. *DS DD* stands for double-sided, double-density; *DS HD* stands for double-sided, high-density; and *ED* stands for extra-density disks. Most disks and their boxes are labeled with the size of the disk.

A 3 1/2-inch disk can be formatted for use in either an IBM-compatible computer using DOS or for an Apple/Macintosh computer. Disks formatted for use in one type of computer cannot be used in the other; a Macintosh-formatted disk, for example, cannot be used in an IBM-compatible PC.

If you don't have the disk box to check for a disk's capacity, there are a couple of other ways you can determine it.

If the original label is still intact on a 5 1/4-inch disk, the letters *HD* or *DD* should be displayed. You can also tell the capacity of a 5 1/4-inch disk by looking at the center hole where the magnetic material is exposed. If the disk is double-density, it has either a darker black or a white ring around the edge of the hole. A high-density disk has no ring.

You can find the capacity of a 3 1/2-inch disk by looking in the upper-right corner of the disk for the letters *HD*, *DD*, or *ED*. Alternatively, you can usually find the capacity written on the *shutter* (the sliding metal "door"). Even if no information is written on the disk, you can still determine its capacity. A high-density 3 1/2-inch disk has an extra square hole punched in it on the side opposite the write-protect hole. If the disk is extra-density, the extra hole is placed higher than on a high-density disk.

Disk	Storage Capacity
5 1/4-inch DS DD	360K (kilobytes)
5 1/4-inch DS HD	1.2M (megabytes)
3 1/2-inch DS DD	720K
3 1/2-inch DS HD	1.44M
3 1/2-inch ED 4MB	2.88M

Notice that the capacity designation of the disk is not the actual capacity of the disk. The ED 4MB disk, for example, holds only 2.88M of data. As you format a disk, DOS uses some of the disk space for sector-identification and error-checking information. A 3 1/2-inch DS HD, therefore, may be labeled to hold 2M of data, but you can only store 1.44M of data on that disk after DOS takes the space it needs.

Drive Capacity

In addition to knowing the capacity of a disk, you must understand the capacity of your disk drive. For example, you can't format a high-density disk in a low-density drive. Here are some guidelines for formatting disks depending on the capacity of the disk and the drive:

◆ A 5 1/4-inch DD disk can be formatted as 360K in a 360K or 1.2M disk drive.

◆ A 5 1/4-inch HD disk must be formatted as 1.2M in a 1.2M disk drive.

◆ A 3 1/2-inch DD disk must be formatted as 720K in a 720K, 1.44M, or a 2.88M disk drive.

◆ A 3 1/2-inch HD disk must be formatted as 1.44M in a 1.44M or 2.88M disk drive.

◆ A 3 1/2-inch ED 4MB disk must be formatted as 2.88M in a 2.88M disk drive.

more ▶

The FORMAT Command

To format a floppy disk, you use the FOR-MAT command. Be extremely careful when you use this command—particularly when you type the drive letter. Before you press Enter to continue with the formatting procedure, always double check the command. If you type the wrong drive letter, you could accidentally format a disk in the wrong drive. And if you accidentally type the drive letter for your hard disk (C, for example), DOS will format the hard disk instead of the floppy disk. Naturally, DOS warns you that you're about to erase all data from the disk and asks if you want to continue. If you aren't paying attention, you may answer yes and wipe out the data on your hard drive.

Here's the syntax of the basic FORMAT command:

FORMAT *<drive>*

TIP

If you can't remember the various switches for the command, type **FORMAT /?** at the system prompt and press Enter.

Specifying the Disk Size

If the capacity of the disk matches the capacity of the disk drive—a high-density disk in a high-density drive, for example—you don't have to use a size switch with the FORMAT command. If you format a low-density disk in a high-density drive, however, you must use a size switch.

To tell FORMAT the size of the disk, you type the size switch plus the disk capacity. For instance, to format a 360K disk, the switch is /F:360; to format a 1.44M disk, the switch is /F:1.44. Here's the syntax of the FORMAT command including the size switch:

FORMAT *<drive>* /F:*<size>*

Quick and Unconditional Formats

Another handy switch to use with the FORMAT command is the /Q (quick) switch, which performs a *quick format*. The quick switch formats a previously format-ted disk very fast; you cannot use this command on an unformatted disk. With a quick format, DOS clears the directories but does not check for bad sectors or delete existing files.

Finally, you can use the /U switch to per-form an *unconditional format* on a disk. This format completely erases all information on the disk and the data cannot be retrieved with the UNFORMAT command. Use this switch when the data on the disk is private or secured and you don't want anyone else to be able to retrieve it.

Naming the Disk

As part of the format process, DOS requests a *volume* label (name) for the disk. If you want to name the disk, type a name from 1 to 11 characters long. If you don't want to name the disk, you can skip the name by pressing Enter after DOS prompts you for a name. For more information about volume labels, see the article "Adding a Volume Label."

Completing the Format

When the format is complete, DOS displays a report showing the maximum space on the disk, the space still available for storage, and the number of bad sectors. DOS ends the procedure by asking if you want to for-mat another disk. If you indicate that you want to format another, DOS formats the disk with the same specifications used in the previous format.

Format a Floppy Disk

1. Insert the floppy disk in the drive.

2. At the system prompt, type **FORMAT** and press the space bar.

3. Type the drive letter followed by a colon (usually **A:** or **B:**).

4. Type the appropriate switches. If you don't need to specify any switches, skip to step 5.

5. Verify that the drive letter and switches for the command are correct.

6. When you are sure the command is correct, press Enter.

7. When DOS prompts you to specify a volume label, type the desired name or press Enter to skip the name.

8. When DOS asks whether you want to format another disk, type **N** or press Enter for no; type **Y** for yes.

Troubleshooting

If you accidentally format a disk that you didn't want to format, use the UNFORMAT command immediately, before you perform any other operation. For more information about UNFORMAT, see the article "Unformatting a Floppy Disk" later in this section and "Unformatting Your Hard Disk" in the "Hard Disks" section.

```
C:\>format a: /f:1.44 /u
Insert new diskette for drive A:
and press ENTER when ready...

Formatting 1.44M
   t complete.

Volume label (11 characters, ENTER for none)?

   1457664 bytes total disk space
   1457664 bytes available on disk

      512 bytes in each allocation unit.
     2847 allocation units available on disk.

   e Serial Number is 2E6A-12E4

Format another (Y/N)?n


C:\>
```

Accidents happen! If you accidentally format a floppy disk containing data you need, you may be able to recover some or all of the data with the UNFORMAT command.

When you reformat a floppy disk, DOS issues a message saying `Checking existing disk format. Saving UNFORMAT information`. DOS stores that information on the disk to use if you need to restore the data on the disk. Don't assume, however, that you can reformat a disk and then simply use UNFORMAT later if you want the data back; UNFORMAT doesn't work that way.

The UNFORMAT command completely rebuilds a disk's "filing system," which may cause some data to be lost or corrupted during the process. In addition, if you have saved any data to the disk since it was formatted, some or all of the original data may have been overwritten. Finally, the amount of data the UNFORMAT command can recover depends on which switches you used with the FORMAT command. If you used the /U (unconditional) switch, you cannot unformat the disk.

The UNFORMAT Command

UNFORMAT rebuilds the system area of the drive, essentially unformatting the disk. After you unformat a hard disk, you must restart the system; however, you don't have to reboot after unformatting a floppy disk. Here's the syntax of the UNFORMAT command:

UNFORMAT *<drive>*

To unformat a disk in drive A, for example, you type **UNFORMAT A:** and press Enter.

UNFORMAT Switches

There are several switches available with the UNFORMAT command. Here are two switches you are most likely to use:

◆ The /L (list) switch instructs UNFORMAT to perform a search of the disk without writing any changes to the disk until UNFORMAT prompts you; you can then either unformat the file or not. A search report lists the files and directories likely to be recovered if you proceed with the unformat. This search may take several minutes to complete.

◆ The /TEST (test) switch tests the disk to see if the files can be unformatted successfully and shows you how the information will be re-created. The test does not write changes to the disk until UNFORMAT prompts you. This test may take several minutes to complete. The /TEST switch provides a report at the end of the test.

TIP

Add the UNFORMAT command to your system disk just in case you accidentally format your hard disk. For more information about a system disk, see the article "Creating a System Disk" in the "Hard Disks" section.

Unformat a Floppy Disk

1. Insert the floppy disk in the drive.

2. At the system prompt, type **UNFORMAT** and press the space bar.

3. Type the drive letter followed by a colon (usually **A:** or **B:**).

4. Type the appropriate switches. If you don't need to specify any switches, skip to step 5.

5. Verify that the drive letter and switches for the command are correct.

6. When you are sure the command is correct, press Enter.

   UNFORMAT displays a message explaining the process and asks you to confirm that you want to continue.

7. Press Y to continue or N to cancel.

8. Remove the disk from the floppy drive.

9. Press Ctrl+Alt+Del to restart the computer.

Troubleshooting

If you decide to cancel the UNFORMAT list (/L) or test (/TEST), press Ctrl+C; then type **N** and press Enter when you're prompted.

```
Using drive A:

Are you sure you want to do this?
If so, press Y; anything else cancels.
? y

Searching disk...
100% searched, 1 subdirectory found.
Files found in the root: 0
Subdirectories found in the root: 1

Walking the directory tree to locate all files...
Path=A:\
Path=A:\SUBDIR.1\
PKUNZIP.EXE       29378  2-01-93  2:04am
READ.ME            5303  6-20-91  9:07am
Path=A:\

Files found: 2
Warning!  The next step writes changes to disk.

Are you sure you want to do this?
If so, press Y; anything else cancels.
? N
```

In this example, the line UNFORMAT A: /L has scrolled off the top of the screen so that you can see the results of the command.

Data on floppy disks is just as important as data on the hard disk. Make backup copies of your floppy disks to guarantee you won't lose important data.

Floppy disks can become damaged or worn out, and files can become corrupted just as they can on a hard disk. In order to protect the data on your floppy disks, you should make copies, or backups, of your floppies.

To protect the program disks, you should also make copies of the original disks that came with any software you use, such as word processing, spreadsheet, database, or other programs. Application programs are expensive, so protect your investment! Some program disks are copy-protected so you can't back them up; others include special instructions for making backups. Most, however, allow you to make copies. If your program disks aren't copy-protected and include no special instructions for making a backup, make copies as you would any other floppy disk.

Using the DISKCOPY Command

You can make an exact replica of a floppy disk by using the DISKCOPY command. DISKCOPY copies an original (*source*) disk to a second (*target*) disk by using one disk drive or two disk drives. Both the source and the target disk must be the same size and capacity; therefore you cannot use DISKCOPY to copy data from a 3 1/2-inch disk to a 5 1/4-inch disk. The DISKCOPY command works only on floppy disks; you cannot use DISKCOPY for a hard disk. If you have only one disk drive, DISKCOPY is a perfect way to make floppy disk copies.

Here's the syntax for the DISKCOPY command:

DISKCOPY <*source*> <*target*>

For example, to copy the contents of the disk in drive A to another disk that you will insert in drive A later, first insert the source disk in drive A. Type **DISKCOPY A: A:** and press Enter. When DISKCOPY prompts you, insert the target disk in drive A and press Enter. Depending on the disk and drive types, you may need to switch the disks several times, but DISKCOPY prompts you each time.

TIP

If you're using one floppy drive to copy two disks, label the disks source and target before you begin the DISKCOPY procedure so you don't get the two disks mixed up.

DISKCOPY notifies you when the process is complete by asking if you want to copy another disk.

TIP

To save time, you can begin the DISKCOPY procedure at the system prompt of the source disk and just enter **DISKCOPY** as the command. For example, at the system prompt A:\>, type **diskcopy**. DOS prompts you to insert the source disk and then prompts you when it's ready for the target disk.

Copy a Disk

1. Insert the source disk in the source drive. If you are copying from one drive to another, insert the target disk in the target drive.

2. At the system prompt, type **DISKCOPY** and press the space bar.

3. Type the source drive letter, followed by a colon (usually **A:** or **B:**), and press the space bar.

4. Type the target drive letter, followed by a colon (usually **A:** or **B:**).

5. Verify that the drive letters for the command are correct.

6. When you are sure the command is correct, press Enter.

   DISKCOPY copies the disk and prompts you to change disks in the drive as necessary.

7. Follow any on-screen prompts. When the DISKCOPY procedure is complete, DOS displays a message asking if you want to copy additional disks.

8. Press **Y** to continue or **N** to cancel.

Troubleshooting

DISKCOPY destroys all information on the destination disk; don't use a disk for the destination disk that contains data you want to keep.

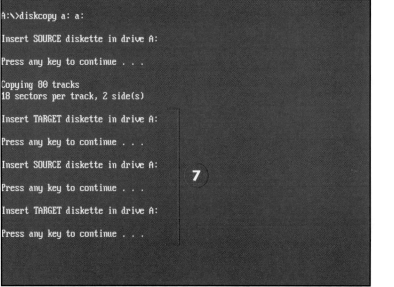

```
A:\>diskcopy a: a:

Insert SOURCE diskette in drive A:

Press any key to continue . . .

Copying 80 tracks
18 sectors per track, 2 side(s)

Insert TARGET diskette in drive A:

Press any key to continue . . .

Insert SOURCE diskette in drive A:

Press any key to continue . . .

Insert TARGET diskette in drive A:

Press any key to continue . . .
```

Copying Notes

You can copy the contents of a floppy disk to another disk drive by using the XCOPY command. For example, to copy everything on the floppy disk in drive A to a disk in drive B, type **XCOPY A:*.* B:** and press Enter.

After you make copies of floppy disks, label the disks with the date, the number in the series (such as *1 of 2* or *2 of 2*), and the word *Backup* or *Copy*. Then store the disks in a safe place until you need them again. You may or may not want to update these disks later, depending on the type of data or program files that the disks contain.

Write-protect your source disk in case you accidentally insert the source disk when you are prompted for the target disk.

To avoid copying fragmented files, run DEFRAG on your source disk before you use DISKCOPY; otherwise, DISKCOPY copies the fragmented files.

What good is a copy of a disk if the the copy doesn't accurately reflect the data contained on the original? Compare the copy to the original disk just to be sure they're the same.

Using the DISKCOMP (disk compare) command, you can compare a copy of a floppy disk to the original to verify that the disks are identical. If DISKCOPY finds that the contents of the two disks aren't the same, you can make another copy or backup immediately, to ensure that your data is safe.

The DISKCOMP Command

DISKCOPY compares the first disk you specify to the second disk you specify. It doesn't matter which disk was the original and which was the copy. DISKCOMP works only on floppy disks; you cannot compare two hard disks or a hard disk and a floppy disk. For DISKCOMP to work, the disks must be the same size and capacity. You can compare the disks by using one disk drive or two disk drives.

Here's the syntax for the DISKCOMP command:

DISKCOMP *<source>* *<target>*

For example, to compare the contents of the disk in drive A to another disk that you will insert in drive A later, insert the first disk in drive A. Type **DISKCOMP A: A:** and press Enter. When DISKCOMP prompts you, insert the second disk in drive A and press Enter. Depending on the disk and drive types, you may have to switch the disks several times, but DISKCOMP prompts you each time.

When the compare process is complete, DISKCOPY indicates whether the compare was okay or differences were found in the two disks. The program then asks if you want to compare another set of disks.

TIP

To save time, you can begin the compare process at the system prompt of the disk drive and just enter **DISKCOMP** as the command. For example, at the A:\> prompt type **diskcomp.** DOS then establishes both the source and target disks as A and prompts you to insert each disk as the data is compared.

Use DISKCOMP to compare only floppy disks that were copied with DISKCOPY. DISKCOMP is not effective on two disks that contain the same information arranged differently. The comparison reports each sector on the destination disk that does not *exactly* match that same sector on the source disk. Thus, if the data is arranged differently on the source and target disks, a DISKCOMP comparison is useless.

TIP

As an extra bonus to using DISKCOMP, the command recognizes an unformatted destination disk and formats it automatically as part of the copying process.

Compare Two Floppy Disks

1. Insert the first disk in the drive. If you are comparing one drive to another, insert the second disk in the second drive.

2. At the system prompt, type **DISKCOMP** and press the space bar.

3. Type the first drive letter, followed by a colon (usually **A:** or **B:**), and press the space bar.

4. Type the second drive letter, followed by a colon (usually **A:** or **B:**).

5. Verify that the drive letters for the command are correct.

6. When you are sure the command is correct, press Enter.

   DISKCOMP compares the disks and prompts you to change disks in the drive as necessary.

7. Follow any on-screen prompts.

   When the compare process is complete, DISKCOMP displays a message showing the results. The program then asks if you want to compare additional disks.

8. Type **Y** to continue or **N** to cancel.

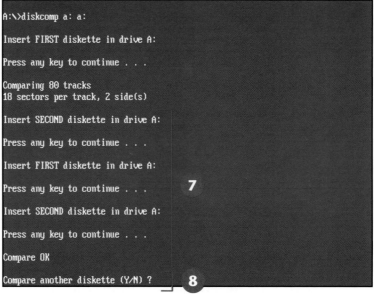

Troubleshooting

If at any time you want to back out of the comparison process, press Ctrl+C; DISKCOMP will terminate at the next logical stopping point.

Is the data on that floppy disk important? Write-protect the disk so that nothing happens to your files!

Suppose that you just backed up a database containing 10,000 customer files. You definitely want to protect that backup in every way possible. Files and programs stored on floppy disks are always in jeopardy—it's very easy to overwrite or erase the data on the floppy by accident. But you can protect a floppy disk—from an accidental COPY, DELETE, or FORMAT command, for example—by write-protecting the disk. Both 3 1/2- and 5 1/4-inch disks can be write-protected.

Note: *Even though the disk is write-protected, the computer still can read and use the contents of the disk.*

How Does Write Protection Work?
A floppy disk drive reads and writes data to a floppy disk with its read/write head. The drive uses an apparatus similar to a pin to determine whether the disk is write-protected. When you instruct the computer to read a disk, it does so without checking the disk's write-protect notch. However, when you ask a program to write to a disk—such as when you're saving, revising, or deleting a file—the disk drive first inserts this "pin" into the write-protect notch of the disk to determine whether it is open or closed. If the notch is open in a 5 1/4-inch disk, or closed in a 3 1/2-inch disk, the program writes to the disk. If the reverse is true, the program issues a message telling you it cannot write to the disk.

By covering the notch of a 5 1/4-inch disk or opening the notch of a 3 1/2-inch disk, you can maintain the integrity of your data because the program cannot write to your floppy disk.

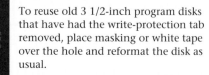

TIP To reuse old 3 1/2-inch program disks that have had the write-protection tab removed, place masking or white tape over the hole and reformat the disk as usual.

Tabs and Notches
To write-protect a 5 1/4-inch disk, locate the notch on the side of the disk. Cover the notch with one of the write-protect tabs on the sheet of disk labels included with your box of disks. If you need a quick write-protect tab for a 5 1/4-inch disk, you can use masking or white tape.

To write-protect a 3 1/2-inch floppy disk, locate the write-protect tab on the back of the disk, in the corner. Slide the tab so that a "window" is open in the plastic. Any time you want to write to the disk, you can slide the tab back to its original closed position.

Write-Protect a 5 1/4-Inch Floppy Disk

1. Remove the disk from the disk drive or sleeve.

2. With the label side of the disk facing you, place a write-protect tab over the write-protect notch on the side of the disk.

3. Fold the tab around to the back of the disk, so that the tab covers the entire write-protect notch.

4. Seal the tab tightly.

Write-Protect a 3 1/2-Inch Floppy Disk

1. Remove the disk from the disk drive or sleeve.

2. With the label side of the disk facing down, move the write-protect tab to the safe position, which opens a "window" in the notch.

Troubleshooting

◆ Be careful when you apply tape to the notch of a 5 1/4-inch disk; make sure that the tape covers just the notch and does not touch the magnetic material of the disk. You could damage the data on a disk with tape.

◆ If a 5 1/4-inch disk gets stuck in the disk drive, remove it and apply a new piece of tape or a write-protect tab. The tab could be loose on one end, making it catch in the disk drive.

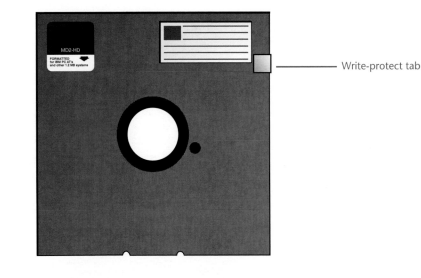

Write-protect tab

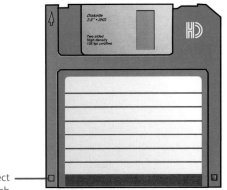

Write-protect notch

```
A:\>del *.rep

Write protect error writing drive A
Abort, Retry, Fail?
```

If you write-protect a disk and then try to change the files on the disk, you get an error message like this.

Part Three

Section 6—Memory

Memory is the place where the computer stores information it's working on. When you type letters in WordPerfect or sales figures in Excel, for example, the stuff you type isn't committed to paper; it's displayed on-screen and stored in the computer's memory until you save the file to disk.

Section 7—Configuring

Could your computer run faster? Hold more information? How do you add more peripheral equipment to your computer setup? This section provides the answers. When you *configure* the computer, you adjust basic files like the CONFIG.SYS and AUTOEXEC.BAT to accommodate your equipment and your work.

Section 8—Customizing

When DOS saves files, it marks them with the current system date and time. If your computer's clock needs an update, use the information in this section to fix it! You also learn how to change the way the DOS prompt appears, change the keyboard to type Portuguese or other language characters, create macros to speed up your DOS work, and use many more special DOS features.

Section 9—Batch Files

Sometimes you do the same things over and over. Maybe you begin each day by updating the system clock, copying the day's project files from a \WORKING directory to a \REPORTS directory, and starting 1-2-3. With a *batch file*, you can combine a bunch of commands in one place; then you just run the batch file. This section tells you all you need to know about creating your own batch files and building custom menus.

Think of the computer's memory as the activity center of the system. The more memory your computer has, the more quickly your computer can process data and access programs.

People often confuse disk space with memory. Simply put, *disk space* is where files are stored; *memory* is where programs run.

Suppose you have a 212M hard disk with 8M of RAM. The 212M is disk space—that is, storage. You store program and data files on the hard disk; you can back-up, defragment, or double the space of the hard disk. But what you end up with is still storage space. Think of your disk as a filing cabinet. The 8M of RAM, on the other hand, represents the tools (programs) and the files you have removed from the filing cabinet to work on. These are "active." When you are done with them, you return them to the filing cabinet to be stored until next time.

DOS and applications software packages use the computer's memory to operate. But DOS (and some other programs) can manage memory so that applications run more efficiently. To understand how to manage the memory on your computer, you need to begin with a basic understanding of memory.

TIP For more information on disk space, see the section "Hard Disks."

Random-Access Memory (RAM)

RAM (*random-access memory*) makes up the bulk of the computer's memory and is the portion of memory the computer can read and write to. In the RAM, information is read, analyzed, and used. RAM is temporary memory; when you turn off the computer, the memory is cleared and starts clean each time you start the computer.

RAM is stored on *chips* in the computer, and you can add RAM chips to add memory. Computers come with a standard amount of RAM—512K, 640K, 1M, 2M, 4M, and so on—and each computer has a limit to how much RAM you can add. If programs run slowly, or if it seems to take forever for the screen to redraw or a file to open, your computer may benefit from more RAM.

Read-Only Memory (ROM)

ROM (*read-only memory*) is the other kind of computer memory. ROM stores computer instructions that cannot be updated or overwritten—such as how to load the operating system and how to control hardware devices. ROM resides permanently in the computer and isn't lost when you turn off the computer.

Conventional versus Upper Memory

When the personal computer was first designed, engineers assigned 1M of RAM as the system's memory. They divided the 1M of RAM into two parts: the first 640K was used for RAM, and the rest—384K—was used for ROM. The term *conventional memory*—or *low-DOS memory*—describes the first 640K; *upper memory* describes the memory above the 640K reserved for RAM. At the time, memory was quite expensive and no software programs used more than 640K to run, so the arrangement seemed reasonable.

Now, more people use PCs, software programs use more memory, and memory prices are extremely low—making it possible for more computer users to buy additional memory. Unfortunately, the early limitation of 640K to run DOS and software programs is still with us. Consequently, other solutions to memory limits have been developed.

TIP For more information about CONFIG.SYS, see the "Configuring" section.

Upper-Memory Blocks (UMBs)

Much of the 384K assigned to the upper-memory area is unused. ROM stores instructions for controlling devices—such as the keyboard, mouse, display, and so on; but these instructions use only a small part of the upper-memory area; the rest is "free" space.

Unused parts of the upper-memory area are called *upper-memory blocks (UMBs)*. If you create UMBs from unused upper memory, you can access the memory to hold device drivers and memory-resident programs, thus freeing space in conventional memory.

Conventional Memory

DOS programs require conventional memory to run: conventional memory is where DOS loads and runs your programs. But the entire 640K area of conventional memory isn't available just for programs. DOS loads and runs itself in conventional memory. DOS also uses conventional memory to open files, to run devices loaded with CONFIG.SYS, and to store any memory-resident programs (see following sidebar).

Computer Measurements

◆ **Bit**. The smallest amount of data that can be stored; one value.

◆ **Byte**. Eight bits, the smallest collection of bits the computer can work with; one character, such as the letter A or the number 1.

◆ **Kilobyte (K)**. Approximately 1,000 bytes (actually 1,024 bytes) or half a page of text.

◆ **Megabyte (M)**. Approximately 1,000,000 bytes (actually 1,048,576 bytes) or a small graphic image.

◆ **Gigabyte (G)**. Approximately 1,000,000,000 bytes (actually 1,074,741,824 bytes).

All in all, 640K of conventional memory isn't enough to run programs effectively. If it seems that you never have enough conventional memory, you're in good company. Nobody ever has enough conventional memory.

more ▶

Memory-Resident Programs

Memory-resident programs, also called *TSRs* for terminate-and-stay-resident programs, load into conventional memory and are available at the touch of a key. When you finish with the TSR, it remains in memory, waiting to be called again.

Because memory-resident programs use valuable space that DOS and other programs need, they are not as popular as they once were. With the advent of programs such as Windows, memory-resident programs are not as essential as they used to be. With Windows, you can easily open, switch between, and use many programs at one time while using little RAM; TSRs enable you to switch between two or three programs but they are memory hogs.

Most of today's TSRs are utilities that you can load and unload with ease, allowing you to direct your system's use of RAM. One example of a DOS utility that is memory-resident is SMARTDrive disk caching. (For more information, see the article "Using SMARTDrive" in the "Hard Disks" section.)

Expanded Memory

Expanded memory comes in the form of an expansion card added to your computer's memory. Although expanded memory is RAM, it isn't the same as conventional memory; programs cannot run in expanded memory.

Instead, software that's compatible with *expanded memory specification (EMS)* can access the memory for storing data—such as a spreadsheet or a huge database. Not only does the software have to be compatible with EMS for it to work, your computer must be compatible. To be compatible with EMS, your computer must have EMS-compatible memory and a special device driver known as an *expanded memory manager (EMM)*. A device driver is a set of instructions that DOS uses to access specific devices—in this case the memory expansion card. For more information about device drivers, see the article "Configuring Devices" in the "Configuring" section.

Expanded memory is one solution to conventional memory limitations; however, it is slower than directly addressing conventional memory.

Extended Memory

In computers with processors that are 286-based or higher, *extended memory* is additional memory beyond the original 1M of conventional memory. Extended memory, then, is an increase in a computer's conventional memory. A 286 microprocessor can access up to 16M of RAM; 386 and 486 microprocessors can make even greater use of extended memory by accessing up to 4096M of RAM.

Extended memory simulates expanded memory in 386 and higher processors with the use of a device driver called an *extended memory manager*. Although not all programs can take advantage of extended memory, Windows and Lotus 1-2-3 Release 3.1 are two programs that can use it.

Some software programs can access extended memory for storage; DOS, however, has limitations in using extended memory. To take advantage of extended memory, DOS tricks the computer into thinking that some of the extended memory is located in the upper-memory area reserved for ROM. The first 64K of extended memory is called the *high-memory area (HMA)*.

For DOS to access the high-memory area requires a PC with a 286 or higher processor and extended memory. In addition, you must have a device driver to control and access the high-memory area. DOS includes the driver that accesses the high-memory area; it's called HIMEM.SYS. For more information, see the article "Optimize with HIMEM.SYS" later in this section.

Don't worry if you don't completely understand how the memory in your computer works. This article has provided an introduction to the different types of memory in your computer and the purpose of each; the remaining articles in this section should give you a better understanding of how memory works.

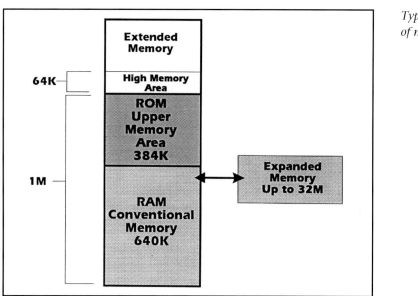

Types and amounts of memory.

How do you know how much memory your computer has? You can find out with the MEMORY command.

To best use the optimization features that DOS offers, you have to know how much memory your computer has and how that memory is divided. You can use the MEMORY command to display a detailed list of your system's memory.

The MEMORY command may mean little to you now, but the more you learn about configuring and optimizing your system, the more you will use this command.

The Memory Report

The report generated by the MEMORY command is a list of how the memory in your computer is being used. The report includes details of memory types, how much total memory is available, how much memory is used, and how much is free. In addition, the memory report shows the size of the largest program you can load into conventional memory, the largest free upper-memory block, and whether DOS is loaded in the high-memory area.

The MEMORY Command

Here's the syntax for the MEMORY command:

MEM <*switches*>

You can use the /C (classify) switch with the MEMORY command to list DOS programs and device drivers that are currently loaded, some of which load when you start the computer. In addition to the basic memory report, the classify switch displays a list of programs loaded and the type and amount of memory each program uses. To use the classify switch, type this command:

MEM /C

> **TIP**
>
> To view one screen of the MEMORY report at a time, type the MEMORY command and any of its switches, and then add a space and either type the **|MORE** command or the **/P** switch.

To learn more about how the different types of memory work, experiment by loading device drivers and TSRs into upper memory. Start by loading the largest drivers and programs first by placing them at the beginning of the AUTOEXEC.BAT or CONFIG.SYS file. Use the MEMORY command to check the results. Then try loading programs and drivers in a different order to see how you can get the most from your memory.

> **TIP**
>
> Use the LOADHIGH command for TSRs in the AUTOEXEC.BAT file; use DEVICEHIGH for drivers in the CONFIG.SYS file to conserve conventional memory. Use the MEM /C command to see if the drivers and programs loaded correctly.

Display Memory

1. At the system prompt, type **MEM**.

2. If you want to use any switches, press the space bar and type the appropriate ones.

3. Press Enter.

Troubleshooting

- If you're running DOS under MS Windows 3.0, DOS won't display the upper memory when you use the MEM /C command. You must first exit Windows and go to the DOS system prompt.

- If your computer doesn't have more than 1M of extended memory, DOS will not display the status of extended memory.

- If you are not using a UMB provider, such as EMM386, DOS will not display the status of upper memory.

```
C:\>mem

Memory Type       Total =   Used +   Free
-------------     -----     ----     ----
Conventional       640K     115K     525K
Upper               67K      10K      57K
Adapter RAM/ROM      0K       0K       0K
Extended (XMS)*    1341K    1341K      0K
                   -----    -----    -----
Total memory       2048K    1466K     582K

Total under 1 MB    707K     125K     582K

Total Expanded (EMS)           1728K (1769472 bytes)
Free Expanded (EMS)*            160K  (163840 bytes)

* EMM386 is using XMS memory to simulate EMS memory as needed.
  Free EMS memory may change as free XMS memory changes.

Largest executable program size   525K  (537248 bytes)
Largest free upper memory block    53K   (54320 bytes)
MS-DOS is resident in the high memory area.

C:\>
```

The first page of a sample memory report generated by using the /C switch and the |MORE command.

```
Modules using memory below 1 MB:

Name      Total      =  Conventional  +  Upper Memory
-------   -----         ------------     ------------
MSDOS     17389  (17K)    17389  (17K)       0   (0K)
SETVER      800   (1K)      800   (1K)       0   (0K)
HIMEM      1120   (1K)     1120   (1K)       0   (0K)
EMM386     4144   (4K)     4144   (4K)       0   (0K)
SMARTDRV  29536  (29K)    29536  (29K)       0   (0K)
DBLSPACE  44416  (43K)    44416  (43K)       0   (0K)
COMMAND    3168   (3K)     3168   (3K)       0   (0K)
SAVE      17424  (17K)    17248  (17K)     176   (0K)
MODE        480   (0K)        0   (0K)     480   (0K)
SHARE      5248   (5K)        0   (0K)    5248   (5K)
CVFLOPPY   4080   (4K)        0   (0K)    4080   (4K)
Free     596128 (582K)   537440 (525K)   58688  (57K)

Memory Summary:

Type of Memory      Total     =      Used     +      Free
--------------      -----            ----            ----
Conventional       655360   (640K)  117920  (115K)  537440  (525K)
-- More --
```

- DOS program
- Memory-optimization utilities
- DOS disk-caching program
- TSR
- Free memory

Smart use of conventional memory is one key to computer speed and efficiency. You can free some conventional memory by enabling your system to use the high-memory area.

To use the high-memory area, you must have an extended memory manager—a driver that provides access to the high-memory area to programs that can use it and controls the way the programs address extended memory. DOS includes an extended memory manager called HIMEM.SYS.

HIMEM.SYS is a device driver, so you can't load it at the system prompt. Instead, you load HIMEM.SYS as a device in your configuration file (CONFIG.SYS).

Updating the CONFIG.SYS File for HIMEM.SYS

To use the HIMEM.SYS extended memory manager, you have to add a DEVICE statement to your CONFIG.SYS file. A device is hardware, such as a mouse, a printer, or memory. To effectively use a device, you must give DOS the information it needs to access and manage the device with the help of a device driver. HIMEM.SYS is a device driver that provides a standard way for your programs to address the extended memory of your system. You tell DOS to use HIMEM.SYS by adding a DEVICE statement to your CONFIG.SYS file.

A DEVICE statement simply tells DOS that anything following the word DEVICE is a device. To be most efficient, the DEVICE statement for HIMEM.SYS must be inserted in the CONFIG.SYS file *before* any other DEVICE statements that use extended memory, such as SMARTDrive or EMM386.

TIP

Before you make any changes to your CONFIG.SYS file, make a backup of your original CONFIG.SYS and be sure you have a system (bootable) disk.

To revise your CONFIG.SYS file, open CONFIG.SYS in MS-DOS Editor and insert the HIMEM.SYS DEVICE statement before any other DEVICE statements involving extended memory.

You must reboot your computer for changes to the CONFIG.SYS file to take effect. To reboot your computer, press Ctrl+Alt+Del.

Loading DOS in High Memory

To free even more conventional memory, you can run DOS in the high-memory area (HMA) after loading the HIMEM.SYS extended memory manager. To run DOS in HMA, add the following line to your CONFIG.SYS after the HIMEM.SYS statement:

DOS=HIGH

To enable DOS to load memory-resident programs and device drivers into the upper-memory blocks, thereby freeing more conventional memory, you can add the UMB (upper-memory blocks) statement to the preceding DOS statement, like this:

DOS=HIGH, UMB

Combining HIMEM.SYS and EMM386

You can use HIMEM.SYS in conjunction with EMM386 to run DOS in extended memory. Combining these two memory managers enables you to use parts of the upper-memory area if you have a 386 or 486 computer. For more information, see the article "Optimize with EMM386.EXE" later in this section.

TIP Use both HIMEM.SYS and EMM386.EXE in configuration files; together, the two present powerful memory optimization.

Add HIMEM.SYS to CONFIG.SYS

1. Use DOS Editor to open your CONFIG.SYS file (located in the root directory of your hard disk).

2. Add the following line to CONFIG.SYS, *before* any other DEVICE statements that use extended memory:

   DEVICE=C:\DOS\HIMEM.SYS

   If your system has DOS loaded in any directory besides C:\DOS, be sure to add the correct path when you type the preceding statement.

3. Save the changes and exit DOS Editor.

4. Reboot the computer so that the DEVICE command can take effect.

HIMEM statement

```
 File  Edit  Search  Options                                    Help
                        CONFIG.SYS
DEVICE=C:\DOS\SETVER.EXE
DEVICE=C:\DOS\HIMEM.SYS
DEVICE=C:\DOS\EMM386.EXE RAM HIGHSCAN WIN=FB00-FDFF WIN=F800-FAFF
buffers=30,0
FILES=40
dos=HIGH, UMB
LASTDRIVE=E
FCBS=16,8
DEVICE=C:\DOS\SMARTDRV.EXE /DOUBLE_BUFFER
SHELL=C:\DOS\COMMAND.COM C:\DOS\ /e:512 /p
DEVICE=c:\cuss12.sys
DEVICEHIGH /L:2,4096 =C:\CUFLOPPY.SYS /D1:2
STACKS=9,256
DEVICEHIGH=C:\DOS\DBLSPACE.SYS /MOVE




MS-DOS Editor  <F1=Help> Press ALT to activate menus      N 00001:001
```

Use MS-DOS Editor to edit the CONFIG.SYS file.

Load DOS into high memory

Troubleshooting

◆ If you add the DEVICE statement to your CONFIG.SYS and you don't have extended memory, DOS will display this error message each time you boot: ERROR No available extended memory was found.

◆ If you are using a third-party memory manager and you try to load HIMEM.SYS, DOS displays the following error message: ERROR An Extended Memory Manager is already installed.

Optimize with HIMEM.SYS 139

Still trying to free up conventional memory? Here's another idea.

The EMM386 extended memory manager uses extended memory to simulate expanded memory. What that means to you is a more efficient computer. In addition, EMM386.EXE can create upper-memory blocks (UMBs) that can be used for device drivers and memory-resident programs, leaving more conventional memory free.

EMM386.EXE is added to the CONFIG.SYS file; it cannot be used at the system prompt. To decide whether you should add EMM386.EXE to your CONFIG.SYS, ask yourself these questions:

◆ Do you have a 386 or 486 computer with extended memory?

◆ Do you have any programs that require expanded memory—such as a spreadsheet?

◆ Will you be using UMBs for device drivers or memory-resident programs?

If you answered "Yes" to all of these questions, you can, and should, use EMM386.EXE.

Updating the CONFIG.SYS File for EMM386

To add EMM386.EXE to your CONFIG.SYS file, you have to insert a DEVICE statement—just as you did for HIMEM.SYS. You must add the EMM386.EXE statement *after* the HIMEM.SYS statement. Make sure that you use the EXE extension for EMM386.EXE—as opposed to the

SYS extension that HIMEM uses. Also, be sure that you have a backup copy of your original CONFIG.SYS file before you make any changes to it.

After you add EMM386.EXE to your CONFIG.SYS file, you must reboot your computer for the changes to take effect. To reboot your computer, press Ctrl+Alt+Del.

Caution: *Have a system disk handy—just in case your system doesn't reboot properly.*

The EMM386.EXE Options

Programmers use many EMM386.EXE options that are beyond the scope of this book. However, you can optimize your memory by adding EMM386.EXE to your CONFIG.SYS with either the RAM option or the NOEMS option.

The RAM option creates UMBs and simulates expanded memory. The default amount of simulated expanded memory is 256K. Use the RAM option if you have programs that can use expanded memory—we all can use extra UMBs!

The NOEMS option creates UMBs only, reserving extended memory instead of using it for expanded memory simulation; some programs work more efficiently with extended memory. Use this option if you use programs that don't require expanded memory or if you use Microsoft Windows 3.1. Windows 3.1 works more efficiently with the NOEMS option because that option offers the maximum amount of extended memory.

TIP You must have HIMEM.SYS in your
CONFIG.SYS to use EMM386.EXE.

Add EMM386.EXE to CONFIG.SYS

1. Use DOS Editor to open your
CONFIG.SYS file (located in the root
directory of your hard disk).

2. Add one of the following commands to
CONFIG.SYS, *after* the HIMEM.SYS
statement:

DEVICE=EMM386.EXE RAM

or

DEVICE=EMM386.EXE NOEMS

3. Save the changes and exit DOS Editor.

4. Reboot the computer so that the command takes effect.

Troubleshooting

If your system doesn't boot properly after
following these steps, use a system disk to
reboot. Open DOS Editor again and study
your CONFIG.SYS file to see if you made
any typing errors. Correct any errors, save
the file, and reboot the computer.

```
  File  Edit  Search  Options                                  Help
                              CONFIG.SYS
  DEVICE=C:\DOS\SETVER.EXE
  DEVICE=C:\DOS\HIMEM.SYS
  DEVICE=C:\DOS\EMM386.EXE NOEMS
  DOS=HIGH,UMB
  STACKS=9,256
  FILES=40
  BUFFERS=32
  REM LASTDRIVE=H
  SHELL=C:\DOS\COMMAND.COM C:\DOS\  /p
  DEVICE=C:\MOUSE.SYS




  MS-DOS Editor   <F1=Help> Press ALT to activate menus    N 00001:001
```

*EMM386 statement
with NOEMS option.*

If you're looking for an easy way to optimize your computer's memory, forget adding memory managers to your CONFIG.SYS file and use MemMaker instead.

The MemMaker program is included with DOS and can help you make the best use of your memory. MemMaker moves as many programs and device drivers to upper memory as possible, freeing that ever-popular conventional memory.

MemMaker is a fairly automatic program; you just have to agree with it now and then. You can run MemMaker any time you add a new program or change your configuration. It's quick and easy to use.

MemMaker Options

When you enter the MEMMAKER command at the system prompt, MemMaker displays a welcome screen telling you about the program and offering suggestions on when to use it. Highlighted text on the screen represents an option. To accept the option, press Enter; to change the option, press the space bar.

The second screen offers you either the Express or Custom Setup. Unless you really know what you're doing, choose the Express Setup. MemMaker then displays a screen asking if you have programs that use expanded memory. If you aren't sure, check the reference manuals that come with your programs. Alternatively, choose No; you can always run MemMaker again if you find you need expanded memory.

The MemMaker Process

After you specify the options you want, MemMaker displays a message saying it will reboot your computer; press Enter. MemMaker tests and configures your system, writes changes to the CONFIG.SYS and AUTOEXEC.BAT files, and then displays another message indicating that it will reboot your computer. Press Enter again. Watch your screen carefully as the computer boots, noting any error messages that appear.

MemMaker displays a screen asking you to choose No if you saw an error message or Yes if your system appeared to be working properly. If you choose No, MemMaker cancels all the configuration changes it made and returns you to the system prompt. If you choose Yes, indicating your computer was operating properly, MemMaker displays a report telling you how much conventional memory, upper memory, and expanded memory you had both before and after you ran the program. Press Enter to exit.

> **TIP**
> If you chose No and MemMaker cancelled its alterations to your system, you can try adjusting your configuration files and running MemMaker again.

Optimize Memory with MemMaker

1. At the system prompt, type **MEMMAKER**.

2. Press Enter.

3. At the Welcome screen, read the text and then press Enter to continue.

4. Choose Express Setup.

5. Follow the directions on-screen, and answer each prompt that MemMaker displays.

Troubleshooting

If at the end of the setup you experience problems with your system or you don't like what MemMaker did, you can undo the changes by typing **MEMMAKER /UNDO** at the system prompt and pressing Enter.

The MemMaker Welcome screen.

```
Microsoft MemMaker

Welcome to MemMaker.

MemMaker optimizes your system's memory by moving memory-resident
programs and device drivers into the upper memory area. This
frees conventional memory for use by applications.

After you run MemMaker, your computer's memory will remain
optimized until you add or remove memory-resident programs or
device drivers. For an optimum memory configuration, run MemMaker
again after making any such changes.

MemMaker displays options as highlighted text. (For example, you
can change the "Continue" option below.) To cycle through the
available options, press SPACEBAR. When MemMaker displays the
option you want, press ENTER.

For help while you are running MemMaker, press F1.

             Continue or Exit? Continue

ENTER=Accept Selection  SPACEBAR=Change Selection  F1=Help  F3=Exit
```

MemMaker asks if your programs use expanded memory.

```
Microsoft MemMaker

If you use any programs that require expanded memory (EMS), answer
Yes to the following question.  Answering Yes makes expanded memory
available, but might not free as much conventional memory.

If none of your programs need expanded memory, answer No to the
following question.  Answering No makes expanded memory unavailable,
but can free more conventional memory.

If you are not sure whether your programs require expanded memory,
answer No.  If you later discover that a program needs expanded
memory, run MemMaker again and answer Yes to this question.

Do you use any programs that need expanded memory (EMS)? Yes

ENTER=Accept Selection  SPACEBAR=Change Selection  F1=Help  F3=Exit
```

Adding Memory

If you're going to buy memory for your computer, don't rely solely on a salesperson for information.

When you're buying memory for a computer, understanding the basics is very important. Some salespeople are knowledgeable and helpful; others know very little but still want to make the sale. If you order memory from a mail-order house, you're pretty much on your own. If you're ordering from a place that deals only with memory, however, you may be able to get competent help. At least have an idea of what you're looking for in computer memory so you'll have a fighting chance to get what's right for your computer.

TIP
If you have a 386 or higher computer, the best advice is to buy as much RAM as you can afford. If you have 4–8M of RAM, many programs will run faster and more efficiently.

Before You Shop
Before you shop for memory, find out how much memory you have, how much memory you need, and what kind of memory your computer uses. You should be able to find all the information you need to buy memory just by reading the documentation that came with your computer. That same information should tell you how much memory you can add to your computer.

As you're reading your computer's documentation, look for the speed and capacity of the memory, which is how RAM chips are graded. *Speed* is measured in *nanoseconds* (*ns*)—one-billionth of a second. 130ns is fairly slow; 70ns is faster. The capacity of a chip tells you how many bits it holds—usually 64K, 256K, 1M, or 4M.

Additionally, you have to find out the *style* of the memory chip. There are several styles of chips: SIMMs, DIPs, and SIPs, for example. The style refers to how the chip is inserted into your computer, and how the chips are clustered.

SIMM (which stands for Single In-line Memory Module) is currently the most common RAM chip. SIMMs usually come as three or four chips soldered to a card that plugs into a SIMM socket. A *DIP* (Dual In-line Package) is a single chip that plugs into a socket in your computer. Finally, a *SIP* (Single In-line Package) contains nine chips and plugs in with tiny prongs.

TIP
If you're purchasing an expanded memory card, find out how much expanded memory your software needs; then make sure the card is LIM EMS 4.0 compatible. LIM EMS is the expanded memory specification that's most current and allows for the best use of your expanded memory.

Buying and Installing Memory
The simplest method of purchasing memory is to go to the dealer who sold you the computer. He or she should know what kind of computer you have and what type of memory you need. The dealer may even install the memory for you and charge you an hourly rate. It should take no longer than a few minutes to install the memory.

You can install the memory yourself. If you purchase the memory through a mail-order house, you'll have to install it, or have someone knowledgeable do it for you. Instructions come with the memory you buy through the mail. Installation is fairly easy; just be careful you don't damage the chips by dropping them, bending them, forcing them, and so on.

Before you hand over the money for memory, ask the salesperson these questions:

◆ Will all the chips be the same brand? Chips also should be all the same speed.

◆ If a chip is bad, will they provide a replacement at no charge? Chips are easily damaged, so be sure you can get a replacement.

◆ If you're installing the chip yourself, ask whether instructions are enclosed.

Troubleshooting

◆ If you install the memory yourself, be very careful not to damage the chips or the card; stores will not refund your money or give you a new card if you damage it while you are installing it.

◆ Inspect all cards you purchase for bent edges, metal legs, scratches, and loose chips before you install it.

◆ If you install a card and find that it does not work, first try removing it and re-installing. If it still does not work, take it back to the place you purchased it.

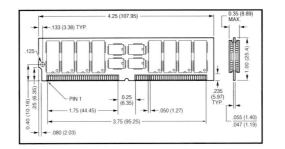

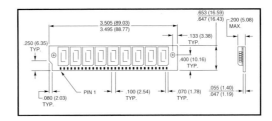

A SIMM chip is a tiny expansion card that plugs into your computer to let you take full advantage of the computer's memory potential.

Installation Tips

◆ Turn the computer off and unplug it before you remove the cover.

◆ Before you insert the chip into the computer, touch the metal housing of the computer with your hand or finger to discharge any static electricity that has built up. Static can ruin your memory chip.

◆ Don't touch the metal legs on a DIP or SIP, or the metal edge connectors of a SIMM. You'll damage the chip.

◆ After installation, leave the computer's cover off while you check the memory so you don't have to unscrew all those screws again if there's a problem.

◆ When you turn your computer on, you must go through Setup to tell the com-puter how much memory you added. To access Setup, insert the Reference disk that came with your computer and reboot. Follow the directions on the screen.

◆ If you get a `Parity error` message, one of the chips may be bad or inserted improperly. Turn off the computer and unplug it before you adjust the chips.

To make the most of your system resources, you can enter special configuration commands in your computer's CONFIG.SYS file.

Configuration files govern how the operating system—DOS—interacts with software and hardware. The CONFIG.SYS is a system file containing special commands that DOS reads during the boot process. The CONFIG.SYS file is located in the root directory of the boot disk—either a hard disk or a floppy system disk. Because the CONFIG.SYS file is a text file (or ASCII file), you can change it and add to it using the MS-DOS Editor.

Changing your configuration file is not at all hard; however, getting your system to work after you change the file can be difficult. You have to be willing to experiment with the configuration commands, test your programs using the new CONFIG.SYS file, and then tweak the file a little more.

 TIP In addition to the following suggestions, consider adding HIMEM.SYS and EMM386 to your CONFIG.SYS file to optimize your system's memory.

Configuration Commands

The commands used in a CONFIG.SYS are called *configuration commands*; these commands tell DOS how to run your system. When you install DOS, it creates a CONFIG.SYS file with some generic commands to run your system. In addition, many application programs change the CONFIG.SYS when installed. You can control the way that DOS handles your system by adding or changing configuration commands in your CONFIG.SYS.

TIP Changes you make to CONFIG.SYS could prevent your computer from booting. If you have not yet created a system disk, refer to the article "Creating a System Disk" in the section "Hard Disks" and make a system disk now. That way, if you do have a problem with changes made to your CONFIG.SYS file, you can boot from the system disk and copy the old CONFIG.SYS file back to your hard disk.

This article describes a number of configuration commands you may want to add to or change in your CONFIG.SYS file. If you're unsure about modifying your CONFIG.SYS file, you may want to learn more about DOS and configuration files before attempting a change. For more information about any command, see Appendix B, "Command Reference."

BREAK

BREAK controls how often DOS checks for the key combination Ctrl+C, which stops a command. The default setting is BREAK OFF, which means that DOS checks for Ctrl+C only while it reads from the keyboard or writes to the screen or printer. If BREAK is on, DOS checks for Break commands during other operations.

TIP MemMaker changes your CONFIG.SYS file to optimize your memory and devices, customizing the configuration for your system.

BUFFERS

Using buffers can speed your computer. *Buffers* specify an amount of RAM that DOS reserves for holding data when reading or writing to disk. The amount of buffers you use depends on the type of programs you run and the size of your hard disk. You can specify from 1 to 99 buffers. Buffers take up memory, however, so you may have to adjust the amount of buffers if your computer starts running slower. A few suggestions follow:

◆ If your hard disk size is 80M or less, use 20 to 30 buffers (**BUFFERS=20**). Specify 20 buffers if you use a simple word processing program; specify 30 buffers if you use several programs—word processing, spreadsheet, office manager, and so on.

◆ If your hard disk size is from 80M to 120M, you can increase buffers to 40 and see faster, more efficient work from your computer. You may even want to increase the buffers to 50 if you use a desktop publishing program or Windows.

◆ If your hard disk size is 120M or more, set your buffers to 50 for maximum efficiency.

COUNTRY

The COUNTRY setting configures DOS to use international time, dates, currency, and so on.

Set buffers to no more than 50 for the most effective use of the BUFFER command; setting more than 50 buffers uses more memory without increasing speed.

DEVICE and DEVICEHIGH

DEVICE loads a device driver into memory. DEVICEHIGH loads a device driver into an upper memory block. See "Configuring Devices" for more information.

DOS

If you haven't already loaded DOS into high memory, and you have a 386 or higher processor, load DOS high by adding the command **DOS=HIGH** to your CONFIG.SYS file. When DOS is in the high memory area, about 14K of conventional memory is freed. In addition, you can enable DOS to use upper memory blocks by adding the command **UMB** (**DOS=HIGH, UMB**).

DRIVPARM

DRIVPARM defines the operating characteristics—such as the total number of drive heads, whether the drive is removable, the total number of sectors per track in a drive, and so on—of an existing disk or tape drive.

FCBS

FCBS specifies the number of file control blocks (FCBs) that DOS can have open at one time. FCBs are small blocks of information that help DOS keep track of file usage. Most new application programs don't require FCBs, and you're unlikely to need the FCBS command in your everyday use of DOS.

FILES

FILES specifies the number of files that can be opened simultaneously. You can set FILES anywhere from 8 to 255. The default is 8; however, this is very seldom enough. If you use a word processing program, for example, setting FILES to 20 is probably sufficient (**FILES=20**). If you use Windows, a database, or a spreadsheet program, increase the number of files to 30. If you use Windows and a desktop publishing program, increase the number of files to 40. You probably don't need any more than 40 files set; the more files you specify with the FILES command, the more memory is used.

INSTALL

INSTALL loads a TSR (memory-resident program) into memory each time your computer starts, and keeps it in memory until you turn off your computer.

more ▶

LASTDRIVE

LASTDRIVE sets the highest number of disk drives you can access, using the values A through Z. LASTDRIVE is usually set to the one after the last drive being used; for example, if you use disk drives A, B, and C, LAST-DRIVE is usually set to D or E.

NUMLOCK

NUMLOCK (MS-DOS 6.0 only) sets the NumLock key on or off when your computer starts.

REM

REM precedes a line in the CONFIG.SYS file to turn off the line. You can also use this command to add remarks to the CONFIG.SYS. Any statement beginning with REM is ignored when DOS reads the configuration file.

SET

SET (MS-DOS 6 only) specifies how the environment looks or behaves. You can change how the system prompt looks by using SET, for example. Many SET commands are also used in the AUTOEXEC.BAT file. For more information about the AUTOEXEC.BAT file, see the article in this section "Editing AUTOEXEC.BAT."

SHELL

SHELL specifies the location and name of the command interpreter—a file containing

internal commands such as dir, del, date, and time. COMMAND.COM is DOS's default command interpreter; however, you could use a third-party command interpreter instead.

STACKS

STACKS specifies the amount of RAM set aside for DOS to store information when a hardware interrupt occurs. Two numbers are used: the first number indicates how many stacks are set aside (from 8 to 64); the second number specifies the size of each stack (from 32 to 512). A common value for setting stacks is 8, 512 or 9, 128. Naturally, the more stacks you set aside and the larger each stack is, the more memory they use. For more information about memory, see the section "Managing Memory."

SWITCHES

SWITCHES blocks enhanced keyboard functions to make your keyboard function like a conventional keyboard. Some programs cannot interpret input from an enhanced keyboard.

CONFIG.SYS Guidelines

When editing your CONFIG.SYS, keep the following items in mind:

◆ Load HIMEM.SYS before you load any other device or command that uses extended memory because HIMEM.SYS is the extended memory manager. Load EMM386.EXE after HIMEM.SYS.

◆ Load device drivers that can use the upper memory area into upper memory so that you can save conventional memory for your application programs. But don't load HIMEM.SYS or EMM386.EXE into upper memory because both are memory managers that cannot run in the upper memory area.

◆ Type **rem** in front of any memory-resident programs or device drivers that you don't need. If you're not using the TSRs or devices, they are taking up unnecessary memory.

◆ Changes you make to CONFIG.SYS could prevent your computer from booting. Before you edit your CONFIG.SYS, copy it to your system disk, just in case you have a problem with the changes you make. If you do have a problem, boot from the system disk.

Note: You may have to try several configuration changes before your computer boots.

◆ Instead of deleting a command in CONFIG.SYS, use the REM command to deactivate the command, just in case you want to refer to it at a later date.

TIP

To see what's in your CONFIG.SYS without editing it, at the system prompt, type the command **type config.sys** and press Enter. You may need to specify the path to the CONFIG.SYS file if it's in a different directory.

Edit CONFIG.SYS

1. Start the MS-DOS Editor (see the section "MS-DOS Editor" for details on using Editor).

2. Open the CONFIG.SYS file.

3. Edit the file as desired.

4. Choose Save from the File menu to save the file.

5. Choose Exit from the File menu to return to the system prompt.

6. Reboot your computer by pressing Ctrl+Alt+Del.

Troubleshooting

◆ Be sure to use the correct syntax for each configuration command. If you don't use the correct syntax, DOS cannot carry out the command.

◆ If your computer doesn't start when rebooted (no system prompt appears), use your system disk to boot the computer. Then access the hard disk and edit the CONFIG.SYS file.

◆ If the computer boots but you get error messages, and you're not sure which commands are causing the problem, copy your original CONFIG.SYS from the system disk to the hard disk.

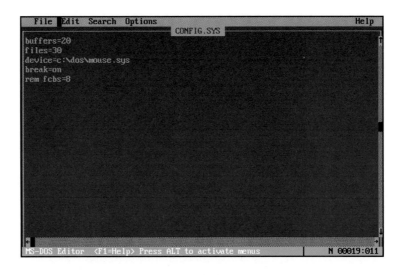

A basic CONFIG.SYS file.

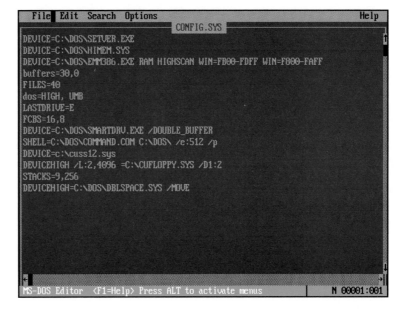

A fine-tuned CONFIG.SYS file.

A large part of fine-tuning your system configuration deals with how DOS handles your devices—the printer, mouse, floppy drives, and so on.

Your computer is made up of input and output devices. *Input devices* include any device that enables you to put information into your computer—such as the keyboard, mouse, or floppy disk drive. *Output devices* are those that the computer sends information to—a printer or floppy disk drive, for example.

In addition to these devices, you have channels for communication—ports. *Ports* are the connections between one computer and another or between a computer and a device. Ports are *serial* (COM1, COM2, etc.) or *parallel* (LPT1, LPT2, etc.), which describes how the information is transferred.

Device Drivers

A *device driver* is a file that contains a set of instructions that gives DOS what it needs to run a device or access certain hardware. When you use a mouse or a printer, for example, you must load a device driver to tell DOS how to use it. If you've ever loaded a software application, you know that it asks what kind of printer you use. When you specify a printer, the application may load a printer device driver that DOS uses to access that printer. You don't want to load all printer drivers when you only need one; that takes up too much disk space.

TIP
You can use DEVICEHIGH to load TSRs and device drivers into high memory. Use LOADHIGH (or LH) to load a TSR into upper memory from the command prompt.

Device Statements

A *device statement* is a command line that tells DOS which driver you need for the current work session. You normally don't enter a device statement at the system prompt; instead, you place the statement in your CONFIG.SYS file. When you place a device statement in your configuration file, DOS loads the drivers you need each time you start your computer.

Device drivers you place in your CONFIG.SYS file, like commands, must be written in a format that DOS can understand. Use the DEVICE command to tell DOS to load the driver. Next, enter the path to the device driver file, the device driver's file name and extension, and any switches. To use the HIMEM.SYS driver in your CONFIG.SYS, for example, enter the following statement:

DEVICE=C:\DOS\HIMEM.SYS

This statement tells DOS to use the HIMEM.SYS extended memory manager device. For more information about HIMEM.SYS, see "Optimizing Memory with HIMEM.SYS."

Device Names

DOS assigns names to each device; you must use DOS's device names when you specify a device in a command or statement. The following table shows the device names you can use.

Use a Device Driver

1. Start the MS-DOS Editor (for details on using Editor, see the section "MS-DOS Editor").

2. Open the CONFIG.SYS file.

3. Edit the file, using the following syntax for device drivers:

   DEVICE=<*PATH*>\<*DEVICENAME*>

   or

   DEVICEHIGH=<*PATH*>\<*DEVICENAME*>

4. Choose Save from the File menu to save the file.

5. Choose Exit from the File menu to return to the system prompt.

6. Reboot your computer by pressing Ctrl+Alt+Del.

Device driver statements

```
 File  Edit  Search  Options                                    Help
                          CONFIG.SYS
DEVICE=C:\DOS\SETVER.EXE
DEVICE=C:\DOS\HIMEM.SYS
DEVICE=C:\DOS\EMM386.EXE RAM HIGHSCAN WIN=FB00-FDFF WIN=F800-FAFF
buffers=30,0
FILES=40
dos=HIGH, UMB
LASTDRIVE=E
FCBS=16,8
DEVICE=C:\DOS\SMARTDRV.EXE /DOUBLE_BUFFER
SHELL=C:\DOS\COMMAND.COM C:\DOS\ /e:512 /p
DEVICE=c:\cuss12.sys
DEVICEHIGH /L:2,4096 =C:\CUFLOPPY.SYS /D1:2
STACKS=9,256
DEVICEHIGH=C:\DOS\DBLSPACE.SYS /MOVE



 MS-DOS Editor  <F1=Help> Press ALT to activate menus          N 00001:001
```

DEVICEHIGH statements

This CONFIG.SYS file—which is tailored specifically to Windows 3.1 use—includes several DEVICE statements and DEVICEHIGH statements.

Name	Device	Description
AUX	Auxiliary	Input or output device referring to COM1 or COM2—serial ports.
COM1, COM2, COM3, COM4	Communications	Serial ports for input or output.
CON	Console	Keyboard for input; display for output. Which one DOS uses depends on the type of command used with the device name.
LPT1, LPT2, LPT3	Line printer	Parallel printer ports for output.
PRN	Printer	Output device on the parallel port, unless you specify otherwise.

Loading Devices into High Memory

If the following requirements are met, you can use the DEVICEHIGH command to load device drivers into the high memory area, conserving conventional memory:

◆ Your computer has a 386 or higher processor.

◆ HIMEM.SYS and EMM386 statements are in your CONFIG.SYS file.

◆ DOS=HIGH, UMB is in your CONFIG.SYS file.

When entering the device statement in your CONFIG.SYS file, simply substitute DEVICEHIGH for DEVICE. Some drivers may not work with the DEVICEHIGH statement. You can find out if a driver will work by first entering the statement in your CONFIG.SYS file and then rebooting your computer. Use the MEMORY command (MEM /C) to check which devices are loaded into the high memory area.

Are there any commands you want DOS to carry out automatically? If so, put them in the AUTOEXEC.BAT file.

When you install DOS, it creates an AUTOEXEC.BAT file for you. In addition, many application programs add to your AUTOEXEC.BAT file when you install them. You can add any command to your AUTOEXEC.BAT file that you want DOS to execute when you first turn on your computer. You can change directories, list files, start DOS Shell, and even change your system prompt to say What can I do for you today?

When you place commands in the AUTOEXEC.BAT, you're setting up your system's defaults, tailoring your system to what you need to do your work. You can save time by adding the commands you use every day to your AUTOEXEC.BAT and letting DOS carry out those commands automatically.

TIP Before you edit AUTOEXEC.BAT, save it to your system disk or save it under another name, just in case you run into a problem.

What is the AUTOEXEC.BAT?

The AUTOEXEC.BAT file is a batch program. A *batch program* speeds your work by performing multiple commands when you enter the name of the program. However, with the AUTOEXEC.BAT, you don't even have to type the name of the file. When you boot your computer, DOS checks the root directory for the CONFIG.SYS; then it checks for an AUTOEXEC.BAT.

Most system configurations contain an AUTOEXEC.BAT because it's an easy way to give DOS several commands about your system. An AUTOEXEC.BAT usually contains commands that specify the style of the prompt, a temporary directory for programs that use a temporary directory, a path that DOS searches for commands, and so on.

 TIP For more information about batch files, see "Creating Batch Files."

AUTOEXEC.BAT Commands

This article describes a number of commands you may want to add or change in your AUTOEXEC.BAT file. For more information about any command, see Appendix B, "Command Reference."

Although you can use almost any command in a batch program, there are some common commands you'll most likely want to use. Descriptions and examples of common commands you can use in your AUTOEXEC.BAT follow.

PROMPT

The PROMPT command tells DOS what sort of system prompt you want. The normal system prompt is c:\>; however, it can be anything you want. You could tell DOS to prompt you with Have a nice day. You can introduce yourself, ask a question, or use a variety of characters as your system prompt.

The following table shows some common settings.

Type this...	To display this
$q	= (equal sign)
$$	$ (dollar sign)
$t	current time
$d	current date
$p	current drive and path
$v	DOS version number
$g	> (greater than sign)

In addition to or instead of character combinations, you can use words or sentences. The syntax for PROMPT is

PROMPT <TEXT>

Within <text>, you can place a character combination—for example, the prompt format C:\WORD> is written as follows:

PROMPT pg

Or you can use an actual sentence:

PROMPT How can I help you?

TIP

No matter what your prompt, add a space after the text string. That way, your cursor won't crowd the prompt when you enter commands.

PATH

The PATH command sets the path you want DOS to follow when searching for executable files—EXE, COM, or BAT. PATH tells DOS in which directories to search. When you type **wp** at any prompt, for example, does WordPerfect start? That's because the path to WordPerfect is in the PATH statement in your AUTOEXEC.BAT. The same idea works when you enter a DOS command; because of the path—for example, C:\DOS—DOS knows where to go to find the COM or EXE file. The syntax for a path statement is:

path <drive:\path;drive:\path>

You can add as many paths to your AUTOEXEC.BAT as you want—up to 127 characters. Separate paths with a semicolon (;). Here's a typical PATH statement:

C:\;C:\DOS;C:\WINDOWS;C:\WP60

more ▶

ECHO

Set to OFF, ECHO prevents the display of the commands from the AUTOEXEC.BAT file as DOS runs and executes them. Set to ON, ECHO displays the commands.

A great way to display a message at the prompt is with the ECHO command. The problem with using **PROMPT** for How can I help you? is that the text is *always* there, every time you press Enter. With ECHO, you can turn the display of the command lines of the batch program on or off. Generally, you may want ECHO off; however, you may want to send yourself a message each day.

When you want one command line of the batch program not to show, begin that line with the @ (at) sign. If you don't want any DOS commands in the batch program to show, use ECHO OFF. If you want to display a message, begin the line of the message with ECHO. For example, **ECHO Don't forget to smile!** could be the last command in your AUTOEXEC.BAT.

Other Popular AUTOEXEC.BAT Commands

Following are some common DOS commands you can also use in your AUTOEXEC.BAT file:

◆ **CD.** Change directories to C:\DOS, or any directory you want, by including the CD command in your AUTOEXEC.BAT. If you regularly work from your REPORTS directory, for example, you can change to the directory as the system boots with the command **CD\REPORTS**.

◆ **CLS.** Clear Screen (CLS) is a handy command to add to an AUTOEXEC.BAT; using the CLS command clears the command from the screen immediately after it is executed.

◆ **DATE.** DATE displays the request for a date; DOS can put a date stamp on newly created or updated files. DATE is not necessary if your computer has a battery-operated system clock that keeps the date current.

◆ **DIR.** The DIR (Directory) command, when listed in your AUTOEXEC.BAT, displays the current directory. You also can add the /w and /p switches to this command.

◆ **DOSSHELL.** Use this command to pull up the DOS Shell when the computer boots, rather than the system prompt.

◆ **TIME.** Want to be sure your computer's clock is correct? TIME displays a request for the time. This command is not necessary if your computer has a battery-operated system clock.

AUTOEXEC.BAT Guidelines

When editing your AUTOEXEC.BAT, keep the following items in mind:

◆ AUTOEXEC.BAT must be the name of the file.

◆ The AUTOEXEC.BAT must be in the root directory of the hard disk.

◆ The AUTOEXEC.BAT is a text file (ASCII).

◆ An AUTOEXEC.BAT file can contain any command you can type at the system prompt.

◆ An AUTOEXEC.BAT file can contain the name of any program, as long as you can start that program from the system prompt—such as an EXE file.

◆ Because DOS executes the AUTOEXEC.BAT file one line at a time, you can only include one command or program name per line.

TIP

To view your AUTOEXEC.BAT without editing it, at the system prompt, type the command **type autoexec.bat** and press Enter. You may need to specify the path to the AUTOEXEC.BAT file if you're working in a different directory.

Edit AUTOEXEC.BAT

1. Start the MS-DOS Editor (for details on using Editor, see the section "MS-DOS Editor").

2. Open the AUTOEXEC.BAT file.

3. Edit the file as desired.

4. Choose Save from the File menu to save the file.

5. Choose Exit from the File menu to return to the system prompt.

6. Reboot your computer by pressing Ctrl+Alt+Del.

Troubleshooting

Before you edit AUTOEXEC.BAT, save it to your system disk or save it under another name, just in case you run into a problem.

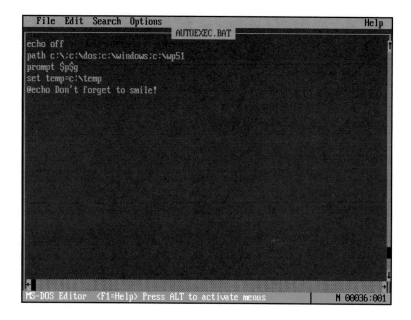

A typical AUTOEXEC.BAT file.

You can customize your system even more by using different configurations for different types of work.

By using multiple configurations, you can get the most from your computer—setting up your CONFIG.SYS, and even your AUTOEXEC.BAT, in different ways for different work sessions. (For details on multiple AUTOEXEC.BAT configurations, see the next article.)

Suppose that you need to work in Windows today. You can use a configuration that suits Windows—set a path just for Windows work, tweak the EMM386.EXE with switches for Windows, set up a temporary directory in the Windows directory, and so on. On the other hand, the days you work in DOS, you can access a configuration especially for those programs.

TIP For safety purposes, save your original CONFIG.SYS file under a new name or to a system disk before you begin.

Creating a Configuration Menu
When you create a CONFIG.SYS for multiple configurations, you use only one CONFIG.SYS file. You can create a new CONFIG.SYS or work from your existing CONFIG.SYS. Changing the CONFIG.SYS to create the configurations is a two-part process:

◆ Decide what the differences in configurations will be, depending on the programs you'll use in each configuration.

◆ Decide which configurations remain the same—for example, buffers and files or loading DOS into high memory.

Now you're ready to begin. You'll need a menu for DOS to display during startup. The menu enables you to choose which configuration you'll use during the current session; you may want to use Windows and DOS as two configuration choices, for example. In your CONFIG.SYS, you identify the menu by placing the word MENU in brackets; then identify the two menu choices as MENUITEMS.

Your next step is to define common configurations—such as devices, buffers, shells, and so on (any configuration commands that both choices can use). Identify the common configuration commands with the heading COMMON in brackets.

Now define each choice, placing the choice names—Windows and DOS, for example—in brackets as a heading for the choices. Below each heading, define the configuration commands specific to the heading.

Save the file and try it out. When you reboot your computer, DOS displays a menu of the headings you specified in your CONFIG.SYS file. Choose the configuration you want to use for this session.

If your computer doesn't start or doesn't operate properly, you may have mistyped a command in the CONFIG.SYS. Reboot your computer using your system disk, and edit the file.

Create a Configuration Menu

1. At the system prompt, type **edit config.sys.**

2. Press Enter.

   MS-DOS Editor opens and displays the CONFIG.SYS file.

3. Add this line at the top of the file:

   [MENU]

4. On separate lines, type the name of each configuration or heading that will appear in the menu, using this format:

   MENUITEM=<*HEADING*>

5. Type this heading for the configuration commands common to all configurations:

   [COMMON]

6. Type or cut and paste any commands you want below the common heading.

7. Type the name of the first configuration heading in brackets; followed by those configuration commands specific to the first heading.

8. Type the name of the second configuration heading in brackets, followed by its specific configuration commands.

9. Save the file, overwriting the old version.

Commands common to both configurations

Startup menu

```
 File   Edit   Search   Options                              Help
                                CONFIG.SYS
[MENU] 3
MENUITEM=WINDOWS 4
MENUITEM=DOS

[COMMON] 5
DEVICE=C:\DOS\SETVER.EXE
DEVICE=C:\DOS\HIMEM.SYS
BUFFERS=30,0
FILES=40
DOS=HIGH, UMB
SHELL=C:\DOS\COMMAND.COM C:\DOS\ /e:512 /p

[WINDOWS] 8
DEVICE=C:\DOS\EMM386.EXE RAM HIGHSCAN WIN=FB00-FDFF WIN=F800-FAFF
SET PATH=C:\WINDOWS;C:\DOS
SET TEMP=C:\WINDOWS\TEMP

[DOS]
DEVICE=C:\DOS\EMM386.EXE NOEMS
SET PATH=C:\;C:\DOS
SET TEMP=C:\TEMP

MS-DOS Editor  <F1=Help> Press ALT to activate menus      CN 00021:017
```

Commands for DOS session

Commands for Windows session

10. Exit Editor.

11. Reboot your computer by pressing Ctrl+Alt+Del.

    The completed configuration menu displays the following options:

    ```
    MS-DOS 6 Startup Menu

    1. WINDOWS

    2. DOS

    Enter a choice: 1

    F5=Bypass startup files    F8=Confirm
    each CONFIG.SYS line [N]
    ```

If one AUTOEXEC.BAT lets you customize your configuration, just think what two AUTOEXEC.BATs can do!

After changing your CONFIG.SYS file to reflect new configurations, you can also alter the AUTOEXEC.BAT with specific commands to enhance the CONFIG.SYS configurations. You can specify the mouse driver and load a TSR for use with DOS programs, for example. When working in Windows, you don't need the TSR; but you may want to alter the path for a specific directory and load a mouse driver in Windows. (Remember that multiple configurations are available with MS-DOS 6 only.)

TIP For safety purposes, save your original AUTOEXEC.BAT file under a new name or to a system disk before you begin.

Altering the AUTOEXEC.BAT

To create the new AUTOEXEC.BAT file, you may want to use some of the commands in your original file, so open AUTOEXEC.BAT in MS-DOS Editor. Begin editing by placing all commands that both configurations have in common at the beginning of the file.

After the common commands, you must include a statement telling DOS to reference the configuration being used.

DOS checks to see which configuration you chose and then moves to the matching heading in your AUTOEXEC.BAT. If the configuration is Windows, for example, DOS should perform commands below the Windows heading.

TIP Make the most of multiple configurations by defining an AUTOEXEC.BAT specifically for the programs you use. You may, for example, use all desktop publishing programs—graphics, screen capture TSRs, publishing programs, and presentation programs—some days; then on other days you change to mathematically based programs—such as spreadsheets, accounting programs, and databases. Tweak your AUTOEXEC.BAT until you create the best working environment for both of your worlds.

Use the same heading that you used in the CONFIG.SYS file and list commands specific to that heading. At the end of the first heading commands, you enter a statement telling DOS to go to the end so that it skips the second set of configuration commands.

You next enter the second heading and its specific commands. At the end of the file, enter an END statement.

Modify the AUTOEXEC.BAT

1. At the system prompt, type **edit autoexec.bat**.

2. Press Enter.

MS-DOS Editor opens and displays the AUTOEXEC.BAT file.

3. Type or cut and paste all common commands at the beginning of the file.

4. At the end of the common commands, enter the following command:

GOTO %CONFIG%

5. Type the heading exactly as it appears in the CONFIG.SYS file, without the brackets. The heading must be preceded with a colon (:). Type the following, for example:

:WINDOWS

6. Type any commands specific to the first configuration heading.

7. At the end of the first heading's commands, type the following on a line by itself:

GOTO END

8. Type the heading for the second configuration.

9. Type the specific commands.

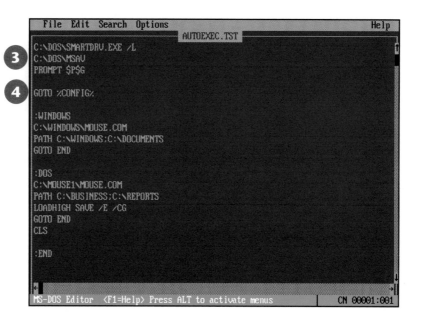

```
 File  Edit  Search  Options                              Help
                        AUTOEXEC.TST
C:\DOS\SMARTDRV.EXE /L
C:\DOS\MSAV
PROMPT $P$G

GOTO %CONFIG%

:WINDOWS
C:\WINDOWS\MOUSE.COM
PATH C:\WINDOWS;C:\DOCUMENTS
GOTO END

:DOS
C:\MOUSE1\MOUSE.COM
PATH C:\BUSINESS;C:\REPORTS
LOADHIGH SAVE /E /CG
GOTO END
CLS

:END


 MS-DOS Editor  <F1=Help> Press ALT to activate menus      CN 00001:001
```

10. At the end of the commands, type the following:

GOTO END

11. At the end of the file, type the following:

:END

12. Save the file, overwriting the old version.

13. Exit Editor.

14. Reboot the computer by pressing Ctrl+Alt+Del.

Troubleshooting

If you have problems with your computer when you reboot, you may have mistyped a command or left out a step. Use your system disk to reboot, open the AUTOEXEC.BAT file in Editor, and go over the file. Correct any mistakes, save the file, and reboot the computer.

For better file management, let DOS stamp the correct date and time on each file you save or update.

If you have a battery-operated system clock that automatically keeps the time, then you don't have to worry about the date and time unless your battery goes out. If your system doesn't have an internal clock, then you should use the DATE and TIME commands.

It's especially important for backup purposes that you use current date and time stamps with your files. A backup procedure often checks the date on a file to see if it has changed since the last backup. You can also search and sort files according to their dates.

Changing the Date and Time

The DATE and TIME commands are similar in the way you enter them and in the way that DOS responds. When you enter either command, DOS displays the current date or time and then asks you to enter a new date or time. If the date or time displayed is correct, you press Enter to accept it and go on your way.

If what DOS displays isn't correct, you enter a new date or time. Type the date as month, day, year in the format mm-dd-yy, unless you're using the format for a country other than the U.S. (see information about the COUNTRY command in the following sidebar). Separate the numbers with hyphens, slashes, or periods. DOS registers the correct day of the week for you.

TIP

You can set the Date and Time commands in your AUTOEXEC.BAT file so DOS automatically displays the prompts each time you start your computer. See the article "Editing AUTOEXEC.BAT" in the "Configuring" section for more information.

If the time is incorrect, enter the new time. Type just the hour and the minutes; you don't have to worry about putting in the seconds. For example, if it's 4:42 pm, type **4:42p** and press Enter. DOS takes care of the rest.

Set the Date and Time

1. At the system prompt, type **DATE**.

2. Press Enter.

3. Enter the new date, or press Enter to accept the current date.

4. At the system prompt, type **TIME**.

5. Press Enter.

6. Enter the new time, or press Enter to accept the current time.

```
C:\> date
Current date is Wed 06-16-1993
Enter new date (mm-dd-yy):

C:\> time
Current time is  4:49:46.66a
Enter new time:

C:\>
```

The DATE and TIME commands.

Setting an International Date

DOS makes provisions for using another country's date and currency format with the COUNTRY command. Over 30 countries can be listed with the COUNTRY command; each country has its own code that DOS identifies with the country. For example, the code for the United States is 001.

Your computer is probably set to the format for the United States, and you usually won't have reason to change it. If you want to change the country setting, however, add the command **COUNTRY=<code>** to your CONFIG.SYS file. Be sure to replace *<code>* with one of the country codes in the following list.

Only a partial listing is shown here; for a complete list, see your DOS reference manual.

Belgium	032
Brazil	055
Canada	002
Denmark	045
France	033
Germany	049
Italy	039
Latin America	003
Spain	034
United Kingdom	044

Changing the Environment

Using the SET command, you can set up a temporary directory, change the way your directory displays, and make changes to your path and prompt.

The SET command lets you change your environment—your work space on the computer. For example, you can change the system prompt to say Happy Birthday for just one day. Or, you can list your directories in a wide format for just one day. You can perform both of these tasks, and more, with the SET command.

DOS enables you to use the SET command at the system prompt for changes that last only until you turn your system off or revise the SET command. You also can use the SET command in your AUTOEXEC.BAT file for changes that are permanent.

Using the SET Command

To use the SET command, you enter the command at the system prompt. Following the command you type the variable, which designates the part of the environment you want to change, such as the prompt or the path. After the variable, you type an equal sign followed by the value, which is the actual change to the environment (for example, *Happy Birthday*).

The SET command remains effective until you turn your computer off or until you enter a new SET command for the same variable. You can turn off a value by entering the SET command, the variable, and the equal sign, with no value designated. For example, type **SET PROMPT=** and press Enter; Happy Birthday is replaced with C>. If you want the fancier C:\> prompt, type **SET PROMPT=PG** and press Enter.

An interesting environment variable is the Directory Command (DIRCMD). DIRCMD enables you to set the directory command (DIR) to display a certain way each time you type the command.

Suppose that you type **DIR /W** to view a wide list of a directory. You could use the SET command to make the directory list that way every time you type DIR. You can use any of the directory switches, such as the switches for attributes, sort order, and so on. To use **SET** with DIRCMD, at the system prompt, type **SET DIRCMD=/W** and press Enter.

Use the SET Command

1. Type this command at the system prompt:

SET *<variable>*=*<value>*

(Specify the variable and the value, of course.)

2. Press Enter.

```
C:\>set prompt=Happy Birthday!

Happy Birthday!
Happy Birthday! set prompt=$p$g

C:\>
```

— Enter command

— New prompt
— Change prompt back to normal

Directory lists wide

```
C:\> set dircmd=/w

C:\> dir

 Volume in drive C is MS_DOS_6
 Volume Serial Number is 0FE8-272D
 Directory of C:\

[DOS]           [OLD_DOS.1]     [WINDOWS]       [COLLAGE]       [BUSINESS]
[REPORT05]      [BUDGET]        COMMAND.COM     WINA20.386      CONFIG.OLD
AUTOEXEC.OLD    AUTOEXEC.BAK    CONFIG.BAK      KTCCACHE.EXE    SFINSTAL.DIR
CONFIG.NEW      CUFLOPPY.SYS    CUSS12.SYS      SPEED200.EXE    FILEINFO.FI
AUTOEXEC.QFX    AUTOEXEC.BAT    CONFIG.SYS      CONFIG.OLE      [MOUSE1]
MOUSE.SYS       CHKLIST.MS      AUTOEXEC.TXT    CONFIG.REA      AUTOEXEC.REA
AUTOEXEC.TST    CONFIG.TST
        32 file(s)      247440 bytes
                      14213120 bytes free

C:\>
```

— Enter command

Need an umlaut or an acute accent? Do you want to type a letter in French, German, or how about Hungarian? You can change your keyboard to enable you to do just that.

Using the KEYB command, you can change your keyboard to type the characters for over 20 languages. The KEYB command configures the keyboard for a specific language; the Keyboard program changes the characters and their arrangement on your keyboard.

Suppose that you want to type a letter in French. You can change the keyboard to French, type the letter in your program, and change the keyboard back when you're finished.

 TIP Your printer may not be able to print the characters from other languages.

Changing the Keyboard

Use the KEYB command at the system prompt to temporarily change your keyboard so that it displays and prints characters in another language. At the system prompt, enter the command and the code representing the appropriate country.

When you use the keyboard after changing to another language, you may notice that some keys are rearranged. Some rearrangement is often necessary to make room for new characters. In addition, some keys will not produce a character; these are called *dead keys*.

Dead keys usually represent an accent mark of some sort. To use a dead key, first press the key and then type the letter it should accent. If in that language it would be incorrect to accent the letter you type, your computer will beep. It takes some experimenting with the new keyboard layout, but if you're familiar with the language, you should have no problem.

To change the keyboard back to United States characters, enter the command plus the keyboard code for the U.S. When you use a foreign language, you can switch back to the U.S. code at any time by pressing Ctrl+Alt+F1. While in the U.S. code, you can switch back to the foreign code by pressing Ctrl+Alt+F2.

Change the Keyboard

1. At the system prompt, type **KEYB** **<*keyboard code*>**.

   Be sure to replace <keyboard code> with the code for the appropriate country.

2. Press Enter.

Troubleshooting

If DOS displays the `Bad command or file name` error when you use the KEYB command, you need to find the KEYBOARD.SYS file. DOS only looks for the file in your DOS directory. If the file has been moved to another directory, DOS assumes it doesn't exist. When you find the KEYBOARD.SYS file, move the file to your DOS directory.

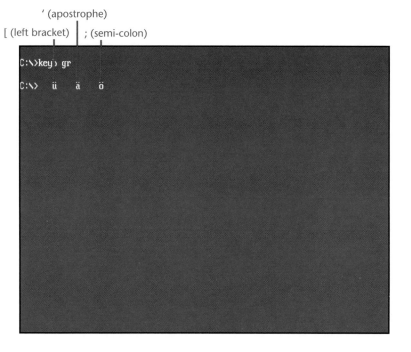

' (apostrophe)
[(left bracket)   ; (semi-colon)

```
C:\>keyb gr

C:\>  ü   ä   ö
```

Changing the keyboard to represent German characters.

Shortcut Keys

Switch to U.S.	Ctrl+Alt+F1
Switch to other language	Ctrl+Alt+F2

Keyboard Codes

Country	Code	Country	Code
Belgium	be	Netherlands	nl
Brazil	bf	Norway	no
Canada (French)	cf	Poland	pl
Czechoslovakia	cz	Portugal	po
Denmark	dk	Spain	sp
Finland	su	Sweden	sv
France	fr	Switzerland (French)	sf
Germany	gr	Switzerland (German)	sg
Hungary	hu	United Kingdom	uk
Italy	it	United States	us
Latin America	la		

If you're tired of typing the path to a subdirectory on drive A over and over again, use the APPEND command.

The APPEND command works much like the PATH command; however, APPEND enables you to access data files as well as program files. Using APPEND, you set a search path for DOS—one path or several paths—that DOS can use to search for a data file you specify.

Suppose that you're working in a database program and you're constantly opening files from drive A. The files in drive A are in the CUSTLIST directory and the PROSPECT subdirectory. Every time you open a file, you have to type the complete path to the subdirectory. If you use the APPEND command, however, you only have to type the path once. DOS remembers it during your work session.

TIP

When you use the APPEND command, your files can be safely read; but when DOS writes to the disk, the APPEND command can cause problems. APPEND causes DOS to make a copy rather than write over the original file.

Appending a Path

You can append a path to make accessing files easier for you and your programs. APPEND tricks DOS into thinking appended directories are actually the current directory. Your program can then read the files without you having to enter a path each time you access the file.

To use APPEND to create a path to your data files, type the command at the system prompt followed by the drive and the path to the files. You can append several paths at one time by separating them with semicolons.

To check what path has been assigned to APPEND, type the command by itself at the system prompt. To end APPEND, type the command followed by a space and a semicolon.

A Word of Caution

Here are some important things to remember when you use the APPEND command:

◆ Use caution when you write to files that APPEND has located for you. APPEND tricks programs into reading files from any location; however, it does not trick the programs when they write changes back to the disk. Changes made to a file are saved to a copy in the current directory rather than in the directory the files originated from. You'll end up with an updated file in the current directory and the original file in the original directory.

◆ You can use APPEND with directories located on network drives.

◆ Don't use APPEND with Windows or with the Windows Setup program.

Append a Path

1. At the system prompt, type the following:

APPEND *<drive>**<path>*

For example:

APPEND A:\CUSTLIST

or, if A is the current drive:

APPEND \CUSTLIST

2. Press Enter.

3. To check the status of **APPEND**, type APPEND and press Enter.

4. To cancel the appended path, type the following and press Enter:

append ;

Troubleshooting

Remember that the APPEND command works best when it reads from the disk. When it writes to the disk, the APPEND path does not tell the program where to save the file, so DOS saves it in the current (or program) directory. You'll end up with an edited version and an original version of the same file, which could cause confusion.

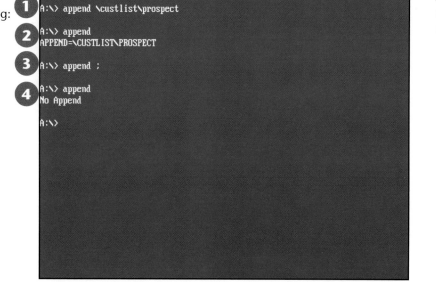

```
1  A:\> append \custlist\prospect

2  A:\> append
   APPEND=\CUSTLIST\PROSPECT

3  A:\> append ;

4  A:\> append
   No Append

   A:\>
```

Appending the path to one subdirectory on drive A.

```
A:\> append \custlist\business;\custlist\personal

A:\> append
APPEND=\CUSTLIST\BUSINESS;\CUSTLIST\PERSONAL

A:\>
```

Appending two or more paths by separating them with semi-colons; DOS searches the paths in the order that you enter them in the APPEND statement.

CUSTOMIZING

If your directory structure includes long, involved paths to files, you can use the SUBST command to make access easier.

The SUBST command assigns an alias name to a path, which makes the path faster and easier to access. The alias name is a drive letter—one that isn't already assigned to your hard disks or floppy disks. When you use SUBST, you can type the alias drive letter rather than typing the path to your files.

> **TIP**
>
> The alias drive letter created with the SUBST command is called a virtual drive. It isn't a real drive, but DOS treats it as if it were.

Consider using the SUBST command in these situations:

◆ Use SUBST to replace long paths, replacing the path with a one-letter drive alias.

◆ Use SUBST with application programs that accept only drive letters and not paths.

Substituting a Drive Letter for a Path

To use the SUBST command, you enter the command at the system prompt followed by the drive letter representing the alias. Then you enter the drive and path to be replaced temporarily by the alias. The SUBST command only remains in effect until you turn your system off or disconnect the substitution.

To use SUBST, you first must enable your system to use the drive letter chosen for the alias. For example, if the alias you choose is K, DOS must be told to recognize K as a drive. To notify DOS of this drive letter, you have to include the LASTDRIVE statement in your CONFIG.SYS file.

DOS assumes your LASTDRIVE is E unless you change it. The letter representing the LASTDRIVE tells DOS how many drives you have. For example, E means DOS recognizes five drives. If you're using drives A, B, and C, then you can use drive D or E as the substitute drive. If you're using drives D and E, you must alter the LASTDRIVE statement to include more drives. See the article "Editing Your CONFIG.SYS File" in the "Configuring" section for more information about altering the file.

If you want to disconnect the drive and path that you substituted with the SUBST command, simply enter the command again at the system prompt, but this time add the /D (disconnect) switch.

> **Warning!**
> Because SUBST creates a virtual drive, you cannot use these commands with SUBST:
>
> | | | |
> |---|---|---|
> | ASSIGN | DISKCOPY | MIRROR |
> | BACKUP | FDISK | RECOVER |
> | CHKDSK | FORMAT | RESTORE |
> | DEFRAG | JOIN | SYS |
> | DISKCOMP | LABEL | |

Use the SUBST Command

1. At the system prompt, type the following and press Enter:

SUBST *<drive1:>* *<drive2:\path>*

For example, to use the alias D: in place of the path C:\BUSINESS\REPORT, type:

SUBST D: C:\BUSINESS\REPORT

2. To view substituted paths, enter this at the system prompt:

SUBST

3. To disconnect the substituted paths and drives, type this at the system prompt:

SUBST *<drive1:>* **/D**

For example: **SUBST D: /D**

Troubleshooting

◆ Do not use SUBST with Windows or a network drive.

◆ If you plan to print a document from DOS, disconnect the SUBST command first or you'll receive an error.

```
C:\> type config.sys
DEVICE=C:\DOS\SETVER.EXE
DEVICE=C:\DOS\HIMEM.SYS
DEVICE=C:\DOS\EMM386.EXE RAM HIGHSCAN WIN=FB00-FDFF WIN=F800-FAFF
buffers=30,0
FILES=40
dos=HIGH, UMB
LASTDRIVE=E
FCBS=16,8
DEVICE=C:\DOS\SMARTDRV.EXE /DOUBLE_BUFFER
SHELL=C:\DOS\COMMAND.COM C:\DOS\ /e:512 /p
DEVICE=c:\cuss12.sys
DEVICEHIGH /L:2,4096 =C:\CUFLOPPY.SYS /D1:2
STACKS=9,256
DEVICEHIGH=C:\DOS\DBLSPACE.SYS /MOVE

C:\>
```

— LASTDRIVE statement in CONFIG.SYS file

```
C:\> subst d: c:\business\report

C:\> subst
D: => C:\BUSINESS\REPORT

C:\> subst d: /d

C:\> subst

C:\>
```

— Substitute drive for path

— Check substitutions

— Disconnect substitution

— Check substitutions

If you use the same files over and over again during a work session, you can help DOS find and access those files faster with Fastopen.

Fastopen is a DOS program that speeds up the process DOS uses to find and open files you use regularly. Fastopen is a cache, of sorts. A *cache* is a reserved space in memory that holds frequently used information until you need it again. Fastopen holds in cache the locations of files you use during a particular session, enabling DOS to find those files faster than if it had to search the disk.

Suppose that you're working on several reports today. You open one, edit it, and close it. Then you open another, print it, and close it. Now you need to open the first report again. Without Fastopen, DOS searches the disk for the path you specify; with Fastopen, DOS goes first to the cache, finds the file quickly, and opens it in a flash.

Starting Fastopen

To use the Fastopen program, you enter **FASTOPEN** at the system prompt, followed by the drive you want the program to track and the number of files you want Fastopen to keep track of. Fastopen can work only with hard disks and remains in effect until you turn off your computer.

> **TIP**
>
> You can include the Fastopen program in your AUTOEXEC.BAT file using the same syntax you use when you enter it at the system prompt. In your AUTOEXEC.BAT file, if you use **LOADHIGH** in front of the FASTOPEN command, DOS loads the program into upper memory.

Choosing a File Number

When you specify the number of files, you can use any number from 10 to 999. Each time you open a new file, Fastopen stores the file name and path in the cache. When the cache is full, Fastopen begins replacing file locations, beginning with the first file you opened.

For optimum use of Fastopen, choose a number from 50 to 200 for the number of files that the program tracks. If you use a number less than 50, Fastopen's cache fills quickly. As you open more files than the cache can hold, Fastopen discards some to make room for more. Therefore, when you need to open a file that Fastopen has discarded, the program has to take the time to read the file from the disk again, thus reducing its effectiveness.

If you use a file number greater than 200, Fastopen has to wade through files to find the one you want—just as DOS wades through the disk to find files. You don't save much time this way.

Each file stored in the cache takes up about 48 bytes; limit the number of files you assign to Fastopen so you don't take too much memory away from your other programs.

If your computer has expanded memory, you can use the /X switch to create the cache in expanded memory rather than conventional memory.

When Not To Use Fastopen

Do not use Fastopen with any disk but a hard disk.

Do not use Fastopen with a network.

Do not open more than one Fastopen program per session.

Do not use Fastopen with Windows or DOS Shell.

When Fastopen is open, do not run DoubleSpace (or other disk compression programs) or Defrag (or other disk defragmenting programs).

Load Fastopen

1. Type CD DOS to change to the DOS directory.

2. At the system prompt, type the following and press Enter:

   FASTOPEN.EXE *<drive>*=*<number of files>* **/X**

   For example, to use Fastopen to track 100 files on drive C and create the cache in expanded memory, type this:

   FASTOPEN.EXE C:=100 /X

Troubleshooting

If your system seems to be running slow after you work with FASTOPEN for an hour or two, you may have assigned too many files to the cache. Lower the number by one quarter and try again.

```
C:\> c:\dos\fastopen.exe c:=200

FASTOPEN installed

C:\>
```

Loading Fastopen from the root directory of the hard disk; 200 files will be stored in conventional memory.

```
 File  Edit  Search  Options                              Help
                      ╔══════ AUTOEXEC.BAT ══════╗
C:\DOS\SMARTDRV.EXE /L
C:\mouse1\mouse.com
PATH C:\DOS;C:\WINDOWS;C:\WP51
PROMPT $P$G
CLS
C:\DOS\FASTOPEN.EXE C:=200 /X
set TEMP=C:\WINDOWS\TEMP
cls
@echo Don't forget to smile!



MS-DOS Editor   <F1=Help> Press ALT to activate menus      CN 00001:001
```

Fastopen loaded in AUTOEXEC.BAT file

In DOS, you often have to enter many complicated commands. The Doskey program can help you keep track of those commands and recall them with the touch of a key.

Doskey is a memory-resident program—using only about 4K of memory—that records each command you type at the system prompt. You can display the commands, recall commands, and even edit commands, after you load the Doskey program.

Suppose that you type several commands containing long paths and then discover you need the same command again—this time with one or two minor changes. If you had Doskey loaded before you entered the commands originally, you may be able to recall the specific command you need.

You can even create your own commands—called macros—with Doskey. For more information, see the article "Creating Macros" later in this section.

Using Doskey

To use Doskey, you first must load it into memory by entering DOSKEY at the system prompt. Then as you enter commands, Doskey records those commands.

If you have a 386 or higher processor, use the LOADHIGH command to load Doskey into upper-memory blocks, which saves conventional memory.

You can view the list of commands that Doskey has recorded by pressing the F7 key. If the list is quite long and you don't want to scroll through it, press F9 and Doskey prompts you with Line number:. Type the line number for the command you want to recall and press Enter. Line number: disappears and the recalled command takes its place on your screen.

Doskey assumes 512 bytes as a storage area, enough to store about 25 to 30 commands.

If the list of recorded commands is short, press the up-arrow key until the command you want to recall appears at the system prompt. The first time you press the up arrow, Doskey displays the last command you entered; the second time you press the arrow key, Doskey displays the next-to-the-last command you entered, and so on.

To edit a command, use Doskey to recall it and then edit it using the special Doskey editing keys (see the following sidebar). You can do this all without typing the command a second, third, or even fourth time.

TIP

A shortcut for recalling a command is to type the first two or three letters of the command and then press F8. Doskey fills in the remaining characters with the most recent command that matches the first two or three letters you entered. For example, type **MEM** and press F8; Doskey displays the **MEM /C|MORE** command you entered earlier.

TIP

Normally in DOS, when you type over a command each character you type replaces a character. If you press the Insert key, however, you can insert characters rather than typing over exiting ones.

TIP

Whether or not you use Doskey, you can always recall the last command you typed simply by pressing F3.

Making Doskey Automatic

You can load the Doskey program automatically every time you start your computer by typing the line **DOSKEY** anywhere in your AUTOEXEC.BAT file. If your processor is a 386 or higher, consider adding the LOADHIGH command in front of the DOSKEY command so that DOS loads Doskey into upper memory. For more information about the AUTOEXEC.BAT file, see the article "Editing your AUTOEXEC.BAT File" in the "Configuring" section.

more ▶

Use Doskey

1. At the system prompt, type the following and press Enter:

DOSKEY

2. To edit a command, recall it from Doskey's memory using the appropriate function key—F7, F8, or F9. Then use the Doskey editing keys to adjust the command as necessary.

3. Press Enter to complete the command.

Doskey Editing Keys

Key	Action
Left arrow	Moves cursor back one character at a time
Right arrow	Moves cursor forward one character at a time
Ctrl+right arrow	Moves cursor forward one word at a time
Ctrl+left arrow	Moves cursor back one word at a time
Home	Moves cursor to the beginning of the line
End	Moves cursor to the end of the line
Del	Deletes the character under the cursor

Doskey loaded into upper-memory blocks

```
Modules using memory below 1 MB:

Name        Total       =  Conventional  +  Upper Memory

MSDOS       17389  (17K)    17389  (17K)        0  (0K)
SETVER        800   (1K)      800   (1K)        0  (0K)
HIMEM        1120   (1K)     1120   (1K)        0  (0K)
EMM386       4144   (4K)     4144   (4K)        0  (0K)
SMARTDRV    29536  (29K)    29536  (29K)        0  (0K)
DBLSPACE    44416  (43K)    44416  (43K)        0  (0K)
COMMAND      3168   (3K)     3168   (3K)        0  (0K)
MOUSE       10480  (10K)    10480  (10K)        0  (0K)
SAVE        17392  (17K)    17248  (17K)      144  (0K)
MODE          480   (0K)        0   (0K)      480  (0K)
SHARE        5248   (5K)        0   (0K)     5248  (5K)
DOSKEY       4144   (4K)        0   (0K)     4144  (4K)
CUFLOPPY     4080   (4K)        0   (0K)     4080  (4K)
Free       581552 (568K)   526976 (515K)    54576 (53K)

Memory Summary:

Type of Memory     Total     =     Used      +     Free
-- More --
```

Use the command LOADHIGH DOSKEY if your processor is a 386 or higher.

Troubleshooting

To clear a command that you just recalled, press Esc rather than Enter.

Shortcut Keys

F7	Display recently recorded commands
Alt+F7	Deletes all commands stored in Doskey memory
F8	Displays commands that contain the first few letters you type
F9	Prompts for line number of command

```
C:\>
1: mem /c|more
2: cls
3: dir c:\business\*.doc
4: fastopen c:=100 /x
5: cls
6: dir *.exe
7: dir *.com
8: type autoexec.bat
9: cls
C:\> dir c:\business\*.doc
```

Pressing F7 displays the commands that Doskey has recently recorded. Then press the up-arrow key until you see the command you want to recall.

What would you say if you found a way not only to save time, but to save keystrokes when you enter commands? Great, right?

DOS provides a way to save time and keystrokes. You can shorten commands that involve long paths or many switches. You can combine several commands you use often into a one-word command that takes only a second to initiate.

Suppose that several times a day you format a 3 1/2-inch double-density disk in a high-density drive. Each time you format the disk, you enter this command at the system prompt:

FORMAT A: /U /F:720

You can create a much shorter command to perform this same task and call it something like *FDD* for *format double density*. Every time you type **FDD** at the system prompt, DOS asks you to insert your disk and then formats it accordingly.

This shortcut command that you can create is called a *macro*. A macro is a set of keystrokes or commands to which you assign a name. Usually, the keystrokes are long and involved, and the macro name is short and to the point. You save time and keystrokes by using macros, and Doskey helps you easily create them.

TIP

For more information about Doskey, see "Tracking Commands."

Creating a Macro with Doskey

Macros can contain one command or several commands; they are limited only by DOS's 127-character limit for a command line. You create a macro by typing the DOSKEY command, the name of the macro, and then the commands in the order you want them carried out. You run the macro by entering the macro name at the system prompt.

When you name your macros, make sure that you use a name you can remember. You can use any keyboard characters for macro names except these:

>	greater than
<	less than
|	pipe
=	equal sign
	space

You can use any DOS commands and include replaceable parameters, as well. *Replaceable parameters* are parts of a command that must be filled in when you type the macro name—such as a directory name or drive letter—because those parameters change from command to command.

To represent a replaceable parameter within the macro, use $1 for the first replaceable parameter, $2 for the second, and so on, up to $9. If you want to create a macro in which one command lists a directory, you can use $1 as a fill-in—DIR $1, for example. When you run the macro, you enter the macro name and then type the directory name. If within that same macro you have another replaceable parameter, you can use $2 to represent it, $3 for the next parameter, and so on.

TIP Macros are only stored in memory as long as your computer is turned on. When you turn off the computer, you lose your macros. You can, however, save your macros to a file to use again and again. See the article "Saving Macros" later in this section.

Macros can contain more than one command. You can create a macro that changes the directory and then lists it, or one that clears the screen, checks the disk, pauses, and then displays memory. The combinations are limited only by 127 characters and your imagination.

When you use more than one command in a macro, separate the commands with $T, rather than with spaces. If, for example, you create a macro to clear the screen, change the directory, and list the directory one screen at a time, separate each of the commands with $T.

To display a list of macros, use the /M (macros) switch with the DOSKEY command. To delete a macro, type the DOSKEY command , the macro name, and an equal sign (=).

more ▶

Example of Macro Containing Three Commands

DOSKEY CDLIST=CLS$TCD\$1$TDIR /P

DOSKEY is the program name.

CDLIST is the macro name.

Equal sign (=) separates the macro name from the first command name.

CLS is the clear screen command.

$T separates two commands.

CD\$1 means to change the directory to a replaceable parameter.

$T separates commands.

DIR /P lists the directory one screen at a time.

When you run the macro, type

   CDLIST *<directoryname>*

For example, **CDLIST C:\BUSINESS**.

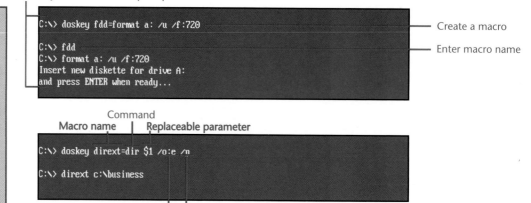

Doskey reads macro and prompts for disk

```
C:\> doskey fdd=format a: /u /f:720

C:\> fdd
C:\> format a: /u /f:720
Insert new diskette for drive A:
and press ENTER when ready...
```

Create a macro

Enter macro name

Command
Macro name | Replaceable parameter

```
C:\> doskey dirext=dir $1 /o:e /m

C:\> dirext c:\business
```

Sort order Pause

```
C:\> doskey /m
FDD=format a: /u /f:720
DIREXT=dir $1 /o:e /p
CHECK=chkdsk$tpause$tmem /c /p
CDLIST=cls$tcd\$1$tdir /p
```

Use the /M switch to list macros.

Create a Macro

1. At the system prompt, type the following and press Enter:

DOSKEY
***<macroname>=<command>*T$**
 <command>

2. To display a list of the macros you have created, type the following and press Enter:

DOSKEY /M

3. To delete a macro, type the following and press Enter:

DOSKEY *<macroname>*=

Troubleshooting

Press Ctrl+C to stop a single macro command. If your macro contains more than one command, you must press Ctrl+C once for each command.

Don't spend all day creating macros that save you time and keystrokes only to lose them by turning off your computer. Save them to a file.

When you create macros with Doskey, the macros are saved only to memory, not to disk; they will be lost when you turn off your computer. You can, however, save the macros to a file and use them over and over.

One problem with creating macros with Doskey is that you must create them each time you start your computer. Even if you saved the macros to a file, you still must enter all the keystrokes for each macro again. To make re-creating the macros easier, however, you can save the macros to a batch file that automatically re-creates them for you in a matter of seconds. That way, instead of entering each macro each time you start your computer, you enter the name of the batch file and it does the rest automatically. A batch file is similar to a macro; it contains commands that DOS executes when you enter the batch file name. A batch file has a BAT extension. For more information about batch files, see the section "Batch Files."

Saving Macros to a File
To preserve your macros, you first must save them to a text file, edit that file ever so slightly, and then save the file with a BAT extension. The process is quick, easy, and well worth the time you save by using the macros.

To save the macros to a file, you type the DOSKEY command, a space, the /M switch, the greater than (>) sign, and then type a file name with a TXT extension. The /M (macros) switch lists the macros in Doskey's memory, and the greater than sign (>) redirects the macro list to a text (TXT) file. The text file doesn't exist, so DOS creates it.

Turning Macros into Commands
If you simply view the file, all you have is a list of the macros. You have to turn the macros into commands by adding the word DOSKEY and a space before each macro (this constitutes the "ever-so-slight" editing mentioned earlier). After you make the macros into commands that will be recognized at the system prompt, you save the file as a batch file—a file that will carry out the commands it contains.

To edit the file, start MS-DOS Editor. Open the file, position the cursor in front of the first macro definition, and type

DOSKEY *<space>*

Repeat for each macro definition. Save the file under the same name, but with a BAT extension.

Now, whenever you start your computer, simply type the name of the BAT file you just created, and your macros will be loaded into Doskey's memory. It just takes a second to load it and it saves you a load of work.

Save the Macros

1. At the system prompt, type the following command and press Enter:

DOSKEY /M > <*filename.txt*>

For example, to save the macros created in one session to a file, you type:

DOSKEY /M > MYMACROS.TXT

2. Open MS-DOS Editor, and open the text file you just saved.

3. At the beginning of each line in the text file, type the following:

DOSKEY *(space)*

4. Save the file as a batch file. Use any file name plus a BAT extension.

5. Exit MS-DOS Editor.

6. To use the batch file, type the name of the file—without the extension—at the system prompt.

Troubleshooting

If for some reason your macros or your batch files don't work, carefully re-read this article and the article "Creating Macros" earlier in this section to make sure you haven't omitted a step or made a typographical error.

The macros aren't in command form

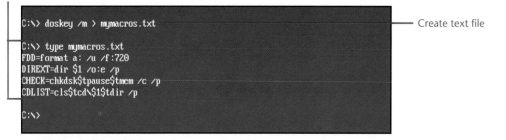

Create text file

Add DOSKEY command

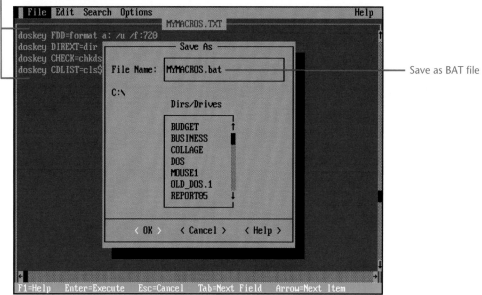

Save as BAT file

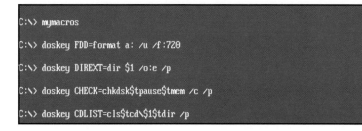

Enter the batch file name, and DOS automatically loads your macros.

Did you ever wish your screen had more color? Ever wish there was a key for a bullet, checkmark, or fraction? You can change all this and more with ANSI.SYS.

You can customize your screen and keyboard in myriad ways using ANSI.SYS. ANSI.SYS is a device driver that gives DOS control over the screen and keyboard devices of your computer. You must load ANSI.SYS into your CONFIG.SYS file before you can customize the screen and keyboard. After loading the device driver, you use special commands to apply the changes to the screen and keyboard.

This article explains the basics of ANSI.SYS—how to install it and create commands—and offers a few examples of changes you can make to your screen and keyboard. ANSI.SYS is a complicated feature and cannot be completely covered in this book.

Installing ANSI.SYS

You first must add the ANSI.SYS program to your CONFIG.SYS file as a device. If you choose, you can load the program into upper memory with the DEVICEHIGH statement. Make sure that you specify the location of the ANSI.SYS program—usually the DOS directory—in the statement. For more information about CONFIG.SYS, see "Editing Your CONFIG.SYS File."

You can use these switches with ANSI.SYS:

◆ **/X** lets you remap the extended keys if your keyboard is a 101-key enhanced. You can't use the /K switch when you use this switch.

◆ **/R** slows the scroll rate of your screen so it's easier to read.

◆ **/K** makes a 101-key enhanced keyboard act as if it were an 84-key keyboard—some programs cannot recognize extended keys. You can't use the /X switch with this switch.

Don't forget to reboot your computer so that the changes to your CONFIG.SYS file will take effect.

Using ANSI.SYS Commands

ANSI.SYS uses special codes that you cannot enter at the system prompt; however, there are several ways to create ANSI commands that DOS can use. The easiest method is to create a batch file. For more information about batch files, see the "Batch Files" section.

You can use MS-DOS Editor to create the batch files. ANSI.SYS commands begin with an Escape sequence, which you can create by pressing and holding Ctrl and typing *P*. Release both keys and press the Esc key (Ctrl+P,Esc). In addition, all ANSI commands end with specific codes—for example, all commands dealing with the screen end with a lowercase *m*.

TIP Within the batch file, you must turn on the ECHO command for each line that contains an ANSI.SYS command.

Changing Your Screen

When you use ANSI commands to customize your screen, you must begin each command with the Escape sequence and a left bracket ([). In addition, the screen commands end with a lowercase *m*. If you use more than one screen attribute code (see the following sidebar), separate the codes with a semi-colon.

For example, to change your screen colors to black text on a yellow background, you would first enter the Escape sequence followed by a left bracket, then the numbers representing the color codes, and, finally, a lowercase *m*:

<Ctrl+p,esc>[30;43m

Typing an Escape sequence, bracket, 0, and *m* changes the screen colors back to normal:

<Ctrl+p,esc>[0m

ANSI Screen-Color Codes

Color	Text Code	Background Code
Black	30	40
Blue	34	44
Cyan	36	46
Green	32	42
Magenta	35	45
Red	31	41
White	37	47
Yellow	33	43

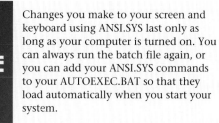

TIP

Changes you make to your screen and keyboard using ANSI.SYS last only as long as your computer is turned on. You can always run the batch file again, or you can add your ANSI.SYS commands to your AUTOEXEC.BAT so that they load automatically when you start your system.

Changing Your Keyboard

The characters on your keyboard are represented by an ASCII code that DOS interprets as a character. The ANSI.SYS driver enables you to assign different codes to keyboard characters so that you can produce fractions, checkmarks, boxes, bullets, and a variety of characters you can't normally access with your keyboard.

Be careful when you reassign the keys on your keyboard. A change in your keys also affects how DOS and your other programs work. In addition, DOS limits the keyboard characters you can use to 200. If you add too many new characters, your system may lock up.

To change the assignment of a key code, you use a batch file of ANSI commands. The keyboard commands start with the Escape sequence followed by a left bracket, then the key codes, and, finally, a lowercase p. Separate the key codes with semi-colons.

You can enter the key codes in one of two ways. If you have a list of ASCII codes, you can use the three-digit decimal code to represent both the character to be replaced and the replacement character. For example, to replace 1/2 with 1/4, enter the codes 171 for 1/2 and 172 for 1/4.

Alternatively, you can use quotation marks and the actual characters. For example, to replace the "at" symbol (@) with the exclamation point (!), enter the symbols as such: "@" and "!".

In most cases, the character you want to use is not represented on the keyboard, so you'll need the ASCII number. You can enter the ASCII character instead of the number, if you want. To reproduce the replacement character, press and hold the Alt key and type the three-digit decimal code on your numeric keypad—for example, Alt+171 produces the fraction ½. You still must include any symbol in quotation marks.

For example, to change the "at" sign (@) on your keyboard to a fraction (1/2), enter this in a batch file:

<Ctrl+p,Esc>[064;171p

or type

<Ctrl+p,Esc>["@";"½"p

Use ANSI.SYS

1. Add the ANSI.SYS statement to your CONFIG.SYS by typing:

DEVICE=C:\DOS\ANSI.SYS /X /K /R

If the ANSI.SYS program isn't in your DOS directory, substitute the correct directory name.

2. Create a batch file of ANSI commands in MS-DOS Editor, using a BAT extension when you save the file.

3. Exit MS-DOS Editor.

4. Enter the name of the batch file at the system prompt to activate the ANSI commands.

Troubleshooting

If your ANSI.SYS changes are not taking effect, make sure you rebooted your computer after entering them.

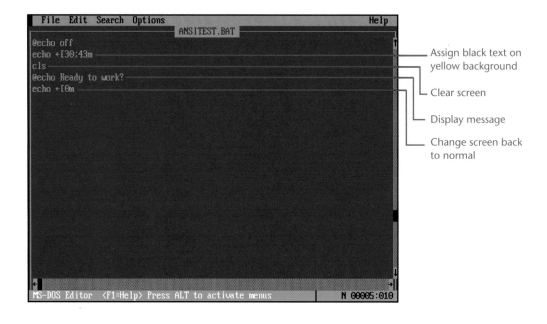

Loading ANSI.SYS into high memory

Assign black text on yellow background

Clear screen

Display message

Change screen back to normal

Some Useful ASCII Characters and Codes

ASCII Character	Decimal Code
♥ (heart)	003
♦ (diamond)	004
♣ (club)	005
→ (right arrow)	016
← (left arrow)	017
→ (right arrow)	026
ü (umlaut u)	129
é (accent e)	130
â (circumflex a)	131
ä (umlaut a)	132
É (accent e)	144
÷ (division)	246
° (degree)	248
✓ (checkmark)	251
■ (square bullet)	254

Characters and Codes

To find out which decimal codes produce which character, look in your program's documentation—most word processing reference manuals include a table of ASCII characters. Alternatively, press and hold the Alt key while you experiment with the numeric key pad. For example, hold Alt and press 001, 002, 003, and so on, up to 255. Write down the ASCII codes for symbols you think you'll use.

Here's the new screen version: black text on yellow background. Esc[0m *changes text and background back to normal.*

Escape code
"At" sign in quotes
Fraction in quotes

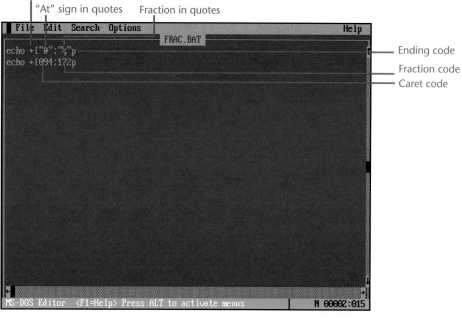

Ending code
Fraction code
Caret code

Are there commands you enter in the same sequence day after day after day? You can combine these commands into a batch file and enter just one word to run those commands.

You can combine commands you often use into a file—called a *batch file* or *batch program*—and type just one word at the system prompt to execute all of those commands. A batch file contains a batch or group of commands. DOS executes each command, in the order that it is entered in the file, one at a time.

Suppose that you want to create a menu that appears when you first start your computer. On this menu are choices for the programs you use during the day—for example, WordPerfect, Q&A, 1-2-3, and Windows. You want to press a number—1 for WordPerfect, for example—and have the program start. You can create the menu using batch files. For more information, see "Creating a Menu."

After you see how easy it is to create and use batch files, you'll find many ways to speed your work with them. To create batch files, you must use special commands and follow specific guidelines. The next article, "Batch Commands," gives you the knowledge you need to create your own, customized batch files.

Batch File Basics

Batch files are text files that you can create in a text editor. Although the way you create the text is different from a letter, for example, many guidelines you follow for creating a text file still apply to batch files:

◆ Batch files must be saved in ASCII; the text must remain unformatted—free of bold, italic, underlined text, and so on.

◆ Use only one command per line in a batch file.

◆ You can use any DOS command that you can enter at the system prompt.

◆ Batch file names must follow conventional DOS file-naming guidelines—eight characters with an extension. You must use the BAT extension.

◆ A batch file name cannot be the same as any DOS command or executable program file.

TIP If you're not familiar with MS-DOS Editor, see the section "MS-DOS Editor."

Create a Batch File

1. Type edit at the system prompt.

2. Press Enter.

   MS-DOS Editor opens.

3. Enter the commands, each on a separate line.

4. Choose Save As from the File menu.

5. Specify a file name that includes the BAT extension.

6. Exit Editor.

7. At the system prompt, type the name of the batch file—with no extension.

8. Press Enter.

Troubleshooting

If your batch file goes awry, press Ctrl+C or Ctrl+Break to stop it. You may have to press the key combination more than once. DOS responds with a Terminate batch job? prompt. Press Y to terminate the job; press N to continue the job.

Batch file name   Replaced parameter

```
C:\> widedir c:\business

C:\> dir c:\business /w /p

 Volume in drive C is MS_DOS_6
 Volume Serial Number is 0FE8-272D
 Directory of C:\BUSINESS

[.]            [..]           [REPORT]       08-19-93.REP   08-20-93.REP
BROCHURE.DOC   COSTGOOD.DOC   DATA01.DOC     DATA01.REP     DATA02.REP
DATA03.REP     INVOICE1.DOC   REPORT.DOC     SALEDELL.123   SALEMARK.123
SALESREP.123
        16 file(s)        120 bytes
                     13918208 bytes free

C:\>
C:\>
```

Directory listed wide

Create a batch file—WIDEDIR.BAT—that lists a directory in the wide format; the replaced parameter is the name of the directory to be listed. This simple batch file saves you several steps and much typing when you display directories in wide format.

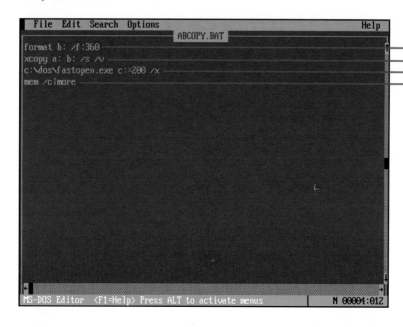

Format a double-density disk
Copy all from A: to B:
Load Fastopen
Check memory

A batch file that formats a disk, then copies files from drive A to drive B works well for quick backups of disks; added punch is added by opening the FASTOPEN program and checking memory.

BATCH FILES

How often do you change and list directories, copy files, or format a disk? How many other commands do you use every day, all day, and wish it were easier? Put those commands in a batch file.

You're probably familiar with your computer's AUTOEXEC.BAT file. The AUTOEXEC.BAT file contains commands—such as PROMPT and PATH—that are executed each time you start your computer. The AUTOEXEC.BAT is a batch file that DOS needs to configure your computer; similarly, you can create batch files to carry out the commands you need.

Suppose that you use the XCOPY command to back up one, two, or more directories to floppy disks every day. Every day you enter the same commands: XCOPY \BUSINESS*.* A:\BUSINESS, XCOPY \REPORTS*.* A:\REPORTS, and so on. You can enter those commands in a batch file called SUBBACK.BAT and at the end of the day, type just one word at the system prompt—**SUBBACK**.

Common Batch Commands

A list of commonly used batch commands follows. More advanced batch commands are available but are not listed or described in this book. For more information, see your DOS Reference Manual.

◆ **@ (at sign)**. When placed at the beginning of a line, the at sign hides the display of that line, even if ECHO is set to ON.

◆ **ECHO OFF**. Prevents the display of each line that of the batch file that follows the command.

◆ **ECHO *<TEXT>***. When placed at the beginning of a line, displays the text on that line.

◆ **PAUSE**. Pauses the batch file execution, displaying the message Press any key to continue.... Pressing any key resumes the processing of the batch file.

◆ **REM**. When placed at the beginning of a line, disables that command. Useful for entering remarks in the batch file.

◆ **CALL**. When placed in a batch file, temporarily interrupts the first batch file to run a second; then returns to the first batch file and continues where it left off.

◆ **GOTO**. Switches to another part of the batch file, skipping some commands, and continues processing from the switch point on. See "Multiple AUTOEXEC.BAT Configurations" for an example.

◆ **CLS**. Clears the screen and positions the cursor in the top left corner of the screen.

Using Batch Commands

To create a batch file, you decide which commands you will use in the file. Because DOS carries out each command one line at a time, you'll want to use a series of commands, just as you would enter at the system prompt. You may want to include the CD (Change Directory) command to get to a deeply buried subdirectory, for example, and then list that directory. Or you may want to check your system's disk and memory. You can format disks, copy files and directories, list directories, and load memory-resident programs; you can do anything in a batch file that you can do from the system prompt.

Use the MS-DOS Editor to create batch files. Enter any commands you want in the file; each command must be on a line by itself. Enter the commands just as you would at the system prompt.

In addition, you can use the special batch commands to control your batch files. PAUSE, for example, is a good command to add when you must insert a disk or check the results of a list. The batch file stops and waits for you to press a key to continue.

When you finish entering the commands, save the file with a BAT extension. You can use any name that follows DOS file-naming conventions, but try to pick one that's descriptive and easy to remember.

To test your batch file, exit MS-DOS Editor to the system prompt and type the name of the batch file—without the extension. Then press Enter. If you discover a problem with the file, go back to Editor and review each command line. Then try again.

TIP
Create a batch file directory—such as C:\BATCH—to hold all of your batch files instead of storing them in your root directory. Then add that directory to your PATH statement in your AUTOEXEC.BAT file.

Using Replaceable Parameters

You can create batch files that include variables, or replaceable parameters. If you use the COPY command in a batch file, for example, you may not always copy the same file; each time you list a directory, you may want to specify a different directory. You can use a symbol for these variables within the batch command and then fill in the blanks when you enter the batch file name at the system prompt.

When specifying replaceable parameters in a batch file, use the percent symbol (%) plus a number from one to nine. You can use up to nine replaceable parameters in each command. To list a directory in wide format and pause after each screen displays, for example, enter the following command:

DIR %1 /W /P

more ▶

BATCH FILES

Batch Commands **189**

DOS Search Sequence

When you enter characters at the system prompt, DOS assumes that you are issuing a command. DOS follows a sequence to search for that command and then executes it.

1. First (in MS-DOS 6 only), DOS looks for a DOSKEY macro. If DOS doesn't find the characters there, it continues the search.

2. DOS checks to see if the command is one of its own built-in commands—COPY, PROMPT, DIR, and so on. If DOS doesn't find the command in this group, it continues the search.

3. DOS next searches for an executable program—first COM files, then EXE files—in the root directory. If DOS finds the program file, it starts it. If the characters you entered are not found, DOS continues the search.

4. Next, DOS checks for the BAT extension—a batch file—in the current directory. DOS searches for the characters you've entered; if DOS finds the batch file, it executes it.

5. DOS continues the search by looking for executable programs in the directories listed in your PATH statement.

6. If DOS must continue to search, it looks again for batch files, but this time it searches the directories listed in your PATH statement.

7. If DOS cannot identify the characters as a command, a program, or a batch file, it displays the message Bad command or file name.

Because of this search sequence, you must be careful when naming your batch files. DOS will never get to a batch file that has the same name as a command or program.

Pause to insert floppy disk

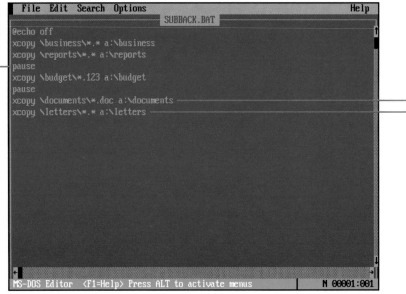

Entering the word SUBBACK is much easier than entering all of these commands.

Copy specific files
Copy all files

A deeply buried subdirectory   List directory by date, one screen at a time

```
 File  Edit  Search  Options                              Help
                          1STQUAR.BAT
@echo off                                                    ↑
cd report                                                    ▓
cd budget
cd annual
cd quarter1
dir /o:d /p
```

```
MS-DOS Editor  <F1=Help> Press ALT to activate menus    N 00001:001
```

Use this batch file when you want to work on reports buried deep in several directories; typing 1stquar is quicker and easier than changing directories four times and listing and sorting the last directory.

Have you ever wanted to use a menu as your start-up screen? You can create your own menu with batch files.

One of the most common uses for batch files is to create a menu for a start-up screen. With a menu, you list the available programs on your computer; with each program name, you provide a number that represents the program. When the user presses the number, the program it represents starts as if by magic.

Creating a menu requires two steps: first, you create the batch file that contains the actual menu; then you create a separate batch file for each entry on the menu. It really isn't hard and it doesn't take very long.

Creating the Menu

It's easiest to create the menu in MS-DOS Editor because you can easily edit the file if necessary. The menu batch file consists mainly of the ECHO command and the text you want to see on-screen. Open the MS-DOS Editor.

TIP Look at the MENU.BAT figure at the end of this article for an idea of how the batch file looks in Editor.

Start by entering the @ECHO OFF command, and then enter CLS to clear the screen. Next, use the ECHO command with a period after it to create blank lines. Create enough blank lines—5 or 6—to place your menu in about the middle of the screen. Here you have to estimate, and you may come back later to enter or delete blank lines.

To enter the menu text that shows on screen, type **ECHO** at the beginning of the line. Then use spaces or tabs to move the text toward the center of the screen. Again, you'll have to estimate and perhaps edit the positioning later. Type the text as you want it to appear on screen—perhaps all caps for a company name, numbers (1, 2, and 3) or letters (A, B, and C) for the software application programs listed on the menu.

You may want to place a blank line between menu items (use ECHO). In addition, you may want to add a line of text at the end of the menu list that gives instructions—such as Choose a number to start the program; then press Enter.

When you finish with the menu, save the file as MENU.BAT by choosing File, Save As. Exit the Editor by choosing File, Exit. DOS Editor closes and returns you to the DOS system prompt.

To display the menu, type the word **menu** at the system prompt. Check to make sure that the menu looks the way you want—that your text is centered, spaces look nice, and so on. Go on to the second part of creating a menu.

Creating the Secondary Batch Files

Your menu looks great; however, nothing happens when you choose a program by pressing a number or a letter. That's because you have to create a batch file for each application choice.

Before you can create the menu, you need to find out two things: which directory the program is in—WordPerfect 6.0 should be in the WP60 directory, for example—and the name of the command that starts the program—WP.EXE, for example. To find the name of the directory the program is in, type **DIR *. |more** at the system prompt and press Enter. The directory should be named so it's easy to identify—WP51 or WP60 for WordPerfect, WORD for MS Word, QUICKEN for Quicken, and so on.

Look at the figure titled 1.BAT at the end of this article for a sample batch file.

At the system prompt, change directories to the the program directory and press Enter. Type DIR *.EXE and press Enter. One or several executable files display. Choose the one that you use to start the program; if you aren't sure, test each one by typing it at the system prompt and pressing Enter.

When you have the name of the directory and of the executable file, start Editor by typing Edit at the system prompt. To create the batch file called 1.BAT, for example, you can start with the @ECHO OFF and CLS commands—one command per line. Next, enter the CD (Change Directory) command with the directory that contains the first program on the menu—CD WP51, for example. Enter the EXE file name that starts the program, such as WP to start WordPerfect. Next add the Change Directory command followed by a backslash (\)—CD\—to change directories back to the root when you exit the program. Last, type MENU, referring to the menu bat; by adding this line last, DOS displays the menu at the system prompt after you exit the program. You're done. Save the file and exit DOS Editor. Test your batch file by entering the number 1 at the system prompt and pressing Enter.

If you placed the MENU.BAT in a directory you created for batch files—such as C:\BATCH, you'll have to use the path to the MENU.BAT in the 1.BAT file. So instead of the last line to the batch file being MENU, it would be **C:\BATCH\MENU.**

Create 2.BAT, 3.BAT, and so on in the same manner. Test your batch files when you're done to make sure they work.

Add the MENU.BAT to your AUTOEXEC.BAT file so that the menu starts each time you start your computer.

more ▶

Create a Menu

1. In MS-DOS Editor, create a batch file that contains the menu as it will look on-screen.

2. Choose Save As from the File menu and save the file as MENU.BAT.

3. Create a batch file for the first program on the menu.

4. Save the file with the name 1.BAT.

5. Repeat steps 3 and 4 for each item on the menu, saving the files with the name 2.BAT, 3.BAT, and so on.

6. Choose Exit from the File menu to leave Editor.

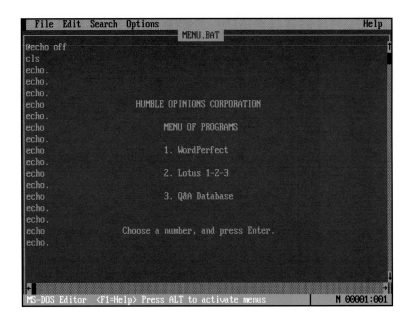

MENU.BAT file in DOS Editor.

Troubleshooting

If you have trouble entering the batch files, refer to the figures in this article for examples.

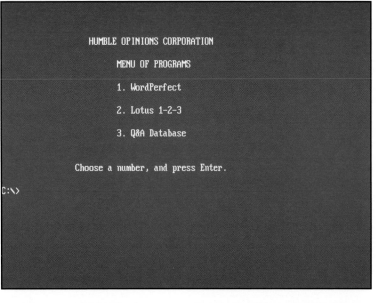

*The menu appears when you type **menu** at the system prompt.*

```
          HUMBLE OPINIONS CORPORATION

          MENU OF PROGRAMS

             1. WordPerfect

             2. Lotus 1-2-3

             3. Q&A Database

          Choose a number, and press Enter.
C:\>
```

Clear screen   Change directories   **Change directories on leaving the program**

The 1.BAT file executes these commands when the user chooses item 1 on the menu.

```
   File  Edit  Search  Options                            Help
                              1.BAT
@echo off
cls
cd wp51
wp
cd\
menu
```

Return to the menu

```
MS-DOS Editor  <F1=Help> Press ALT to activate menus      N 00001:001
```

Start the program

Part Four

IV

Section 10—MS-DOS Shell

MS-DOS comes with some handy programs that can make working with DOS a snap! The MS-DOS Shell may end up as one of your favorites. When you use the Shell, you get an overview of the files and directories on a disk. You can use the Shell to move, copy, delete, and rename files and directories. Need a quick peek at a file to be sure you're opening the right one? Use the Shell. You can switch from one directory to another, and even run many DOS commands or other programs, without ever leaving the Shell. This section provides the details.

Section 11—MS-DOS Editor

MS-DOS Editor is terrific for editing text files and creating batch files. It's particularly useful for making changes in your CONFIG.SYS and AUTOEXEC.BAT files. Editor is like a little word processing program. Type the text you want, then edit at will—cut-and-paste, delete, add new lines. This section takes you through the process of creating new files and editing existing ones with Editor.

Uncomfortable working at the DOS prompt? If you prefer a graphical environment, try MS-DOS Shell.

DOS Shell is a program that uses menus and pictures to do what DOS commands do—but in a friendlier environment. DOS Shell uses menus in place of a system prompt, enables you to perform most of the tasks you can perform at the system prompt, and even lets you do a few things you can't do at the system prompt.

With DOS Shell, you can view directories, files, drives, and more. You can select one file or several and apply a command such as COPY or DELETE, and you can view files in a different order (by name, by date, and so on). In addition, you can view directory, file, and disk information with DOS Shell. And for something you can't do at the DOS system prompt, how about displaying files in two directories at the same time?

DOS Shell is included with MS-DOS versions 4.0, 5.0, and 6.0, although the DOS Shell in MS-DOS 4.0 differs somewhat from the one described in this section. Starting with version 6.2, DOS Shell is no longer available with the MS-DOS product and is available only on the MS-DOS 6.2 Supplemental Disk.

Shell Features

You can use the mouse or the keyboard to maneuver the Shell, or both. Pull-down menus let you access DOS commands with the click of a mouse or the touch of a key.

DOS Shell has its own help system that makes finding answers to your problems easy. The Help feature includes an index for finding specific topics, such as topics related to using the keyboard in the Shell. It even offers you help on Help!

DOS Shell also includes a task swapper. You can have multiple programs open at the same time and move among them for a more efficient work strategy.

You can set DOS Shell to run every time you start your computer, or only when you want it to. You may be more comfortable with the graphical interface of Shell than with the system prompt. If that's true, you can configure your computer so that DOS Shell starts automatically as the computer finishes booting. Alternatively, you can start DOS Shell at the system prompt and exit when you're ready to return to the normal DOS setup.

Starting DOS Shell

To start DOS Shell, you type the **DOSSHELL** command at the system prompt and press Enter. (If your system defaults to DOS Shell at startup, this step is unnecessary. If your system uses a menu, choose the appropriate menu item to access DOS Shell.)

As DOS Shell starts, it reads the disk information—files and directories on the current drive—and reports its progress in the Reading Disk Information dialog box. When finished, DOS Shell displays the opening screen, which contains a list of drives, directories, files, and available programs.

TIP To exit DOS Shell, choose File Exit from the menu or press F3.

Text Mode versus Graphics Mode

Depending on your equipment, you may be able to view the DOS Shell screen either in graphics mode or text mode. The default opening screen of DOS Shell is in text mode. *Text mode* uses keyboard characters rather than pictures. *Graphics mode* is available only on an EGA or VGA display. Graphics mode displays characters and images.

Parts of the Screen

DOS Shell's screen looks completely different than the normal DOS screen. The screen appears as a *window* containing smaller *panes*. The Shell window and the panes have *title bars* describing their contents. At the top of the Shell screen is the title bar containing the name of the program—MS-DOS Shell.

Directly beneath the title bar is the menu bar. The menu bar contains the names of five menus—**F**ile, **O**ptions, **V**iew, **T**ree, and **H**elp—that you can pull down for additional options.

Beneath the menu bar is the name of the current drive and directory, under which are drive letters. The two panes of the window beneath the drive letters contain the *directory tree* and the *file list*. The directory tree displays the directories on the current drive. Subdirectories follow the parent directories and are indented.

The title bar of the file list displays the current drive and directory. The file list displays the files that are located in the directory that is highlighted in the directory tree. Each file is listed with its name, size, and the date it was created or last changed.

The bottom pane is the *Main window* and lists the names of the programs you can run. You can also add your own programs to the list. The bar across the bottom of the screen is the *status bar*, which displays shortcut keys and their functions, as well as the time.

TIP For information about how to move from pane to pane and file to directory, see the article "Getting Around in DOS Shell" later in this section.

more ▶

Start DOS Shell

1. Type **DOSSHELL** at the system prompt.

2. Press Enter.

Switch between Text Mode and Graphics Mode

1. Choose the **O**ptions menu by pressing Alt+O or clicking the name on the menu bar with the mouse.

2. Type **D** for **D**isplay or click Display with the mouse.

The Screen Display Mode dialog box appears.

3. Use the arrow keys or the mouse to highlight the display mode you want.

4. Press Enter.

Graphic images   Window title bar   Menu bar

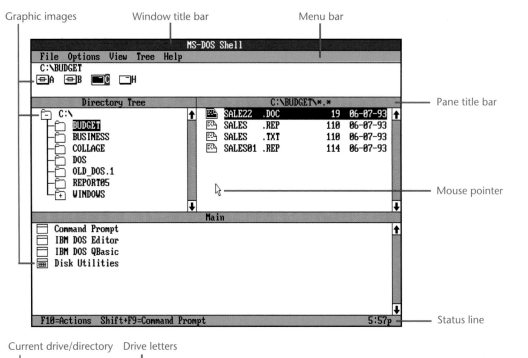

Pane title bar

Mouse pointer

Status line

Current drive/directory   Drive letters

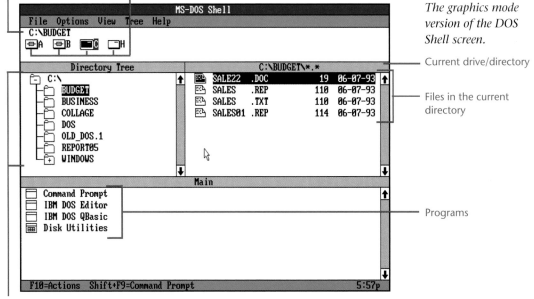

The graphics mode version of the DOS Shell screen.

Current drive/directory

Files in the current directory

Programs

Directories

Troubleshooting

If the Screen Display Mode dialog box seems confusing, don't worry. Choose any one of the graphics modes and then choose Preview. The screen changes while the dialog box remains on-screen. Continue to change modes until you find one you're comfortable with. If by chance, you don't like any of the graphics modes, choose Cancel in the dialog box and the box closes without making a change.

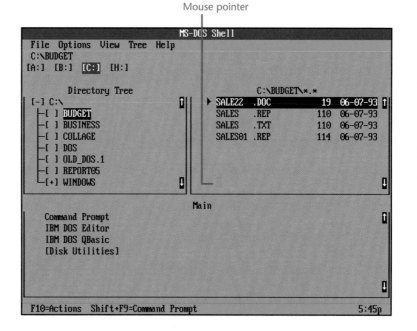

The text mode version of the DOS Shell screen. The DOS Shell screen isn't as attractive in text mode as it is in graphics mode, but it contains the same elements and works in much the same way.

Shortcut Key	
F3	Exit DOS Shell

The Screen Display Mode dialog box works the same way whether it appears in text mode (as shown here) or in graphics mode.

MS-DOS SHELL

DOS Shell can perform many DOS commands with just the touch of a key or a drag of the mouse.

DOS Shell not only enables you to view your directory structure in a different way than at the system prompt, it also lets you manipulate directories and files in a different way. Whether you use the keyboard or the mouse, DOS Shell may be easier for you to use than the normal DOS system prompt.

Getting around in DOS Shell is a matter of moving and clicking the mouse or pressing various keys and key combinations. This article separates keyboard procedures from mouse procedures to make it easier for you to concentrate on the method you prefer.

You may find it more efficient to use a combination of the mouse and the keyboard when you work in DOS Shell.

Moving Around with the Keyboard

As you've already discovered, DOS Shell consists of a window made up of four panes. To move from pane to pane with the keyboard, you press the Tab key. Each time you press Tab, a portion of the active pane lights up. For example, when you press Tab and move to the drive pane, the current drive is highlighted—it changes color or shade. When you press Tab again, the Directory Tree pane is highlighted, as is the current drive letter within that pane. Highlighted panes indicate that the area is current or active, and any action you perform will affect the highlighted pane.

To move around within the current window pane, you press the up- or down-arrow key. Notice that as you change the directory in the Directory Tree pane, the file list changes to show the files contained in the selected directory. Selected files appear in reverse video.

Press Shift+Tab to move to the preceding pane.

Moving Around with the Mouse

If you use a mouse with DOS Shell, navigating the screen and menus is easy. Point the mouse to the pane you want and click the left mouse button. Clicking an item selects it; double-clicking an item activates it (opening a file or directory, for example).

Using the Scroll Bars

You can use the *scroll bars* to view portions of a window pane that won't fit in the window. Scroll bars are located to the right of each window. Click the mouse on the scroll bar's up arrow to move up the list one line at a time; click the down arrow to move down one line at a time. Each scroll bar contains a *scroll box*—a gray box within the otherwise black scroll bar. By clicking and dragging the scroll box, you can move up or down a list more quickly.

Using the Menus

Pressing the Alt key activates the menu bar. When your screen is in graphics mode, each menu name appears with an underlined letter; for example, **F** is the underlined letter in the **F**ile menu name. Press Alt followed by the appropriate underlined letter to pull down a particular menu and display a list of commands.

The commands listed in each menu also have underlined letters you can press to activate the command. Some commands are dimmed, which means you can't access that command at that particular time.

To pull down a menu with the mouse, click the menu name. To choose a command, click the command name.

When you pull down a menu you access commands that relate to the menu name. Following is a summary of each menu:

◆ **F**ile. The File menu contains commands that act on files, directories, and programs in much the same way as normal DOS commands do. For example, you use the File menu to move, copy, and delete files.

◆ **O**ptions. The Options menu enables you to control the way DOS Shell looks and acts. You can change the way you view files and the screen. You can also view information about each file or directory—such as the hidden or read-only attributes, size, number of files within a directory, and so on.

◆ **V**iew. View enables you to view the files in different ways; for example, you can view the files in one directory or two, or you can view files and no directories.

◆ **T**ree. The Tree menu enables you to customize your view of the directory structure by displaying one level of the tree or all levels.

◆ **H**elp. Help offers information about using Shell, commands, the keyboard, and even includes details on using Help.

more ▶

MS-DOS SHELL

Using Dialog Boxes

Often a pull-down menu command is followed by an *ellipsis* (...), which means that a dialog box appears when you choose that command. *Dialog boxes* are on-screen message boxes that either give you information or require information from you. You must accommodate the dialog box before the command can be completed.

Dialog boxes offer several different ways for you to make selections or enter information: *list boxes*, *check boxes*, *radio buttons*, *command buttons*, and *text boxes*. You move around in a dialog box the same way you move around in a window pane or among window panes in the DOS Shell screen: by pressing the Tab key and using the arrow keys, or pointing and clicking the mouse. The following list describes each of these elements in more detail:

◆ **List box**. A list of items from which you can choose by clicking the mouse on a particular item or by using the arrow keys. After an item is *selected*—highlighted—press Enter or choose OK to accept the choice. If you want to exit the dialog box and cancel the choice, press Esc or choose Cancel.

◆ **Check box**. An option with a box next to it. To select a check box option, click it with your mouse or use the arrow keys to move the cursor to the option and then press the space bar. When an item is selected, an X appears in the check box.

◆ **Radio button**. An option with a small open circle next to it. To select a radio button option, click it with your mouse or use the arrow keys to move the cursor to the option and then press Enter. When the item is selected, a small black dot appears in the circle.

◆ **Command button**. An option that either accepts or cancels the actions of the dialog box. To execute the settings in the dialog box, you generally choose the OK command button. To exit the dialog box without incorporating any changes, you press the Cancel command button. If you need assistance in using the dialog box, you press the Help command button.

◆ **Text box**. A box that requires you to type information—such as a file name, directory, and extension—that the dialog box can then act on.

TIP

The difference between a radio button and a check box is that you can choose several check boxes in one dialog box, but you can only choose one radio button.

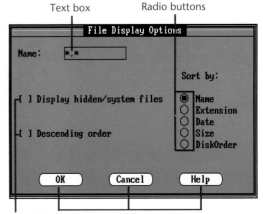

Text box   Radio buttons

Check boxes   Command buttons

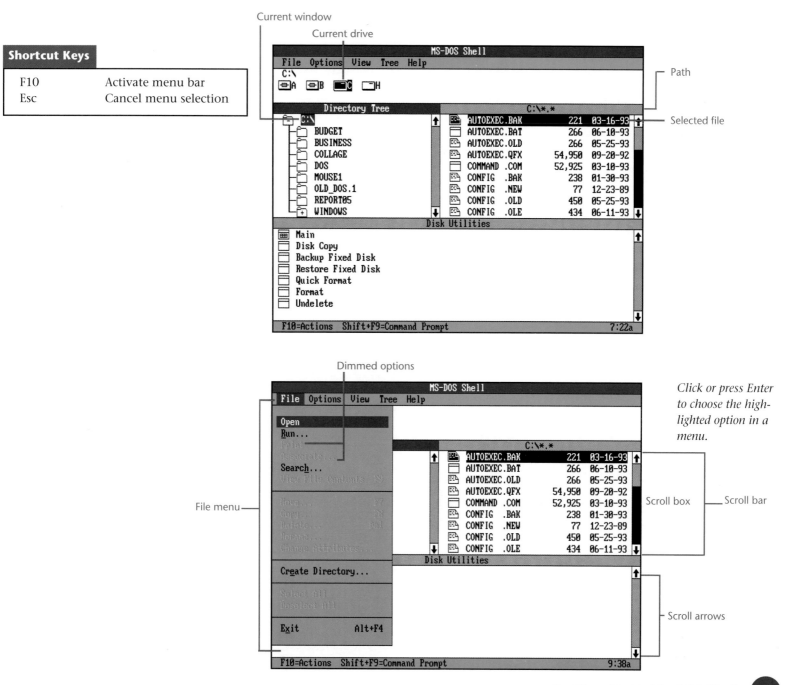

Current window

Current drive

Path

Selected file

MS-DOS Shell

File Options View Tree Help

C:\
⊟A ⊟B ▣C ⊡H

Directory Tree   C:*.*
📁 C:\
    📁 BUDGET   📑 AUTOEXEC.BAK   221 03-16-93
    📁 BUSINESS   AUTOEXEC.BAT   266 06-10-93
    📁 COLLAGE   📑 AUTOEXEC.OLD   266 05-25-93
    📁 DOS   📑 AUTOEXEC.QFX   54,950 09-20-92
    📁 MOUSE1   COMMAND .COM   52,925 03-10-93
    📁 OLD_DOS.1   📑 CONFIG .BAK   238 01-30-93
    📁 REPORT05   📑 CONFIG .NEW   77 12-23-89
    📁 WINDOWS   📑 CONFIG .OLD   450 05-25-93
                       📑 CONFIG .OLE   434 06-11-93
                    Disk Utilities
📊 Main
📄 Disk Copy
📄 Backup Fixed Disk
📄 Restore Fixed Disk
📄 Quick Format
📄 Format
📄 Undelete

F10=Actions Shift+F9=Command Prompt   7:22a

Dimmed options

MS-DOS Shell

File Options View Tree Help

Open
Run...
Print
Associate...
Search...
View File Contents F9

Move...   F7
Copy...   F8
Delete...   Del
Rename...
Change Attributes...

Create Directory...

Select All
Deselect All

Exit   Alt+F4

Click or press Enter to choose the high-lighted option in a menu.

C:*.*
📑 AUTOEXEC.BAK   221 03-16-93
   AUTOEXEC.BAT   266 06-10-93
📑 AUTOEXEC.OLD   266 05-25-93
📑 AUTOEXEC.QFX   54,950 09-20-92
   COMMAND .COM   52,925 03-10-93
📑 CONFIG .BAK   238 01-30-93
📑 CONFIG .NEW   77 12-23-89
📑 CONFIG .OLD   450 05-25-93
📑 CONFIG .OLE   434 06-11-93
Disk Utilities

Scroll box   Scroll bar

File menu

Scroll arrows

F10=Actions Shift+F9=Command Prompt   9:38a

Getting Around in DOS Shell 205

Can't remember how to display subdirectories? Or how to start a program from DOS Shell? Use DOS Shell Help to find out.

DOS Shell Help is an on-line system of information; Help tells you how to use DOS Shell for file and directory management. You can access these topics through DOS Shell Help:

◆ **Keyboard Help**. Describes the keys you use within the DOS Shell screen and its dialog boxes, such as keys to activate menus, select drives, and choose files. Keyboard Help also lists the shortcut keys.

◆ **Commands Help**. Describes each menu—File, Options, View, Tree, and Help—and each menu's commands. Commands Help also presents access to related topics.

◆ **Procedures Help**. Lists information about how to access the file list, program list, and so on, as well as detailing special procedures within each window pane.

◆ **DOS Shell Help**. Explains how to use DOS Shell—menus, commands, dialog boxes, and so on.

◆ **Using Help**. Explains how to use the Help feature.

The Help menu enables you to access help on specific topics, such as the keyboard, Shell basics, and commands. Alternatively, you can choose **I**ndex from the **H**elp menu and then choose any specific help you need. This article discusses how to use the Index, but the other topics in the Help menu work the same way.

Using Help

To use DOS Shell Help, you choose the Help menu and a topic. Index is a general topic that covers all the other help topics. When you select Index, the MS-DOS Shell Help screen appears and displays instructions for moving around in the Help window. To cancel the Help window at any time, just press Esc.

You can use either the arrow keys or the mouse to scroll through the list of topics. If you're using the mouse, click the topic you want to view. If you're using the keyboard, press the Tab key to highlight a topic; press Shift+Tab to highlight the previous topic. Use the arrow keys or PgUp and PgDn to move to the next screen of topics, and then use Tab to move from topic to topic. When you have selected the appropriate topic, press Enter to display another window containing information about that topic.

 You can press Page Up and Page Down to quickly scroll the Help window.

Help offers five command buttons at the bottom of the Help screen: Close exits the Help program; Back takes you to the previous Help screen; Keys opens the Keyboard Help screen in which you choose topics to view keyboard shortcuts; Index takes you to the first screen of the MS-DOS Shell Help Index; and Help gives you help on using Help.

Use Help

1. Choose **H**elp **I**ndex.

   The Help Index window appears.

2. Choose a topic for additional information.

3. Press Esc or choose Close to exit Help.

Troubleshooting

◆ If you have trouble remembering how to get around in Help, choose the Help command button at the bottom of the screen.

◆ If you're in a dialog box or open menu and you need immediate help on that particular topic, press F1.

Shortcut Keys

Esc	Cancel Help
F1	Context-sensitive Help

Getting Dialog Box Help

Most dialog boxes contain a Help button you can choose for more information about the dialog box. When you choose the Help button, a help screen appears that displays information about that dialog box.

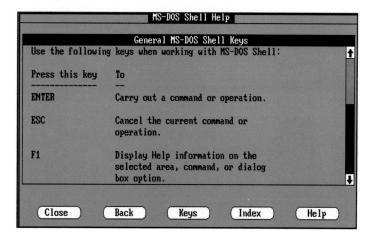

Selected topic

Use the Back command button to go back to the screen immediately preceding the current screen. In this example, choosing Back returns you to the Index screen.

You can display one drive and one directory at a time; or you can display two.

The major advantage to DOS Shell is that it enables you to view the directory structure so that you can see how directories are organized and which files are contained within a directory. After you display a drive, a directory, and its files, you can manipulate the files and directories. For example, you can create new subdirectories, move files from one drive to another, display files in more than one directory at a time, even open programs and view files.

Displaying Drives

To view a drive other than the hard drive, you simply insert a floppy disk and choose that floppy drive from the drive list beneath the menu bar. DOS Shell reads the information and displays the directory tree and the file list of the floppy disk.

Displaying Directories and Subdirectories

The Directory Tree window pane displays the root directory of a drive and shows the names of all the directories located in the root. Notice that the root directory is preceded by a minus (-) sign, which signifies that all directories within the root are displayed. When a directory is preceded by a plus sign (+), it indicates that the directory contains subdirectories that aren't displayed. The subdirectories stemming from a directory are called *branches*.

To display the branch of a directory, use the **T**ree menu. First select, or highlight, the directory and then choose **T**ree. You can choose to expand one branch, expand all branches, or to collapse branches. The **T**ree menu enables you to view any level of your directory structure and to hide the lower levels if they get in your way.

If you're using a mouse, click the directory name to display its files in the file pane. To display subdirectories in a directory, click the plus sign beside the directory name in the Directory Tree.

Displaying Files

In DOS Shell, you can view information about files, such as their size and creation date, just as you can at the system prompt. To move to a specific file in the file list, press the first letter of the file name. If you'd rather view a list of files only, with no directories, choose **V**iew and then choose **A**ll Files.

You can choose to view either a single directory or two directories at the same time, depending on whether you choose the **S**ingle File List or Dual File Lists command from the **V**iew menu. To view two directories at once, choose **V**iew and then choose **D**ual File Lists. With two directories open, you can still work in either Directory Tree or file list as you normally would and use the Tab key to move from pane to pane. The advantage to viewing two directories at the same time is that it is easier to move and copy files from one drive or directory to another when they are both visible.

Display Subdirectories

1. Select a directory name preceded by a plus sign or click the plus sign with the mouse.

2. Choose **T**ree.

3. Choose Expand **B**ranch to expand this directory only or Expand **A**ll to display all subdirectories.

Hide Subdirectories

1. Select a directory name preceded by a minus sign.

2. Choose **T**ree.

3. Choose Collapse Branch.

View Files Only

1. Choose **V**iew.

2. Choose **A**ll Files.

View Two Directories

1. Choose **V**iew.

2. Choose **D**ual File Lists.

Troubleshooting

When you display two directories and their file lists, you must choose **O**ptions, Select **A**cross Directories before you can move or copy between the two displayed file lists.

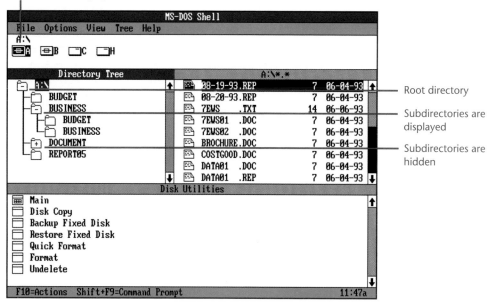

Select drive to display

Root directory

Subdirectories are displayed

Subdirectories are hidden

Viewing files only. Notice that the left-hand column displays specific details about the file highlighted in the right-hand column.

File name and assigned attributes

Drive, number of selected files, file size

Directory name, size, and number of files in directory

Disk volume label, size, available disk space, number of files and directories

Create and Delete

DOS Shell is the perfect place to view your directory structure. It makes it easy to see where you should add and delete directories.

Creating directories is easy in DOS Shell. Suppose you work on the annual budget for your company, so you need a budget directory to store the data you compile. In addition, you would like subdirectories in the budget directory to further divide your work into four quarters. You don't have to exit to DOS and type a bunch of commands. Just open DOS Shell and go to it!

Creating a Directory

To create a directory in DOS Shell, you first must move to the *parent* directory. The parent is the directory that contains the subdirectories. For example, the root directory is the parent to all other directories on your disk.

When the appropriate parent directory is highlighted, choose the **F**ile menu and then choose the Cre**a**te Directory command. Type the name of the new directory, and DOS Shell adds the directory in its proper place. It's that simple.

Deleting a directory is just as easy. Highlight the directory you want to delete. You first must delete all files from the directory. Select the files in the directory and choose **F**ile **D**elete. When the directory is empty, choose **F**ile **D**elete again. DOS Shell displays a confirmation message; choose Yes to delete or No to cancel.

Add a Directory

1. Move to the Directory Tree window pane.

2. Highlight the parent directory.

3. Choose **F**ile.

4. Choose Create Directory.

   The Create Directory dialog box appears.

5. In the New Directory Name text box, type the name of the directory you are adding.

6. Choose OK or press Enter to create the new directory.

   The dialog box closes and returns you to DOS Shell.

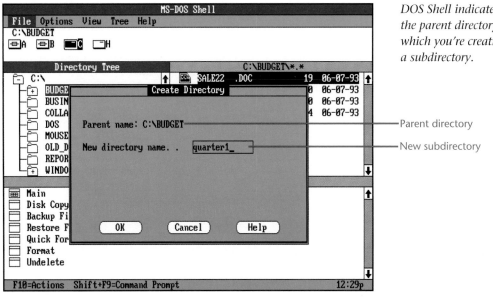

DOS Shell indicates the parent directory for which you're creating a subdirectory.

Delete a Directory

1. Select the directory to be deleted.

2. Delete all files from the directory by moving to the file list pane, selecting the files, and then choosing **F**ile **D**elete. Choose Yes in the confirmation dialog box.

3. Choose **F**ile **D**elete to delete the directory. Choose Yes in the confirmation dialog box.

Troubleshooting

If you decide you don't want a new directory you just created, select the directory in the Directory Tree window pane, choose **F**ile **D**elete. Choose Yes in the confirmation box.

Viewing Files

Need to read a text file right now? Want to view the contents of your CONFIG.SYS file? Check out the file-viewing feature in DOS Shell!

DOS Shell, just like DOS, enables you to view contents of a text file on screen. You can't change the contents, but you can scroll through and read the file.

Suppose that you want to view the contents of a text (ASCII) file that came with your newest application program (for example, a README.TXT file). Text files such as these generally contain information that was not available when the reference manual for the program was written. By reading the text file, you may gain some insight on recent problems or bugs in the program. You can view the text file quickly by using the **V**iew File Contents command on the **F**ile menu in DOS Shell.

To switch the screen between hexadecimal and ASCII, choose the **D**isplay menu from the **V**iew File Contents screen, and then choose either **A**SCII or **H**ex.

Hexadecimal files are numeric files composed of the digits 0 through 9 rather than letters. Hexadecimal files normally are used in computer programming because they are easily converted to a numbering system the computer uses. You probably won't have occasion to view the contents of a hexadecimal file, but you have that capability in DOS Shell.

*Note: If the **V**iew File Contents command is dimmed, you cannot view the selected file type in DOS Shell.*

You can view only text files (ASCII) and hexadecimal files with the View File Contents command. Text files generally have a TXT extension. You may be able to view other files, such as BAT, INI, and HLP, but only if the file is the correct file type (text or hexadecimal). If you are unsure of the file type, select the file and choose File; if the View File Contents command is dimmed, the file is not a text file and you cannot view it from DOS Shell.

Viewing Files

To view a file, you must first select the drive and directory in which the file is located. Next you select the file, choose **F**ile, and then choose the **V**iew File Contents command. Use the Page Up and Page Down keys to scroll to text not in the window. Finally, press the Esc key to exit the view and return to DOS Shell.

Editing Files with Editor

If you want to change the selected file, press Enter (or double-click the file) to open the file in MS-DOS Editor—a text editing program included with DOS. Edit the file as desired and save it. For more information on Editor, see the "MS-DOS Editor" section.

To scroll through a file, use the PgUp or PgDn keys; alternatively, use the mouse to click the words PgUp or PgDn that appear at the top of the screen. You can also use the up and down arrows.

View a File

1. In the Directory Tree, select the directory that contains the file.

2. Move to the file list window pane and select the file.

3. Choose **F**ile.

4. Choose **V**iew File Contents.

5. When you're done viewing the file, press Esc to return to DOS Shell.

Troubleshooting

When you no longer want to view the text file, press Esc to return to DOS Shell.

Shortcut Key	
F9	View File Contents

```
┌──────────────────────── MS-DOS Shell - APPNOTES.TXT ────────────────────────┐
│ Display  View  Help                                                         │
│┌────────────────────────────────────────────────────────────────────────┐ │
││    To view file's content use PgUp or PgDn or ↑ or ↓.                    │ │
│└────────────────────────────────────────────────────────────────────────┘ │
│ APPNOTES.TXT                                                                │
│                                                                             │
│ NOTES ON USING APPLICATIONS WITH IBM DOS VERSION 5.0                         │
│ ===================================================                         │
│                                                                             │
│ This document provides important information not included in the            │
│ IBM DOS User's Guide and Reference or in on-line Help.                       │
│                                                                             │
│ Look through the following table of contents to determine                   │
│ whether your application is included.                                       │
│                                                                             │
│ ATTENTION CODEVIEW AND INTEL ABOVEBOARD USERS                                │
│ +++++++++++++++++++++++++++++++++++++++++++++++++                            │
│ Sections 1.1 and 1.3 contain critical information                           │
│ about using Intel Aboveboard and CodeView with                              │
│ DOS 5.0.                                                                    │
│ +++++++++++++++++++++++++++++++++++++++++++++++++                            │
│                                                                             │
│ For information about installing DOS 5.0 and using hardware                  │
│ ←┘=PageDown   Esc=Cancel   F9=Hex/ASCII                          1:53p       │
└─────────────────────────────────────────────────────────────────────────────┘
```

Viewing the file APPNOTES.TXT.

MS-DOS SHELL

Viewing Files 213

Unlike copying files at the system prompt, you can select many different file types to copy at one time in DOS Shell.

Whether you're copying one or several files, DOS Shell lets you select the files and copy them to another disk or directory. At the DOS system prompt, you can copy like files by using wild-card characters; with the DOS Shell copy feature, however, you can copy files with different names and different extensions all at one time.

Suppose that you want to copy a report file, a formatted cover page, and a spreadsheet file to a disk all at the same time. These files have no characters in common in either their file names or extensions. At the system prompt, you would have to copy them one by one. Using DOS Shell, you can copy them all at once.

Selecting Files

Before you can perform a task, such as copying a file, you must select the file. Highlighting a file selects it. Often you'll want to perform a task on more than one file at a time, so it's helpful to be able to select several files for that purpose.

To select two or more files displayed in a consecutive list, move to the first file to highlight it. Then press and hold the Shift key as you move to subsequent files. When you're finished, release the Shift key and all the files you selected will be highlighted.

Alternatively, you can click the first file with the mouse, hold down the Shift key, and then click the last file in the list that you want to select. All the files between and

including the two files you actually clicked on will be highlighted. Now you can continue with the copy procedure, or any other procedure, and all the files you highlighted will be effected.

To select files that aren't in succession but are scattered throughout the file list, press Shift+F8. The word Add appears in the status bar. Move to the first file and press the space bar to select it. Move to the next file you want to select and again press the space bar. Continue until all the files you want to select are highlighted. Press Shift+F8 to switch back to normal selection.

Alternatively, you can use the mouse to select files that aren't displayed consecutively by holding down the Ctrl key while you click the desired files.

TIP To cancel any selected files, press the up- or down-arrow key or click the mouse anywhere in the window pane.

Copying Files

To copy files, first select one or more files. Then choose the **C**opy command from the **F**ile menu and the Copy File dialog box appears. The selected files appear in the From text box.

The drive and directory in which the files are currently located appear in the To text box. Change to the appropriate drive and directory and press Enter. DOS Shell copies your files in just a few seconds.

Copy Files

1. Move to the drive and directory in which the files reside.

2. Select one or more files to be copied.

3. Choose **F**ile **C**opy.

The Copy File dialog box appears and shows the selected file names in the From text box.

4. In the To text box, change to the appropriate drive and directory.

5. Press Enter or choose OK.

Troubleshooting

If you change your mind about copying the files after you select them, press the up- or down-arrow key or click the mouse once to deselect the files.

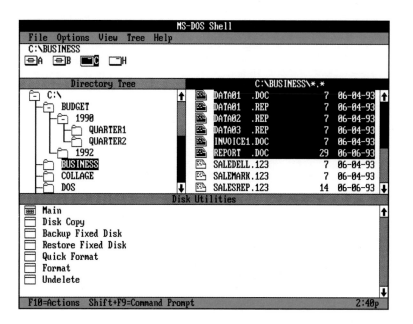

Selected files in succession.

Selected files not in succession.

What in the world is in that file? Why is it in that directory? If you could, you'd probably rename or move many of your files just to make it easier to tell what's in them and to put them where they belong.

It's easy to rename files in DOS Shell. Suppose that you have all your report files named by their dates, but suddenly you have to start generating two reports a day. You have stored most of the report files from previous months on a backup disk, but you still need to keep this month's reports on your hard disk. Rename the files so that you can easily recognize them when you start creating the second set of report files.

In DOS Shell, moving files from one directory or disk to another is just as easy as renaming files; and moving files to another disk is a great way to clean up your hard disk and free valuable disk space.

Renaming Files

To rename a file, you simply select the file and choose the Rename command from the File menu. Don't rename a file with a name that's already assigned in the same directory. Of course if you do, DOS Shell displays a dialog box saying you can't use that name.

Naturally, all file names you use to rename a file must agree with DOS conventions and guidelines—up to eight characters for the name plus an optional three-letter extension. For more information about DOS file-naming conventions, see the article "Naming Files" in the "Files" section.

When you copy a file, you have an original and a duplicate; when you move a file you still have only one file, but it's in a different place. You may need to move files to new or different directories to keep your directory structure organized. On the other hand, you may want to move files to a floppy disk to clean your hard disk and make more room for new files.

Moving Files

Suppose that you finished the business report and found that you no longer need many of the files. You don't want to delete them just in case you need them later, but you don't want to leave them on your hard disk, either. Move them to a floppy disk; this gives you a backup of those files and cleans up your hard disk at the same time!

Before you can move files, you must first select them. You can select one, several, or all files in a directory. After you select the files you want to move, choose the Move command from the File menu. A dialog box appears (similar to the Copy File dialog box that you saw earlier) and displays the names of the files that you selected. Enter the drive and directory to which you want to move the files and choose OK. DOS Shell moves your files for you.

 To select all files in a directory, choose File Select All.

Rename a File

1. Select the drive and directory that contain the file to be renamed.

2. Select the file.

3. Choose **F**ile Re**n**ame.

   The Rename File dialog box appears.

4. Enter the new name for the file and choose OK.

Troubleshooting

If you select more than one file to rename, the Rename command displays each file name in the text box in the order you selected them. Rename the first file, choose OK, rename the second, and so on.

Move a File

1. Select the drive and directory containing the files to be moved.

2. Select the files to be moved.

3. Choose **F**ile **M**ove.

   The Move File dialog box appears and displays the selected files in the From text box.

4. Enter the drive and directory destination in the To box and press Enter or choose OK.

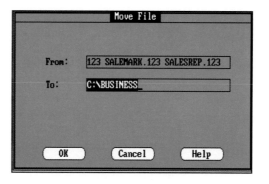

The Move File dialog box.

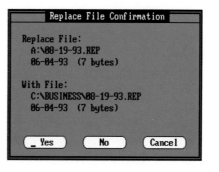

The Replace File Confirmation dialog box.

The Rename File dialog box.

Shortcut Key

F7	Move files

MS-DOS SHELL

Listing your files by their creation dates or alphabetically by their extensions can help you find the file you need—fast.

You can list files in DOS Shell alphabetically by name or extension; by date; by size; or by the order they appear on the disk. Suppose you wanted to find a file created on June 11 or 12, but you couldn't quite remember the name of the file. It would take you a long time to look through the file list; and it's not easy to find files by date. Use the file display options to sort the files for you.

Choosing a Listing Order

You can list files in any of the following orders:

◆ **Name**. Lists files alphabetically by their one- to eight-character file names.

◆ **Extension**. Lists files alphabetically by their three-character extensions, and then by their file names.

◆ **Date**. Lists files chronologically by the date they were created or last updated, oldest date first.

◆ **Size**. Lists files numerically by file size, from the smallest to the largest file.

◆ **DiskOrder**. Lists files chronologically in the order they were saved to disk.

You can also choose to list files in any of these sort orders, but in descending order. If you choose descending order, you get the following results:

◆ **Name**. Lists files in reverse alphabetical order, Z to A, by the eight-letter file name.

◆ **Extension**. Lists files alphabetically from Z to A by extension.

◆ **Date**. Lists the most recent files first.

◆ **Size**. Lists from largest to smallest file size.

You can also choose to display system files and files that have the hidden attribute assigned. Hidden files sometimes are forgotten, so you may want to display them. Many software programs hide system files so that the user is less likely to tamper with them.

To choose the sort order for files, choose the **F**ile Display Options command from the **O**ptions menu. The File Display Options dialog box appears. Choose the appropriate sort order and press Enter.

If you need help with the choices in the dialog box, press F1 to view a help screen, or choose the Help command button.

Change Sort Order

1. Choose **O**ptions.

2. Choose **F**ile Display Options.

The File Display Options dialog box appears.

3. Under Sort by, specify the order you want the files to sort.

4. Choose OK or press Enter.

Troubleshooting

If you change your mind about the options you have chosen, choose C____ the File Display Options dialog box

Choose a sort order in the File Display Options dialog box.

Files sorted by date.

View disk information to see how much space a file or directory takes on your disk. At the same time, you can check how much space is available on your disk.

DOS Shell enables you to view information about a currently selected file, its directory, and its drive. Information including the size of the file, the number of files in the directory, and the available disk space can help you plan your directory structure.

Suppose that one of the directories on your hard disk contains quite a few files. Files in this directory already are difficult to find and organize, but now you're getting ready to start a new project with files that would fit logically in this directory. View the information about the directory to see if you want to do some reorganizing or just assign the new project to a new directory.

TIP

Select several files you want to copy to a disk and view the information dialog box to see if your disk has enough space to hold the files. Check the Selected size and compare it to the size of the floppy disk you're using.

Displaying Information about the Disk

To view the disk information, choose the Show Information command from the **O**ptions menu. The Show Information dialog box appears and contains the following information:

◆ **File**. Displays the file name and any assigned attributes.

◆ **Selected**. Displays the name of the current drive, the number of files selected, and the total size of all the files selected.

◆ **Directory**. Lists the name of the current directory, the disk space taken by all the files in the directory, and the number of files in the directory.

◆ **Disk**. Lists the volume name of the disk, the capacity of the disk, the available space on the disk, and the number of directories on the disk.

TIP

Use the Show Information dialog box to find out how much disk space is left on your hard or floppy disk.

View Disk Information

1. Choose **O**ptions.

2. Choose Show Information.

The Show Information dialog box appears.

3. Choose Close when you've finished viewing the information.

```
                           MS-DOS Shell
    File  Options  View  Tree  Help
  C:\C┌─────Show Information─────┐
  ▣A  │                          │
      │  File                    │
      │   Name : 05FIG.ZIP       │                C:\COLLAGE\*.*
    ┌─┐│   Attr : ...a           │  ▣ 05FIG    .ZIP    169,780  06-12-93 ↑
    │ ││  Selected          C    │  ▣ 05FIG02A.PCX      16,383  06-08-93
    │ ││   Number:          1    │  ▣ 05FIG02B.PCX      15,981  06-08-93
    │ ││   Size :     169,780    │  ▣ 05FIG03A.PCX      11,472  06-08-93
    │ ││  Directory             │  ▣ 05FIG03B.PCX      24,105  06-08-93
    │ ││   Name : COLLAGE        │  ▣ 05FIG03C.PCX      11,754  06-08-93
    │ ││   Size :   2,704,352    │  ▣ 05FIG04A.PCX      10,805  06-08-93
    │ ││   Files :         90    │  ▣ 05FIG04B.PCX      38,957  06-08-93
    │ ││  Disk                   │  ▣ 05FIG04C.PCX      25,488  06-08-93 ↓
    │ ││   Name : MS_DOS_6       │ k Utilities
  ┌─┤│ ││   Size :  36,495,360    │                                        ↑
  │▦ M ││   Avail : 13,500,416    │
  │□ D ││   Files :        578    │
  │□ B ││   Dirs  :         14    │
  │□ R ││                         │
  │□ Q ││  ┌───────┐  ┌────────┐  │
  │□ F ││  │ Close │  │  Help  │  │
  │□ U ││  └───────┘  └────────┘  │
  └────└─────────────────────────┘                                        ↓
  F10=Actions  Shift+F9=Command Prompt                            5:30p
```

The Show Information dialog box describes the selected file, directory, and disk by name, size, capacity, and attributes.

MS-DOS SHELL

You can start your application programs from DOS Shell, and you can even switch between programs without exiting either one.

DOS Shell enables you to open, work in, and even switch between programs while you're in the Shell. Switching between programs means that you can open two programs and move back and forth between them to work without exiting either program.

DOS Shell comes with a few programs already loaded and showing in the Main window pane. You can start these programs from DOS Shell:

◆ **Command Prompt**. Temporarily displays the DOS system prompt so that you can type DOS commands. When you're finished with the command prompt and want to return to DOS Shell, simply type **EXIT** at the prompt.

◆ **DOS Editor**. Opens the MS-DOS Editor for use. For more information about Editor, see the "MS-DOS Editor" section.

◆ **DOS QBasic**. Opens the QBasic program used for BASIC programming.

◆ **Disk Utilities**. A program group. Select this option by pressing Enter or double-clicking with the mouse. A group of programs appears that includes Disk Copy, Backup, Restore, Format, and Undelete.

Starting Programs

To use any program from DOS Shell, you first have to start it. To start a program, highlight the program name and press Enter or double-click it with the mouse. Exit the program as you normally would if the program contains either an Exit or Quit command; otherwise, type EXIT at the command prompt.

If you plan to open and use two programs, you first have to engage the Task Swapper, which enables you to switch between the two programs. When you choose the Enable Task Swapper command from the Options menu, a small dot appears in front of the command, indicating that the command is turned on. If you select the command again, the dot disappears and you have turned it off.

The program list divides into two panes: one titled Main, the other titled Active Task List. You can open a program, such as DOS Editor, and you can switch back to DOS Shell and open other programs. As you open new programs, their names appear in the Active Task List.

You can have several programs open, depending on the amount of memory your computer has, and switch back and forth between DOS Shell and the other programs.

To exit the programs and stop Task Swapping, exit each program as you normally would. Then choose Options to turn off task swapping.

Use Programs

1. To start Task Swapper, choose **O**ptions **E**nable Task Swapper.

2. Open any program in the program list.

3. Press Ctrl+Esc to switch back to DOS Shell.

4. Open another program if desired.

5. Press Alt+Tab (repeatedly, if necessary) to switch between open programs.

6. Exit each program as you normally would.

Troubleshooting

If you have deleted QBasic from your disk, you can't start DOS Editor. Reinstall the QBasic program.

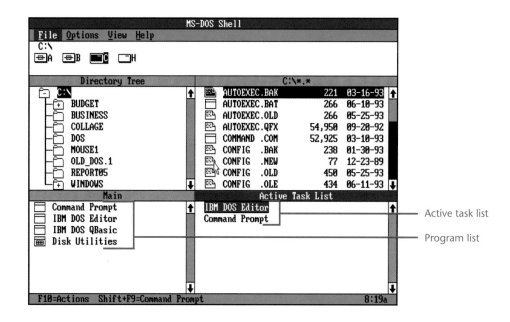

If you want to change CONFIG.SYS, AUTOEXEC.BAT, or another file, you need a text editor. The Editor program provided with DOS is simple to use.

MS-DOS Editor is a basic *text editor*—a simple word processing program that you can use to create and edit text files. Editor has no advanced capabilities such as word wrap, formatting, or graphics; but it's perfect for editing CONFIG.SYS and AUTOEXEC.BAT files, and for creating *batch files*—a set of DOS commands that you can activate by typing one word at the system prompt. (See "Batch Files" for details.) You can even use Editor to type and edit short memos or lists.

Editor is easy to use, especially if you already use a word processing program that has pull-down menus. You'll feel right at home.

Starting Editor

You start the Editor program from the system prompt. You can start Editor and then open a file, or you can start Editor with a file already open. To start Editor, type **EDIT** at the system prompt and press Enter. To start Editor with a file open, add a space and then type the file name. For example, to start Editor with the CONFIG.SYS file ready to edit, type **EDIT CONFIG.SYS** and press Enter. If you want to edit a file not in your current directory, either change directories or use a path to the file.

When the Editor screen appears, you decide whether to view some basic information on using Editor (the *Survival Guide*), or go directly to the editing screen.

TIP

You can view the Help screen when you first open Editor, or you can use the **H**elp menu—located at the right end of the menu bar—any time you need help with Editor.

When the file is on-screen in Editor, you can use the mouse or the keyboard to move around and change the text as you like. For details on editing a file, see the next article in this section, "Editing and Saving Files."

Using Menus

To open an Editor menu, press the Alt key to activate the menu bar. Each menu name then appears with an underlined letter; for example, F is the underlined letter in the **F**ile menu. Press the underlined letter to pull down that menu and display a list of commands.

Commands listed in each menu also have underlined letters that you press to activate the command. Some commands are *dimmed*, meaning that particular command isn't currently available for you to use.

If you use a mouse, making menu selections is easy. To pull down a menu with the mouse, move the mouse pointer (it looks like a solid block) to the menu name and click the mouse. To choose a command, click the command name.

Using Dialog Boxes

Many menu commands are followed by an ellipsis (...), which means that a dialog box appears when you choose that command. Dialog boxes are on-screen message boxes that either give you information or request information from you. You must accommodate the dialog box before the command can be completed. Dialog boxes contain various elements, including list boxes, check boxes, text boxes, and command buttons. For more information about the elements of a dialog box, see the article "Getting Around in DOS Shell" in the "DOS Shell" section.

Opening and Creating Files

Editor is mainly used to edit files, although you can also create new files. To edit a file, you first open the file by choosing **F**ile **O**pen. In the Open dialog box, type the name of the file, including the extension and path if necessary, and choose OK. Alternatively, you can select the file name from a list. The file opens in the Editor screen, and Editor displays the file name at the top of the screen.

To create a new file in Editor, you can start from a blank editing screen or modify an existing file and save it with a new name. To create a new file from scratch, use the **F**ile **N**ew command. Editor displays Untitled at the top of the screen until you specify a name for the file by saving it.

To create a new file from an existing file, open the file, edit it, and then save it with the **F**ile Save **A**s command, giving it a new name. Notice that Editor changes the file name displayed at the top of the screen to the new name you specify.

Scrolling the File

If you are editing a long file, Editor may not be able to display all of the file in the editing screen at one time. You can use the *scroll bars* to view the contents of the file. Scroll bars are located at the right side and bottom of the editing screen. To scroll the file slowly (one line at a time), click one of the *scroll arrows*. To move more quickly, click the scroll arrow and hold down the left mouse button. You can also move quickly through the file by clicking and dragging the *scroll boxes*.

more ▶

Start Editor

1. At the system prompt, type **EDIT**.

If you want to start Editor with a file open, press the space bar immediately after you type EDIT, and then type the name of the file. Be sure to include the path if the file is in a different directory.

2. Press Enter.

3. When the opening screen appears, press Enter if you want to use the Survival Guide. To bypass the Survival Guide and start working with files immediately, press Esc.

Open a File

1. To open an existing file in Editor, choose **F**ile, **O**pen.

The Open dialog box appears.

2. In the File Name text box, type the name of the file you want to open.

3. Press Enter or choose OK.

Menu bar

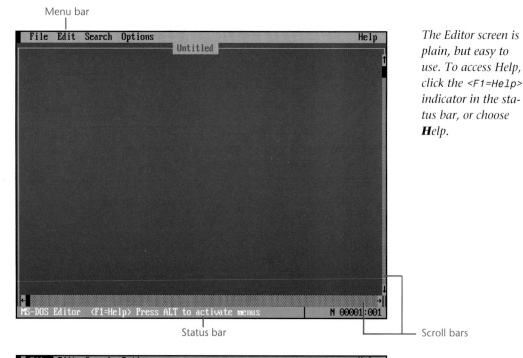

The Editor screen is plain, but easy to use. To access Help, click the <F1=Help> indicator in the status bar, or choose **H**elp.

Status bar

Scroll bars

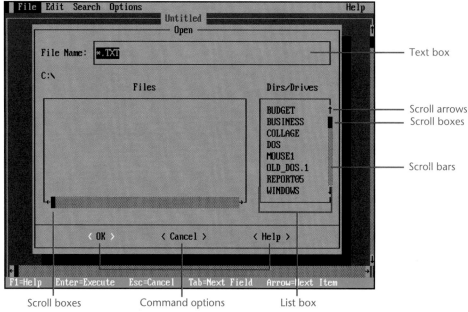

Text box

Scroll arrows
Scroll boxes

Scroll bars

Scroll boxes   Command options   List box

Create a New File

1. Choose **F**ile **N**ew. Editor displays a blank screen.

   If you prefer to work from an existing file, choose **F**ile **O**pen and specify the file you want. Editor displays the file on-screen.

2. Type and edit the file.

3. Save the file, specifying a new name.

Exit Editor

1. Choose **F**ile, E**x**it.

2. Editor closes down and returns to the DOS prompt.

Troubleshooting

◆ If you choose **F**ile **N**ew when you have a modified file on-screen that hasn't been saved, Editor prompts you to save the modified file before clearing the screen. Choose **Y**es to save the file, **N**o to start a new file without saving the old one, Cancel to return to the modified file, or **H**elp to display the Help menu.

◆ If you choose **F**ile E**x**it when you have a modified file on-screen that hasn't been saved, Editor prompts you to save the file. Choose **Y**es to save the file, **N**o to exit without saving, Cancel to return to the file, or **H**elp to display the Help menu.

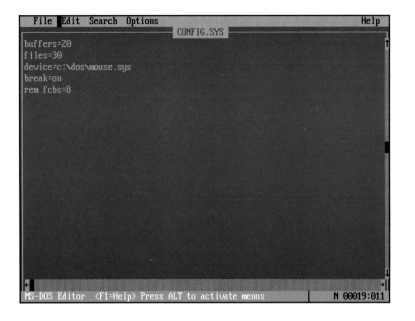

You can type the entries for your file in upper- or lowercase characters, or a combination of the two. Editor doesn't care which case you use.

Shortcut Keys

Alt	Activate menu bar
Esc	Cancel menu selection or dialog box

Make editing your AUTOEXEC.BAT and CONFIG.SYS files quick and easy by using MS-DOS Editor.

To edit a file in Editor, you begin by placing the cursor at the point in the file where you want to work. If you use a mouse, simply click the mouse pointer where you want to add or change text; the cursor moves to that point. To move the cursor with the keyboard, use the arrow keys. Here are some additional ways to move the cursor:

Key	Moves to
End	Last character on line
Home	First character on line
Ctrl+right arrow	Beginning of next word
Ctrl+left arrow	Beginning of previous word
Ctrl+Home	Beginning of document
Ctrl+End	End of document

Selecting Text

When you work in Editor, you first must select text before you can move, copy, or delete more than one character. To select text with the keyboard, position the cursor at the beginning of the text to be selected. Press and hold the Shift key and then move the cursor to the end of the selection and release the Shift key. The text appears in reverse-video. To cancel the selection, press Esc, or press the right- or left-arrow key once.

To select text with the mouse, position the mouse pointer at the beginning of the text. Hold down the left mouse button and drag the mouse block (cursor) down through the text. Release the mouse button at the end of the block of text you want to select. To cancel the selection, click the left mouse button once.

Moving, Copying, and Deleting

After you've selected the text you want to move, copy, or delete, choose the appropriate command for the editing process from the **E**dit menu—Cu**t**, **C**opy, **P**aste, or Cl**e**ar. Cl**e**ar is the same as deleting the text; if you prefer, you can just press the Delete key instead of going to the **E**dit menu.

When you *cut* text, Editor removes the text from the file on-screen but keeps it in memory. The cut text remains in memory until you paste it somewhere else, cut another section of text, or copy text. To cut and paste text, for example, you select the text and choose **E**dit Cu**t**. Then you reposition the cursor and choose **P**aste. The same holds true for using **C**opy and **P**aste. Cut or copied text remains in memory until you cut or copy another block of text, which is then saved in memory on top of the original cut text.

 TIP If you edit a text file, you must save the file to save the editing changes.

Saving a File

When you're done working in Editor, you save the file to disk. If you want to change the file name, or if you created the file in Editor and it doesn't yet have a name, use the **F**ile Save **A**s command to specify the file name and save the file to disk. If you are working with an existing file and you want to save the new version over the old, use the **F**ile **S**ave command.

Caution: *Editor doesn't prompt you to confirm that you want to replace the existing file with a new one.*

more ▶

Select Text

1. Place the cursor at the beginning of the text you want to select.

2. Use the cursor keys or drag the mouse to highlight the text.

Cut and Paste Text

1. Select the text to be cut.

2. Choose **E**dit and then Cut, or press Shift+Del.

3. Reposition the cursor and choose **E**dit and then Paste, or press Shift+Ins.

Copy and Paste Text

1. Select the text to be copied.

2. Choose **E**dit and then Copy, or press Ctrl+Ins.

3. Reposition the cursor and choose **E**dit and then Paste, or press Shift+Ins.

Selected text

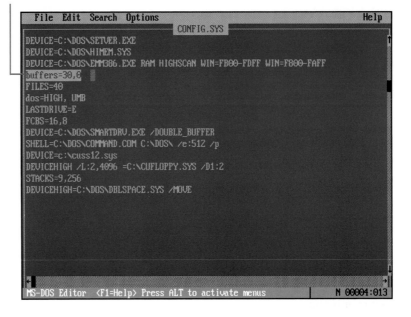

*After you select the text, use the **E**dit menu to cut, copy, or clear it.*

Save a File

1. Choose **F**ile, **S**ave.

   The Save As dialog box appears.

2. Type the new name for the file in the File Name text box.

3. If necessary, specify the drive and directory where you want to save the file in the Dirs/Drives list box.

4. Choose OK or press Enter.

```
┌─────────────── Save As ───────────────┐
│                                        │
│  File Name:  ┌CONFIG.SYS────────────┐  │
│              └──────────────────────┘  │
│  C:\                                   │
│                   Dirs/Drives          │
│              ┌────────────────┐↑       │
│              │  BUDGET        │        │
│              │  BUSINESS      │▓       │
│              │  COLLAGE       │▓       │
│              │  DOS           │▓       │
│              │  MOUSE1        │        │
│              │  OLD_DOS.1     │        │
│              │  REPORT05      │↓       │
│              └────────────────┘        │
├────────────────────────────────────────┤
│   < OK >     < Cancel >    < Help >    │
└────────────────────────────────────────┘
```

Use Save As to save a file under a new name—as a backup, for example.

Troubleshooting

◆ If you are making many changes to a file, save it periodically as you work. You don't want to have to start over if you have a sudden power failure!

◆ When changing CONFIG.SYS or AUTOEXEC.BAT, save the file under another name—CONFIG.BAK or AUTOEXEC.OLD—before you make changes to it, just in case the revised file doesn't work.

Shortcut Keys

Cut	Shift+Del
Copy	Ctrl+Ins
Paste	Shift+Ins
Clear	Del

MS-DOS EDITOR

Part Five

Section 12—Windows

Whether you've never used Windows or are a long-time fan, be sure to check out this section. Windows is a graphical interface that runs on MS-DOS. With Windows, you can run multiple programs simultaneously, and share data between those programs. MS-DOS 6.0 automatically provides a special program group for Windows, with Microsoft Anti-Virus, MS Backup, and Undelete built in. This section explores these programs and also describes how to configure your system to get the best performance from Windows.

Section 13—Viruses

If you've ever caught a virus, you know how easily they spread and how hard they are to get rid of. Computer *viruses*—programs that play pranks or destroy data—are just as bad. More than one thousand viruses have been detected, with more being created every day. This section helps you identify the symptoms of a virus and teaches you some preventive medicine that you can use to keep your computer healthy.

Section 14—Troubleshooting

Many articles in this book contain Troubleshooting ideas, specific to the task at hand. This section discusses how to handle a wide range of DOS-specific problems—what to do when DOS won't start, you can't get new printers or other devices to work, you have disk problems resulting from a virus, and many other potential trouble spots. Pay particular attention to the articles on preventing difficulties with the DOS programs MemMaker and DoubleSpace, and on how to fix problems with FastBack Plus, Norton Utilities, and other programs that you might use with DOS.

If you're an avid Windows fan, you'll be pleased to know that DOS 6 can help make Windows run more efficiently.

DOS includes memory managers and programs that can make Windows run faster and more efficiently. In addition, DOS 6 includes programs you can run in Windows to perform backups, check for viruses, and undelete files. Here's a short description of these three features:

◆ Back up your disk with Microsoft Backup for Windows. You can perform a full, incremental, or differential backup, just as you would at the DOS prompt.

◆ Search and remove viruses with Microsoft Anti-Virus for Windows. This program checks and cleans your disks and generates a status report when it's done.

◆ Use Microsoft Undelete for Windows to easily recover files you've deleted from disk.

During DOS 6 installation, Setup displays a list of programs it can install. For each program—Backup, Anti-Virus, Undelete, and so on—you can choose to install the DOS version, the Windows version, both versions, or neither version. If you, or the person who installed DOS 6, chose to install these programs to Windows, then the DOS Setup program creates a program group called Microsoft Tools and adds it to your Program Manager. Microsoft Tools contains the Windows versions of these DOS programs.

Combining DOS and Windows

DOS has a few problems with Windows. Several DOS commands don't work in Windows; worse yet, they may cause file or disk damage if they are used with Windows. Although DOS offers some ways to make Windows run more efficiently, certain DOS commands used with Windows can lock up your system.

It's important to know what you can and can't do when you use DOS and Windows. Doing the right thing—such as configuring more extended memory—can make Windows run more efficiently. Doing the wrong thing—such as using the CHKDSK (check disk) command from Windows—can destroy data, or, at the very least, lock up your computer.

Following are some tips for running Windows and taking advantage of the DOS features that can enhance your use of Windows.

Using Extended Memory

Windows and Windows-based applications need as much free extended memory as possible. To get more extended memory, use SMARTDrive, HIMEM.SYS, and EMM386.EXE with the RAM switch.

Make sure the previously mentioned devices are not using all your extended memory. Use the **MEM /C** command at the system prompt to see how much extended memory is available and how much is in use. If extended memory is low, use the REM (remark) command to disable the EMM386.EXE statement in your CONFIG.SYS file; then reboot and view the memory again.

Note: *For more information, see "Optimize with HIMEM.SYS" and "Optimize with EMM386.EXE" in the "Memory" section, and "Using SMARTDrive" in the "Hard Disks" section.*

Freeing Conventional Memory

DOS-based applications running in Windows require more free conventional memory. Streamlining your configuration files so that they don't load unnecessary memory-resident programs frees conventional memory. You can also free some conventional memory if you run DOS in extended memory.

Commands To Avoid

When you are running Windows, don't use these commands:

◆ **APPEND**. Tricks a program into thinking its files are located in the current directory rather than in their real directory.

◆ **DBLSPACE**. Disk compression program.

◆ **DEFRAG**. Program that reorganizes files on the disk to optimize disk space.

◆ **EMM386**. Enables or disables the expanded-memory manager.

◆ **FASTOPEN**. Decreases the amount of time it takes a program to access and open files.

◆ **MEMMAKER**. Reconfigures your computer to optimize memory.

◆ **MSCDEX**. Provides access to CD-ROM drives.

TIP

If your processor is a 386 or higher, run your device drivers in the upper-memory area.

◆ **NLSFUNC**. Loads country-specific information for national language support.

◆ **SCANFIX/N** or **/NOPROMPT** or **SCANFIX/A** or **/ALL.** Diagnoses and repairs disk errors.

◆ **SMARTDRV**. Creates a disk cache in extended memory.

◆ **SUBST**. Substitutes a drive letter for a path.

◆ **VSAFE**. Virus detection program.

◆ **CHKDSK /F**. Checks and fixes any problems with the disk.

For more information about any of these commands, see Appendix B "Command Reference."

more ▶

Handling Memory-Resident Programs

Do not run Windows Setup with any memory-resident (TSR) programs running. First of all, the TSRs may be taking valuable memory that Windows Setup needs. Second, some TSRs can cause problems with Setup and lock up your computer, perhaps even corrupt data files.

DOS includes many memory-resident programs that you may not even realize are running. Following is a list of DOS commands that start a TSR. Avoid loading any of these programs before you install Windows:

◆ APPEND   ◆ JOIN

◆ ASSIGN   ◆ MIRROR

◆ FASTOPEN   ◆ PRINT

◆ GRAPHICS   ◆ SUBST

TIP

Check your AUTOEXEC.BAT for these commands. Use the REM (remark) command to disable any TSRs in your AUTOEXEC.BAT until after you have installed Windows.

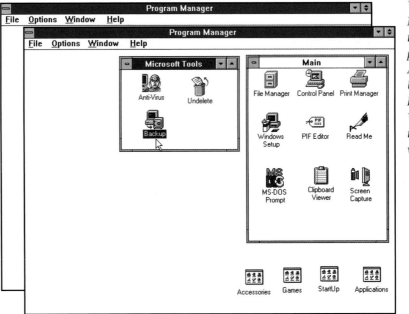

Windows Program Manager displaying the Microsoft Tools program group; Anti-Virus, Undelete, and Backup for Windows appear in the Microsoft Tools window.

Using the DOS Prompt from Windows

In Windows, you've probably noticed the MS-DOS prompt in the Main group window. You can access the prompt by double-clicking this icon. The DOS screen and system prompt appear, with instructions on how to return to Windows.

From the system prompt, you can use most commands you normally use with DOS (refer to the preceding list of commands to see which ones you should *not* use with the DOS prompt from Windows). When you're finished working at the DOS prompt and are ready to return to Windows, keep these things in mind:

◆ Type **EXIT** to return to Windows. If you type **WIN** to start Windows, you'll have Windows open twice, and your computer's memory will be severely taxed.

◆ If you forget to type **EXIT** at the system prompt, and just turn off your computer, you'll lose any unsaved files you were working on in Windows.

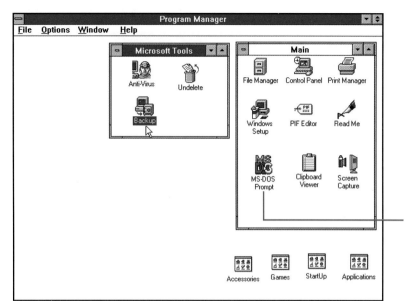

Exiting to the DOS prompt is useful when you need to run DOS-based programs or commands.

Double-click the MS-DOS prompt icon to exit Windows temporarily and go to the DOS prompt.

WINDOWS

Backing Up from Windows

If you're used to the mouse and using programs in Windows, the Windows version of MS Backup is for you!

I f you're the type of computer user who works with Windows programs all day long, you'll find it's now quick and easy to perform your backups in Windows, as well. MS Backup for Windows is similar to MS Backup for DOS in that you can choose a full, incremental, or differential backup. In addition, you can select specific files and directories to back up, you can compare the backup to the original, and you can restore the files.

Windows Backup versus DOS Backup

If you've already used MS Backup for DOS, you have a head start on using MS Backup for Windows. The primary difference between the Windows and DOS programs is the screen. The Windows interface provides you with a different look, but the task is still much the same. For information about the various types of backups, see these articles from the "Hard Disks" section: "Planning Your Backup," "Performing a Full Backup," and "Performing Partial Backups."

Configuring the Backup

The first time you use MS Backup for Windows, Backup configures and tests the compatibility of your computer. Backup displays a dialog box telling you that the program must be configured; choose **Y**es to continue. Follow the directions on-screen to complete the compatibility test and configuration. While testing your drives, Backup displays several dialog boxes: one asks you to remove all disks from the floppy drives, another asks you to choose the drive you want to backup to, and so on.

The configuration process uses one or two floppy disks to perform a test backup. The progress of the backup is displayed on-screen while you wait. When the test backup is complete, Backup prompts you to insert the first test backup disk (if two disks were required) for the compare phase of the test. When testing is complete, you can begin a normal backup.

During configuration, the system defaults that the Backup program uses during the normal backup process are set, such as which floppy drive you'll back up to. Naturally, you can change any of the defaults before you begin a backup.

Making a Backup

To make a backup in Windows, double-click the Backup program icon in the Microsoft Tools window; Backup reads your hard disk. (If you haven't used Backup before, the configuration program runs, as previously described.)

Choose the **B**ackup button from the Backup window. Before you begin the backup, there are a few choices to make:

◆ Setu**p** File. Choose DEFAULT.SET, which contains options set during the compatibility test, or create your own set of backup options.

◆ Bac**k**up From. If you have two or more drives, choose the one you want to back up.

◆ Se**l**ect Files. Choose to display the directory tree. Select individual files and/or directories by holding the Shift key while you click the files you want to back up. If you click a directory while holding down the Shift key, all files in that directory are selected.

◆ Backup T**y**pe. Choose Full, Incremental, or Differential backup. For more information about these three types, see the article "Planning Your Backup" in the "Hard Disks" section.

◆ Backup **T**o. Choose the drive or the path you want to back up to. You can change the drive by choosing the down arrow in the Backup **T**o box.

After selecting the appropriate options, choose Start Backup. The program prompts you to insert disks.

When finished, Backup displays a dialog box that lists information about the backup. Choose OK to return to the Backup window. Choose Quit to end the backup session.

After you complete your backup, you may want to compare or restore your backups. Both are easy tasks with MS Backup for Windows. The following paragraphs touch on the basics of comparing and restoring backup files with MS Backup for Windows. However, the DOS and Windows versions of these tasks are very similar, so for more information, refer to the articles "Comparing the Backup" and "Restoring Data" in the "Hard Disks" section.

Comparing the Backup

To compare the backed up files with the originals, choose the Compare button in the Backup window and the Compare window appears. The Compare window looks similar to the Backup window: you can choose to compare individual files, directories, or the entire backup. It's a good idea to compare the backups to the originals to verify the integrity of your data. If the files don't match, you can repeat the backup immediately.

Select the files or directories you want to compare and choose Start Compare. When Backup completes the comparison, it issues a report.

Restoring Files

Restoring files from a backup is as easy as backing up the files. Choose the Restore button from the Backup window. This window is similar to the Backup and Compare windows. Choose your restore options and then choose Start Restore. Directions on-screen will tell you which disks to insert.

more ▶

WINDOWS

Make a Backup

1. From Program Manager, double-click the Backup icon in the Microsoft Tools window.

   If you have never used MS Backup for Windows, DOS must first configure the program and test for compatibility. Follow the directions on-screen as DOS completes this test.

2. Choose your backup settings or accept the default settings. Choose **S**tart Backup when you are ready to begin.

3. Follow the instructions on-screen that prompt you to insert disks.

   When Backup is finished, it displays a report.

4. Choose OK to return to the main Backup screen.

5. Choose **Q**uit to return to Program Manager.

Troubleshooting

If you have problems with the backup, refer to Appendix A, "Error Messages."

Shortcut Keys

Within the Select Files dialog box:	
Ctrl+/	Select all files
Ctrl+\	Deselect all files

Choose disk to back up

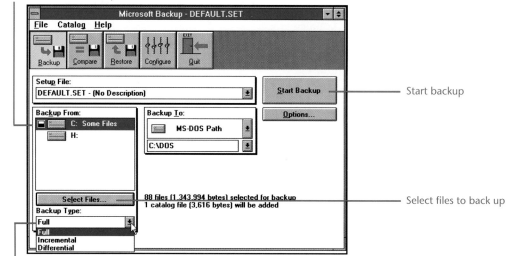

Start backup

Select files to back up

Specify backup type

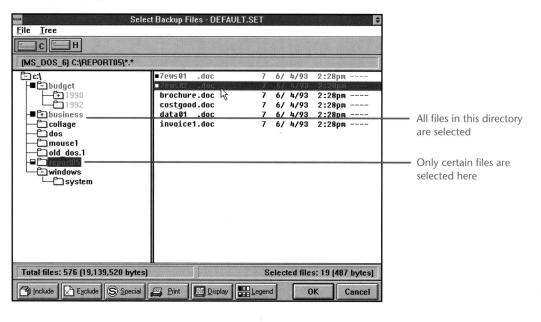

All files in this directory are selected

Only certain files are selected here

Compare the Backup

1. In Microsoft Backup, choose **C**ompare.

2. Choose the Bac**k**up Set you want to compare. Choose **S**tart Compare when you are ready to begin.

3. Follow the instructions on-screen that prompt you to insert disks.

4. When Compare is finished, it displays a report. Choose OK to return to the main Backup screen. Choose **Q**uit to return to Program Manager.

Restore the Backup

1. In Microsoft Backup, choose **R**estore.

2. Choose the Bac**k**up Set Catalog, and choose Start Restore when you are ready to begin.

3. Follow the instructions on-screen that prompt you to insert disks.

4. When Restore is finished, it displays a report. Choose OK to return to the main Backup screen. Choose **Q**uit to return to Program Manager.

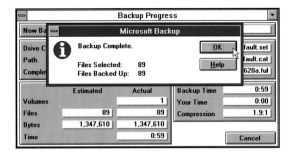

The Backup report.

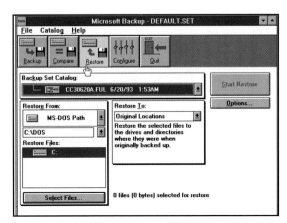

It's a good idea to compare backup files to originals.

Restoring backup files is easy.

WINDOWS

Oops! You didn't mean to delete that file from the hard disk yesterday, did you? You may be able to recover it, using the Undelete program in Windows.

Undelete for Windows works similarly to Undelete for DOS. You choose a drive and a directory, view the files to see which can be restored, then undelete those files you want to recover. The Windows interface makes the program easy to use and to understand.

To undelete files using Undelete for Windows, you first open the Undelete program from the Microsoft Tools window in Program Manager. The Microsoft Undelete screen appears with the current drive and directory displayed—probably C:\WINDOWS.

Selecting Files To Undelete

To change drives, choose the **D**rive/Dir button and the Change Drive and Directory dialog box appears. Either choose the correct drive and directory from the list of Directories, or type the path in the **C**hange to Directory text box. Choose OK or press Enter to accept the change.

The program returns to the Undelete window and displays a list of files that have recently been deleted from the directory you selected. Each file is listed by name—with a question mark as the first character, the condition of the file, size of the file, and the date and time the file was created or last updated.

In the Condition column, any file listed as `Perfect` can be successfully undeleted. A file listed as `Excellent` may be recoverable, and a file listed as `Destroyed` cannot be recovered by the Undelete program. To undelete a file, select it by clicking the file name with the mouse; select more than one file by clicking each file name with the mouse. To deselect a file, click it a second time.

Performing the Undelete

When you've selected all the files you want to undelete, choose the **U**ndelete button. A dialog box appears requesting the first character of the file name. Fill in the missing character and press Enter. If Undelete can recover the file, it replaces the original condition with `Recovered`. If the program cannot undelete the file, it displays a dialog box giving the reason for the problem.

Options

You can find out about any listed file in Undelete by choosing the Info button. The **I**nfo button displays a File Information dialog box that describes the file's size, path, last modified date, condition, and so on.

Use the **S**ort By button to sort the files in the list in order by name, extension, size, condition, and so on.

Use the Find button to search for specific files in the Undelete program.

Undelete a File

1. Double-click the Undelete program icon in the Microsoft Tools window in Program Manager.

2. Choose the **D**rive/Dir button, and the Change Drive and Directory dialog box appears.

3. Choose the appropriate drive and directory.

4. Choose OK or press Enter.

5. Select the file or files to be undeleted.

6. Choose the **U**ndelete button.

7. Enter the first character of each file as prompted.

8. To exit the Undelete program, choose **F**ile Exit.

Troubleshooting

UNDELETE cannot restore deleted subdirectories or any file if you deleted the subdirectory that contained the file.

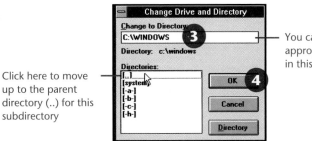

Click here to move up to the parent directory (..) for this subdirectory

You can type the appropriate path in this text box

Destroyed files

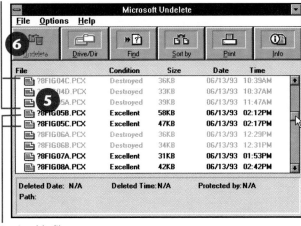

Retrievable files

WINDOWS

Checking for Viruses in Windows

It's easy to scan and clean a disk with MS Anti-Virus. Whether you use the DOS or the Windows version, you should periodically test your system for viruses.

Viruses can destroy data, program files, even your hard disk. If your computer is at high risk for catching viruses—you have copied illegal software or used other people's floppy disks in your computer—then test your computer periodically for viruses.

The MS Anti-Virus for Windows is similar to MS Anti-Virus for DOS. MS Anti-Virus is easy to run and helps you protect your valuable data and programs. For more information on viruses, see the section "Viruses."

Using MS Anti-Virus for Windows

To use Anti-Virus for Windows, double-click the Anti-Virus icon in the Microsoft Tools window in Program Manager. The Anti-Virus dialog box appears.

You can choose the drive you want to scan for viruses by clicking the icon for the appropriate drive. MS Anti-Virus scans the drive and lists the number of directories and files in the Status box.

TIP From the Scan menu, choose Virus List to view a list of viruses and information about each one. Within the Virus List dialog box, you can scroll the list of viruses and view or print more information about each one by choosing the Info command button. To search for a specific virus—such as the Michelangelo virus— enter the first few letters of the virus in the Search for text box.

TIP Choose the Options menu, and then choose Set Options to view a list of alternatives for the Anti-Virus program. You can, for example, turn off the alarm system, verify the integrity of the detect and clean operation, or have the program prompt you while it's detecting viruses.

Choose Detect and Clean to scan the drive for viruses and remove any it finds. MS Anti-Virus displays a progress report as it scans the drive.

If MS Anti-Virus finds a problem, it sounds an alarm and displays a dialog box informing you of the problem. The dialog box displays several options for you to choose, usually with a suggestion as to the best choice.

At the end of the scanning, MS Anti-Virus displays a Statistics dialog box that reports the results of the scan. Choose OK to return to the Anti-Virus screen.

The Status area of the dialog box is updated to show the results of the recent virus search. To exit the program, use the Scan menu.

Check for Viruses

1. Double-click the Anti-Virus icon in the Microsoft Tools window.

2. Choose the drive you want Anti-Virus to scan.

3. Choose Detect and Clean.

4. Follow directions on-screen if a virus is found.

5. At the end of the virus check, a statistics dialog box is displayed. Choose OK to return to the Anti-Virus screen.

6. Choose **S**can E**x**it Anti-Virus to close the program.

Choose drive

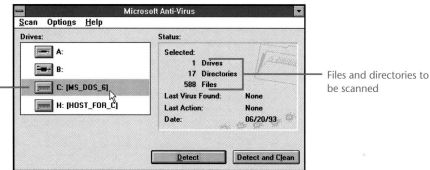

Files and directories to be scanned

At the end of virus scanning, the Statistics report is displayed.

WINDOWS

If your hard disk starts acting strange (you see unexplained error messages, your display flashes garbage, or you lose files), you may have a virus.

A *virus* is a program that hides in a file, infects your computer, spreads to other computers, and can do great damage if not detected and stopped. Viruses are created by hackers who don't realize or don't care about the damage the viruses can do. They create a virus as a joke or out of spite; then the virus is spread unknowingly by other users. A virus is a program that is interwoven with another program such as a game or a word processing program. When you install the program on your hard disk, you install the virus with it. The virus may take action immediately or may lie in wait on your disk, like a time bomb.

Some viruses cause aggravation by displaying messages; others can multiply and destroy some or all of your program and data files. Still other viruses can damage your hard disk by changing the speed at which the disk runs. Furthermore, viruses are made to spread—not only from file to file and directory to directory, but from computer to computer.

TIP

Before you run any new application program (whether you installed it from original disks, borrowed disks, or from a bulletin board), install the program and then scan it for viruses.

Preventive Measures

More than 1,000 kinds of viruses are in existence today, and thousands of variations of those viruses exist. The chances of your computer contracting a virus are lessened, however, if you take precautions.

Viruses are spread by infected files—usually program files. You can get infected files from sources like these:

◆ **Illegal software programs**. Be careful when trading software programs with friends and acquaintances. A software program could have been in many hands before it reached yours. Because a virus may not show up for weeks or even months, you may not find out about the virus until it's too late.

◆ **Disreputable software dealers**. Watch out for ads in the back of magazines offering free or inexpensive programs you've never heard of; you never know how what kind of program you'll get!

◆ **Bulletin boards**. Anyone can upload infected program files to a bulletin board and then advertise it as a free program.

◆ **Bootable floppy disks**. Viruses can hide in executable files, like those on a system disk. Use only bootable disks you create.

Scanning for Viruses

In addition to taking preventive measures, you can use Microsoft Anti-Virus for MS-DOS program to help protect your computer. Anti-Virus can detect and remove more than 800 variations of known viruses from your hard disk or floppy disks, saving your computer before it's too late.

Anti-Virus offers two methods of scanning for a virus: Detect and Detect & Clean. If you choose the Detect method, Anti-Virus scans for viruses and just displays information about them; if you choose Detect & Clean, Anti-Virus removes any viruses it finds.

Anti-Virus scans the disk and presents a report of its progress, displaying the directories and files it is scanning. A box indicates the percent of directories scanned and the percent of files within each directory. When Anti-Virus is done, it displays a report of the disk it scanned, the types of files scanned, and the viruses found, if any.

more ▶

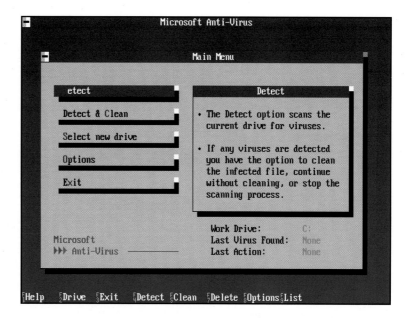

The Microsoft Anti-Virus main menu.

Specify the drive you want to scan by highlighting a drive letter at the top of the screen.

VIRUSES

Scan for Viruses

1. At the system prompt, type **MSAV**.

2. Press Enter.

   The Anti-Virus main menu appears.

3. If you want to check a floppy disk, choose **S**elect New Drive and specify the drive (usually A or B).

4. Choose the anti-virus method you want to use: **D**etect or Detect & **C**lean.

   Anti-Virus displays a report.

5. After you read the report, press Enter or choose OK.

   Anti-Virus returns to the main menu.

6. Choose E**x**it to return to the system prompt.

If Anti-Virus finds a virus, the program sounds a warning tone and displays a warning message.

Because viruses often change important program files, Anti-Virus displays a warning message if it detects changes in these files.

You can detect a floppy disk that is write-protected, but you must remove the write protection if you want to clean the virus.

Troubleshooting

It's possible for viruses to infect the Anti-Virus program as well as other programs on your hard disk. You can save the Anti-Virus files to your system disk—before a virus strikes—and use them to detect and perhaps remove the virus from your hard disk. Copy the following files to your system disk from the DOS directory: MSAV.EXE, MSAV.HLP, MSAVHELP.OVL, and MSAVIRUS.LST.

```
┌─────────────────────────────────────────────┐
│■         Viruses Detected and Cleaned        │
│                                              │
│                Checked    Infected   Cleaned │
│                                              │
│   Hard disks   :    0         0         0    │
│   Floppy disks :    1         1         0    │
│   Total disks  :    1         1         0    │
│                                              │
│   COM Files    :    0         0         0    │
│   EXE Files    :    0         0         0    │
│   Other Files  :    2         0         0    │
│   Total Files  :    2         0         0    │
│                                              │
│   Scan Time    :   00:00:06                  │
│                                              │
│                                    ▐  K  ▌   │
└─────────────────────────────────────────────┘
```

An Anti-Virus report of the drive and files scanned, and the viruses found.

```
┌──────────────────────────┐
│■      IMPORTANT !        │
│                          │
│  Since a virus was       │
│  detected, rebooting is  │
│  recommended to minimize │
│  the possibility of      │
│  further infection.      │
│                          │
│   ▐ eboot ▌   ▐ Exit ▌   │
└──────────────────────────┘
```

If you find a virus, Anti-Virus warns you to reboot for maximum virus protection.

Curious about viruses and what they do? Want to know what a *Trojan horse* is? View the virus descriptions in Anti-Virus.

If Anti-Virus finds a virus on your disk, you can view information about the virus in the Anti-Virus program. In addition, if you're just curious about viruses, you can scroll through the list of more than 1,200 viruses and view information on any viruses you find interesting. Anti-Virus contains a listing of all of the viruses it recognizes.

Suppose that the Anti-Virus program detects the Ogre virus on your hard disk. Before you remove it, you want to find out what exactly an Ogre virus is. You can search the virus list for the virus and view more information about it. The information listed about each virus includes the type of virus and the number of strains of the virus.

Virus Types

The type of virus describes how the virus infects the system. A *boot virus* infects the boot sector by replacing the disk's original boot sector with its own. When the disk is booted with the virus, the virus loads itself into memory and can spread to other disks.

A *file virus* infects the files that run programs. When you start a program, the virus is activated, and the virus spreads to other program files.

A *Trojan horse* is a serious virus. The Trojan horse virus disguises itself as a program; when you run the program, the virus may damage your hard disk and destroy your files. Damage by a Trojan horse virus may be irreparable.

Viewing Virus Information

To open the Anti-Virus program, type MSAV and press Enter. To view the types of viruses, press F9 to display the virus list. The list gives you the virus names, aliases, types, sizes, and number of variations.

To view more information about a virus, select the virus name from the list by highlighting it and press Enter. To search for a specific virus, enter the name of the virus in the text box and press Enter.

TIP

Since new viruses are discovered regularly, you can order updates for the Anti-Virus for MS-DOS from Microsoft. Check your MS-DOS Reference Manual for more information.

View Virus Information

1. At the system prompt, type **msav**.

2. Press Enter.

The MS Anti-Virus welcome screen appears.

3. Press F9 to display the virus list.

4. Highlight the virus you want to learn about.

5. Press Enter to view more information.

The Virus Characteristics dialog box displays details about the virus you specified.

6. After you read about the virus, press Enter to close the dialog box.

7. Choose OK to close the virus list.

8. Choose Exit to return to the system prompt.

Troubleshooting

If you suspect your system contains a virus not listed in the Anti-Virus Virus List, call your local software vendor for help finding an anti-virus program that can detect and clean your system. Norton Anti-Virus is an excellent program, as is Novi by Certus.

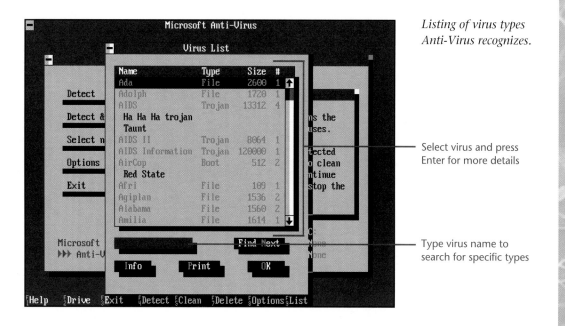

Listing of virus types Anti-Virus recognizes.

Select virus and press Enter for more details

Type virus name to search for specific types

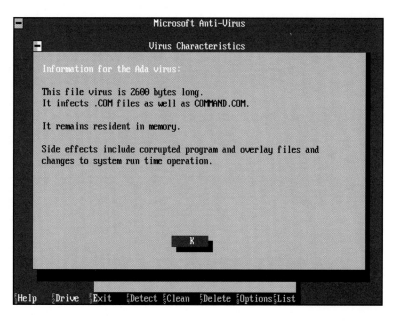

Viewing virus characteristics.

VIRUSES

If you use disks from other people many times each day, you need constant protection from viruses—use *VSafe*.

VSafe is a memory-resident program you can load from the system prompt. VSafe monitors your computer for any activity that appears to be a virus. If VSafe detects virus activity, it displays a warning message.

VSafe is good to use in certain circumstances—for example, if you use disks and programs that come from other computer systems. However, since VSafe is a memory-resident program—also called TSR for terminate-and-stay-resident—it uses quite a bit of conventional, extended, and expanded memory. Because VSafe is a TSR, it slows your system and robs valuable conventional memory from other programs. In addition, VSafe checks all disk and memory activity as you work, thus taking time and speed from other programs.

> **TIP** For more information about memory and TSRs, see the section "Memory."

Running VSafe

To load VSafe, type the command (VSAFE) at the system prompt. You can view VSafe warning options by pressing Alt+V. The warning options describe when VSafe will warn you and what it should check. You can have VSafe check and protect the hard disk boot sector and executable files, for example. Naturally, the more options you choose, the more your system slows.

VSafe Options

Generally, you're safe with the following default options:

◆ **HD Low Level Format**. Notifies you if a virus is formatting your hard disk.

◆ **Check Executable Files** of each program that is opened.

◆ **Boot Sector Viruses** found, VSafe displays a message.

◆ **Protect HD Boot Sector**. Warns if a virus attempts to write to the hard disk's boot sector or partition table.

> **TIP** When using Windows, load the VSafe Manager program so that Windows can display any virus warning messages. See "Checking for Viruses in Windows" for more information.

You can turn off VSafe by entering the VSAFE command with the /U (unload) switch.

> **TIP** Turn VSafe off—vsafe /u—before installing Windows and never use VSafe while Windows is running. You can, however, use a similar memory-resident program with Windows. Add the following line to your WIN.INI file: **load=mwavtsr.exe**, which enables messages about viruses to be shown in Windows.

Use VSafe

To load VSafe, type the following at the system prompt and press Enter:

vsafe

To turn off VSafe, type the following at the system prompt and press Enter:

vsafe /u

Troubleshooting

If your programs seem to run slow, unload VSafe.

Shortcut Key

The default hot key for VSafe is Alt+V.

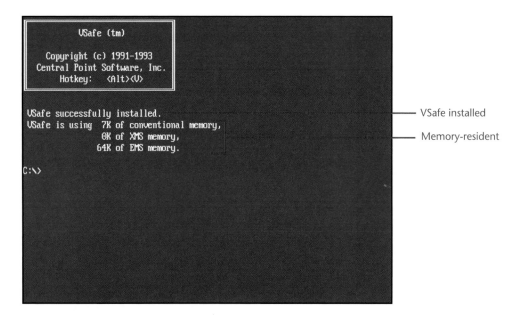

```
        VSafe (tm)

    Copyright (c) 1991-1993
  Central Point Software, Inc.
    Hotkey:   <Alt><V>


VSafe successfully installed.
VSafe is using  7K of conventional memory,
                0K of XMS memory,
               64K of EMS memory.

C:\>
```

VSafe installed

Memory-resident

You're excited about the prospect of using DOS 6 and all its new features; but during installation, something goes wrong.

Although it's unlikely anything will go wrong during the installation of DOS 6, it could happen. Suppose your computer locks up before DOS is completely installed. Fortunately, DOS has a built-in safeguard in case that happens. And there are additional methods you can use to avert disaster during Setup. You may be able to reboot your computer and start again; if not, you can try a special option that enables you to customize Setup to your computer.

Using Uninstall

When you use DOS Setup, DOS creates one or two uninstall disks to protect your files while you're installing DOS. If a problem occurs while you're installing DOS—damaged disk, power failure, and so on—you can use the Uninstall disk to recover from Setup problems and return to your previous DOS version.

When you install DOS 6, the Setup program saves all your previous DOS files to the OLD_DOS.1 directory. In addition, Setup copies these same DOS files to the Uninstall disk, along with your configuration files—AUTOEXEC.BAT and CONFIG.SYS. If you use the uninstall disk, DOS copies these files back to your computer, overwriting any newly installed DOS and configuration files.

Caution: You can't use the uninstall disk if you have reformatted your hard drive, deleted the OLD_DOS.1 directory, or installed a disk-compression program after you installed DOS.

To use the uninstall disk, insert the disk in drive A and perform a warm boot. Follow the instructions on-screen.

DOS Files in Root Directory

If your root directory (usually C:\) contains DOS files, Setup displays the message Root directory of your hard disk contains some of your original DOS files. You must remove the DOS files from the root before you can install DOS 6. Here's how:

◆ Exit Setup by pressing F3 twice.

◆ Create a directory called DOS, if you don't already have one.

◆ Move all DOS files from the root directory to the DOS directory.

◆ Delete the DOS files from the root directory.

> *Caution: When deleting files from the root directory, don't delete the CONFIG.SYS, AUTOEXEC.BAT, or COMMAND.COM files.*

◆ Try running Setup again when your root directory is free of DOS files.

If you're not sure which files are DOS files, print your directory list. See the article "Listing Directories" in the "Directories" section for information about printing the directory list. Compare the printed directory list to the file PACKING.LST on the DOS Setup Disk 1. PACKING.LST contains the names of the files that should be in your DOS directory.

Lock-Up During Install

If your computer locks up or Setup stops during the DOS installation, there are a couple of things you can try before calling Microsoft technical support. The first thing is to remove all disks from your floppy drive and warm boot your computer by pressing Ctrl+Alt+Del. DOS may or may not respond by asking for the uninstall disk.

If DOS prompts you for the uninstall disk when you reboot, insert the disk and press Enter. Follow the instructions on your screen to uninstall DOS 6. You can try to install the program again; if Setup stops again, call Microsoft technical support.

DOS Doesn't Ask for Uninstall

If Setup stops, but DOS doesn't prompt for the uninstall disk, try to access the hard drive by typing **DIR C:** (substitute the appropriate drive letter for **C**). Then take one of these steps to reboot:

◆ If DOS doesn't list the files and directories on the drive, you cannot access your hard disk. If you have a system floppy

disk, insert it into drive A, reboot your computer with the floppy disk, and try to access the hard drive one more time before calling technical support.

◆ If you don't have a system disk, but you see a directory listing, create a system disk by placing a floppy disk in drive A and typing the command **FORMAT A: /S** at the prompt. Leave the disk in drive A and warm boot the computer.

After you reboot the computer, insert the Setup Disk 1 into the floppy drive and type the drive letter plus **SETUP** (for example, type **A:SETUP**); then press Enter. Continue with Setup.

Setup Stops Repeatedly

If Setup stops again, insert the system disk in drive A and reboot. Insert the Setup Disk 1 in the drive again; but this time, type the drive letter (usually **A:**), the word **SETUP**, plus **/I**. The **/I** switch skips Setup's hardware detection and enables you to input information about your computer. Follow the directions on-screen and enter any information DOS prompts you for.

If Setup stops again, call Microsoft technical support.

Not Enough Free Disk Space

If Setup displays the message `There is not enough free space on drive C to install MS-DOS`, note how much additional free disk space Setup needs—Setup indicates which

drive needs the space and how much more it needs.

Exit Setup by pressing F3 twice. At the system prompt, type **CHKDSK** and press Enter to see how much disk space you need to free. You can then back up some files to floppy disks and delete them in order to free disk space. When you've made enough space available, run Setup again.

Incompatible Disk-Compression Program

If you use a disk-compression program, Setup may prompt you with the message `Your computer uses a disk-compression program that is incompatible with Setup`. If you receive this message, you must replace the disk-compression program if you want to install DOS 6.

You can either replace the program with the DOS 6 DoubleSpace program, or you can contact the software vendor for an updated version of the disk-compression program you are presently using. DOS 6 is compatible with most recent versions of disk-compression programs.

Before you replace your disk-compression program, perform a full backup of your hard disk. To replace your program with DoubleSpace, you'll have to format your hard drive and then run DOS Setup. After DOS is fully installed, type **DBLSPACE** at the system prompt and press Enter to install the program.

If DOS doesn't start, all is not lost. This article provides a step-by-step procedure for diagnosing the problem.

If DOS doesn't start, it's most likely a problem with your CONFIG.SYS or AUTOEXEC.BAT file. The problem could be an incompatible device driver, a TSR taking too much memory, or just a bad command. You may be able to fix the problem yourself. Following is a step-by-step procedure you can try before calling for technical support.

The following diagnostic procedure can be used quite successfully with other problems with DOS. You'll see it referred to often in this article.

Diagnostic Process

If you can't start DOS, there may be a problem with a command or statement in your CONFIG.SYS or AUTOEXEC.BAT file. If you're using DOS 6, when your computer starts after you boot it and the Starting MS-DOS... message appears, press the F8 key to view each command in the CONFIG.SYS file.

Pressing the F8 key causes DOS to prompt you. It carries out each command in your CONFIG.SYS. DOS displays the command and a [Y/N] prompt. Type **Y** to accept the command; type **N** to bypass the command. Using this confirmation method, you can test the various configuration commands, and you may be able to discover which command is causing the problem.

At the end of the step-by-step command confirmation of CONFIG.SYS, DOS prompts you to process the AUTOEXEC.BAT file. DOS doesn't go through the AUTOEXEC.BAT commands one by one; you either accept the entire file or bypass the entire file.

Another way to diagnose a problem with your configuration is to completely bypass the CONFIG.SYS and AUTOEXEC.BAT files. If you are using DOS 6, press F5 when you see the message Starting MS-DOS....

EMM386 Problem

If you're having problems starting DOS, another command that could be giving you problems is the EMM386 extended memory manager. To find out, use the diagnostic procedure just described. As you are prompted for each command in the CONFIG.SYS file, press **Y** for each one except the device command that loads EMM386.EXE—DEVICE=EMM386.EXE. When that command appears, press **N**. When DOS prompts you to process the AUTOEXEC.BAT file, press **Y**.

If your computer starts, the problem was with the EMM386 expanded memory manager. Reconfigure the device driver or run MemMaker to do it for you. For more information about EMM386, see the section "Memory."

TSR or Device Problem

If your computer doesn't start, you may have a problem with a memory-resident program (TSR) or a device driver that either the CONFIG.SYS or AUTOEXEC.BAT file loads during startup. You can start your computer and skip both configuration files to see if that could be the problem.

To bypass both the AUTOEXEC.BAT and CONFIG.SYS, reboot your computer. When the message Starting MS-DOS... appears, press F5. DOS should bypass your configuration files and start, displaying a system prompt. If your computer still doesn't start, call Microsoft technical support.

If your computer does start when you bypass both the AUTOEXEC.BAT and CONFIG.SYS files, it means there is most likely a problem in one of the configuration files. Follow the preceding steps for checking each command in your CONFIG.SYS file, pressing **Y** after each prompt. After you have viewed the entire CONFIG.SYS file and you are prompted to process your AUTOEXEC.BAT file, press **N**. If your computer starts, the problem is in the AUTOEXEC.BAT file; if your computer doesn't start, the problem is in your CONFIG.SYS file.

To track down a problem in your AUTOEXEC.BAT file, you can use the Remark command (REM) to temporarily disable one statement at a time. You may need to save the troublesome file under a new name and create a new AUTOEXEC.BAT or CONFIG.SYS file piece by piece if you can't find the problem any other way.

Shortcut Keys	
F8	Process CONFIG.SYS commands one at a time
F5	Bypass CONFIG.SYS and AUTOEXEC.BAT

Installing any new device can cause problems with DOS; here are some tips to solve a couple of those problems.

Installing devices—mouse drivers, network cards, and so on—can cause problems with DOS if your system isn't configured properly or if the drivers aren't compatible with DOS 6. For example, some drivers from earlier versions of DOS aren't compatible with DOS 6. The device may not work, or worse, your computer may stop working.

Here are solutions for two common problems with hardware: installing a new device card and updating your mouse driver.

Mouse Compatibility

When you use DOS Shell, you may see a message that tells you to Check the Mouse Compatibility List. You can choose the option <Use Mouse Anyway>. If your mouse then works in DOS Shell, DOS was able to find a mouse driver it could use for your mouse. This is just a minor inconvenience.

Every time you open DOS Shell, the same compatibility message will appear, which can be annoying after a while. The first step in getting rid of that irritating error message is to check the documentation that came with your mouse. Find the version number for your mouse driver and compare that number to the numbers in the second column of the following list:

Mouse Type	DOS MOUSE.COM Compatible Version
Microsoft	Version 8.20
Logitech	Version 5.01 and later
Genius	Version 9.06 and later
IBM PS/2	Version 8.02
Hewlett-Packard	Version 7.04 and later
Mouse Systems	Version 7.01 and later

If your mouse isn't a compatible version, contact the vendor for an updated version of your mouse driver. If you use a Microsoft mouse or an IBM PS/2 mouse, use the MOUSE.COM file that comes with DOS to update your driver.

To update the driver that comes with DOS 6, open your CONFIG.SYS file and delete the statement that loads MOUSE.SYS as a device; then save the file. Open your AUTOEXEC.BAT file and add **MOUSE.COM** to the file and save the file. Reboot your computer. Your mouse will now work in DOS Shell.

Installing a Hardware Device

When you install a new device card, you may have problems with the EMM386 memory manager. If both the EMM386 and the new card use the same memory address, your computer may lock up when you restart it. Or another problem could result: DOS won't load the EMM386.EXE.

To find out if EMM386 is loaded, type **EMM386** at the system prompt and press Enter. If DOS responds with a status screen ending with EMM386 is active, the memory manager is properly installed; but it may not be configured correctly for the new hardware card. Read the documentation that came with the card and see if there are any special configurations. If you find no special instructions, contact the manufacturer of the device and ask for more information.

If DOS responds with the message EMM386 driver not installed, you may be able to correct the problem by running MemMaker. To get to the point where you can use MemMaker, reboot your computer. When Starting MS-DOS... appears, press F8. As each command in your CONFIG.SYS file appears, press **Y** for each command except the one loading the EMM386; press **N** for that command. Continue confirming the other commands, including the AUTOEXEC.BAT file processing.

Start MemMaker at the system prompt. When the MemMaker Advanced Options screen appears, choose Yes for the prompt Specify which drivers and TSRs to include during optimization? Choose No for Keep current EMM386 exclusions and inclusions? As MemMaker continues the optimization, it prompts you for each device driver and TSR. Press Enter to accept each one. If the EMM386 driver still doesn't work, contact Microsoft technical support.

Check Status of EMM386

```
C:\> emm386

MICROSOFT Expanded Memory Manager 386  Version 4.45
Copyright Microsoft Corporation 1986, 1993

    Available expanded memory . . . . . . . .  1248 KB

    LIM/EMS version . . . . . . . . . . . . .   4.0
    Total expanded memory pages . . . . . . .   108
    Available expanded memory pages . . . . .    78
    Total handles . . . . . . . . . . . . . .    64
    Active handles  . . . . . . . . . . . . .     3
    Page frame segment  . . . . . . . . . . . D000 H

    Total upper memory available  . . . . . .     0 KB
    Largest Upper Memory Block available  . .     0 KB
    Upper memory starting address . . . . . . C000 H

EMM386 Active.

C:\>
```

EMM386 is active

Problems Caused by Viruses

Viruses often cause problems because they damage data and program files. Here are a couple of simple solutions.

You'll encounter few, if any, problems with the MS Anti-Virus program (discussed in the "Viruses" section and in the "Windows" section). You may, however, run into problems with the files that have been infected by viruses. When MS Anti-Virus (new with DOS 6) discovers viruses on your disk, it informs you about the virus and then, if you have instructed it to do so, it removes the virus. Often, however, the virus has already damaged all or part of your files. If you discover problems with programs or data files, you must fix those problems before you can continue with your work.

Here are three common problems—along with some simple solutions—that may occur when viruses infect your files. One problem deals with infected program files; another with Windows system files; and the last problem deals with your computer freezing while it's running MS Anti-Virus.

Infected Program Files

After a program has been infected, it sometimes won't run correctly even after the virus has been removed from the program's files. You could spend hours trying to find which files are damaged or trying to replace some files here and some files there. By far, the simplest, easiest, and quickest solution is to delete all the affected program files and reinstall the program from the original floppy disks or from a non-infected backup.

Windows Doesn't Start

If Windows doesn't start, the system files may be infected. Use MS Anti-Virus for DOS to check the Windows system files. Don't start the program from within Windows; exit Windows and then start MS Anti-Virus for DOS from the system prompt.

If the system files are infected, let MS Anti-Virus remove the virus. If that isn't the problem, refer to your Windows documentation for more information.

Computer Lock Up

If your computer freezes, or locks up, while you're running MS Anti-Virus, part of the directory structure on your disk may be damaged. If you can, quit MS Anti-Virus and reboot your computer. If you can't quit the program, perform a warm boot (Ctrl+Alt+Delete).

After the system boots, run the **CHKDSK /F** command to repair the directory structure; then run MS Anti-Virus again. MS-DOS 6.2 users may prefer to run SCANFIX /A.

Caution: Make sure that you run CHKDSK /F or SCANFIX /A from the true DOS prompt and not from the Windows DOS prompt; it could corrupt your Windows files.

You may experience some problems when you use DoubleSpace to compress the data and program files on your hard disk. Here are some solutions to common problems with DoubleSpace.

DoubleSpace is a disk-compression program offered in MS-DOS 6 and 6.2. It compresses the files on your disk so that you have more disk space to store even more compressed files. Problems can occur if you have incompatible programs on your disk, if you run out of disk space, or if some of your files become corrupted. This article discusses some possible solutions to problems with the DOS DoubleSpace program.

Solving Problems

Any disk-compression program can create problems with your files, programs, and storage space. Here are just a few problems you may encounter when you use DoubleSpace.

Incompatible Disk-Caching Program

Some third-party disk-caching programs may be incompatible with the DoubleSpace program. If you have an incompatible disk-caching program already loaded, DoubleSpace Setup notifies you during installation and stops the installation.

To remedy the problem, check your CONFIG.SYS and AUTOEXEC.BAT files until you find the DEVICE statement that loads the disk-caching program. Then delete that DEVICE statement. You may want to add the SMARTDrive disk-caching program in place of the DEVICE statement. Then run DoubleSpace again. (For information about the SMARTDrive program, see the "Hard Disks" section.)

Compressed Drive Out of Space

If DoubleSpace notifies you that the compressed drive has run out of space, you may be able to easily remedy the situation. You can enlarge the compressed drive, taking space from the uncompressed drive. In addition, you can run the DEFRAG program on your hard disk to optimize and consolidate free space.

You can also change the size of the uncompressed drive to give more room to the compressed drive. See the article "Using DoubleSpace" in the "Hard Disks" section for more information.

You can run DEFRAG to make the most of the space you have. The defragment program consolidates files on your disk, providing more disk space as well as making your disk faster and more efficient. For more information about how DEFRAG works, see the "Hard Disks" section.

It is recommended that when you use DoubleSpace, you run DEFRAG from within the DoubleSpace program (Tools menu, Defragment). That way, DoubleSpace can control how the files are defragmented and where the fragments are stored. You can, however, run the DoubleSpace Defragment program from the command line with the /F switch and accomplish the same thing. To run the defragment program, type the following at the system prompt:

DBLSPACE /DEFRAG /F

The /F switch is for Full Optimization. DEFRAG optimizes your disk by moving the free space to the end of the compressed drive. Be warned, defragmenting a compressed disk can take hours.

Caution: The defragmenting process can take a long time, especially if the disk is nearly full or severely fragmented.

When the Defragment program has finished, run the program again—this time typing **DBLSPACE /DEFRAG**. Running the program a second time consolidates the free space.

Damaged Compressed Volume File

If DoubleSpace displays the message A CVF is damaged, it means DoubleSpace has detected cross-linked files on the compressed drive. *Cross-linked files* are two files or directories that are recorded in the file allocation table as using the same disk space. Cross-linked files can be dangerous because you can lose valuable data and program files if the links aren't fixed.

To correct this problem, change to the compressed drive. At the system prompt, type **DBLSPACE /CHKDSK**. If CHKDSK finds errors, it displays a report telling you which files are cross-linked. Note these file names. MS-DOS 6.2 users should run SCANFIX /C to check DoubleSpace drives for errors.

```
 Drive  Compress  Tools  Help
┌─────────────────── Change Size ───────────────────┐
│                                                     │
│                    Compressed     Uncompressed      │
│                     Drive C         Drive H         │
│                                                     │
│  Current drive size:   32.97 MB     29.84 MB        │
│  Current free space:   12.26 MB     10.15 MB        │
│                                                     │
│  Minimum free space:    2.86 MB      0.54 MB        │
│  Maximum free space:   24.69 MB     14.39 MB        │
│                                                     │
│  New free space:        9.54 MB**  [10.15 ] MB      │
│                                                     │
│  ** based on estimated compression ratio of 2.0 to 1.│
│                                                     │
│     To change the size of drive C, adjust the free space │
│     on drive H.                                     │
│                                                     │
│        ‹  OK  ›   ‹ Cancel ›   ‹ Help ›             │
└─────────────────────────────────────────────────────┘
 DoubleSpace    F1=Help  ALT=Menu Bar  ↓=Next Item  ↑=Previous Item
```

Change the size of the uncompressed drive to give more space to the compressed drive.

Copy the cross-linked files to another directory and then delete the original copies of the files. You may lose some data in the files that were cross-linked.

DoubleSpace Problems 263

MemMaker is a great program for configuring your system's memory automatically; if you have problems with the program, however, read on.

MemMaker changes your configuration files to optimize memory, so most problems dealing with the program stem from your CONFIG.SYS or AUTOEXEC.BAT files. Using the diagnostic process described in the article "DOS Startup Problems" (also found in this "Troubleshooting" section), you may discover the cause of your problems with MemMaker.

Here are two common problems and suggested solutions for dealing with MemMaker. If you receive an error message when you run MemMaker, see Appendix B, "Error Messages," for more information.

Computer Locks Up

If your computer locks up while you're running MemMaker, first try warm booting the computer by pressing Ctrl+Alt+Del. After booting, MemMaker restarts automatically.

At this point, you can choose either to continue MemMaker or to exit the program. If you choose to continue MemMaker, you can specify that the program not be quite so aggressive in its quest for memory. By default, MemMaker uses aggressive settings. The Setup screen does, however, offer an alternative option. Choosing Try again with conservative settings may work better than the more aggressive default settings. If MemMaker runs successfully, follow the instructions on-screen. If your computer locks up again, try using the Custom setup.

 TIP For more information about MemMaker, see the article "Optimize with Mem-Maker" in the "Memory" section.

To use the Custom setup, reboot your computer when it locks up. When the MemMaker screen appears, choose Exit and undo changes and press Enter. Your computer reboots with your old system configuration.

Start MemMaker again. This time, choose the Custom setup instead of the Express setup. Accept any prompts MemMaker suggests until the Advanced Options screen appears. Choose No for Scan the upper memory aggressively? and continue to follow the instructions on your screen. This is a more "aggressive" way to tell MemMaker to take it easy in its quest.

If your computer locks up again, there could be a problem with one of your device drivers, such as the EMM386. See the section "DOS Basics" for more information.

Not Enough Memory
To Continue MemMaker

If you don't have enough free memory to run MemMaker, DOS displays the message `MemMaker cannot continue because there is not enough free conventional memory.` You'll have to free some memory before continuing.

To free some memory by temporarily deactivating the extended and expanded memory managers, press Enter after DOS displays the preceding error message. Your computer will reboot. When the `Starting MS-DOS...` screen appears, press the F8 Key. DOS prompts you to accept or bypass each command in the CONFIG.SYS file as it comes up to be loaded. Press **N** for all commands in the CONFIG.SYS *except* HIMEM.SYS, EMM386.EXE, and SHELL; press **Y** for these three commands. Press **N** for the AUTOEXEC.BAT processing, as well.

When the system prompt appears, type the following and press Enter:

FIND /I "MEMMAKER"
  AUTOEXEC.BAT

Find then displays a line similar to the following:

```
c:\dos\memmaker.exe /session:4494
```

At the system prompt, type this line exactly as it appears on your screen and press Enter. The line displays the path to the MemMaker program and the point at which the program halted. By entering this command, you restart the MemMaker program at that point, but with the additional memory you freed in the previous step. MemMaker will continue its configuration.

If you have other problems with MemMaker, refer to Appendix A, "Error Messages," for more information.

Most of your applications will interact successfully with DOS 6; a few, however, have compatibility problems.

When DOS engineers first created the operating system, they decided they would build each version or upgrade on the most recent release. In other words, instead of developing a brand new operating system with each change and improvement, DOS engineers built on the original DOS. One disadvantage of this process is the memory problem—640K of conventional memory is the limit.

One advantage, however, has been that application programs designed for DOS can usually work with most versions of DOS. Each time DOS releases an upgrade, you don't have to buy all new application programs. What all this means is fewer compatibility problems between your operating system and the programs designed for DOS.

Unfortunately, there are some problems. Luckily, you can either avoid or easily correct most problems. It would be impossible to list all applications and their potential problems with DOS 6, so this article deals with some of the most commonly used programs.

DOS 6 and Applications Programs

You may run into a few problems when running your programs under DOS, and some of the more common difficulties are explained in the following paragraphs. If you are having problems with a program not listed here, consult the documentation that comes with the software. The documentation may give you information about running the program more efficiently with DOS 6. If the application's documentation provides no assistance, try the DOS manual. As a final resort, call technical support for either DOS or your application program.

Fastback Plus

If you use a version of Fastback Plus below 3.0, use the LOADFIX command before running the program. The LOADFIX command loads and executes a program above the first 64K of conventional memory. Fastback Plus can cause the error message Packed file corrupt when loaded in the first 64K, and LOADFIX corrects this problem. Type the following at the system prompt:

LOADFIX FB.EXE

Norton Utilities

If you use a version of Norton Utilities below 7.0 and you have compressed your disk using DoubleSpace, don't use the Clear Space option or the WipeInfo utility. Both are incompatible with DoubleSpace drives and can cause you to lose data.

If you have already used the Clear Space option or the WipeInfo utility in the situation just mentioned, use the DoubleSpace Check Disk command with the /F switch to fix the lost clusters. At the system prompt, type the following:

DBLSPACE CHKDSK /F

MS-DOS 6.2 users can use the ScanDisk command to repair lost clusters. At the system prompt, type the following:

SCANDISK /AUTOFIX

PC Tools

The following PC Tools commands and programs are incompatible with a disk compressed using DoubleSpace:

◆ **DISKFIX /SCAN**. This command can cause lost clusters. Use the DoubleSpace Check Disk /F command (CHKDSK/F) to correct any problems.

◆ **FORMAT**. This command from PC Tools Version 7.1 causes a conflict with the DoubleSpace drive.

◆ **Compress 5.5 and 6.0**. These programs are incompatible with DoubleSpace.

DOS and Windows

Windows, although not an application program, is popular and widely used as a graphical environment for application programs. Windows isn't an operating system; you can't run Windows without DOS or OS/2, for example. However, Windows creates a friendly environment for controlling files and programs, and Windows works well with DOS.

There are a few common problems you may run into when you run Windows with DOS 6. These problems generally have to do with how your system is configured and therefore are easily corrected. Here are some of the problems you may encounter.

more ▶

MemMaker and Windows

MemMaker's purpose is to free conventional memory, even at the cost of extended memory. Windows and Windows-based applications need all the extended memory they can find. Therefore, if you mainly use Windows-based applications rather than DOS-based applications, use the Custom setup when you run MemMaker.

When MemMaker displays the Advanced Options screen, answer No to the question `Optimize upper memory for use with Windows?` This way, when you're not running Windows, more conventional memory is available; when you are running Windows, more extended memory is available.

> **TIP**
> Choose this option if you plan to run DOS-based programs in Windows, so that more conventional memory is available.

For more information about MemMaker and tweaking your configuration files, see the section "Memory."

Windows 3.0 Won't Run in Standard Mode

If you have Windows 3.0 loaded and run it in Standard mode—using either a 286 machine or the Standard mode switch—you may encounter the message `Cannot run Windows in Standard mode`. If you receive this message, check the EMM386 device statement in your CONFIG.SYS file. Windows 3.0 cannot run in Standard mode if the EMM386 DEVICE statement includes either the RAM or the NOEMS switch. Simply remove the switch and try running Windows again.

Corrupted Swap File

Windows creates and uses a permanent swap file as a kind of cache when you're working in Windows. If you have compressed your drive, and the Windows swap file with it, you may receive the message `The permanent swap file is corrupt`.

When you install DoubleSpace—the DOS disk-compression program—it checks for the Windows swap file and places it on the uncompressed drive. But if you install Windows *after* you've installed DoubleSpace, the swap file is installed on the same drive as the rest of the Windows files—the compressed drive. If you receive the message that the file is corrupt, you must move the swap file to the uncompressed drive.

In Windows, when you receive the message `The permanent swap file is corrupt. Do you want to delete this swap file?`, type **Y** for yes and then press Enter. This deletes the file, but now you have to replace it.

Open Control Panel from the Main group window. Double-click the 386 Enhanced icon to display the 386 Enhanced dialog box. Windows must be in 386 Enhanced Mode. Choose the **Virtual Memory** button. A message appears, telling you that the swap file wasn't found and asking if Windows should set the file's length to 0. Choose **Yes**.

The Virtual Memory dialog box appears; choose **Change**. Another Virtual Memory dialog box appears with the suggested Swap file settings. In the **Drive** list box, select the uncompressed drive. In the **Type** list box, select Permanent. Choose OK to close the dialog box and return to the 386 Enhanced dialog box; choose OK again to return to Control Panel.

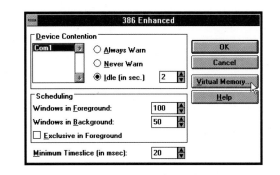

From the Control Panel, choose 386 Enhanced to display the 386 Enhanced dialog box; choose Virtual Memory.

In the Virtual Memory dialog box, choose the uncompressed drive and assign a new size to the drive.

Part Six

VI

Appendix A—Error Messages

DOS displays many messages. Some ask for input, some provide information, and some indicate a problem—whether serious or minor. This appendix presents a list of common error messages, the meaning of each message, and advice on what you should do when you encounter the message. The error messages are sorted in alphabetical order by various categories.

Appendix B—Command Reference

This appendix holds a list of basic DOS commands, with the purpose, syntax, notes, and examples provided for each command. The commands are divided into four groups: Batch commands, Configuration commands, DOS commands, and DOS programs. This appendix is intended to cover only common uses of the DOS commands; for more specific details, consult your DOS manual.

DOS issues messages that notify you of an error, warn you of a problem, or give you general information about the system. Error messages tell you that DOS has a problem with a command. This appendix includes some error messages that you may encounter as you work with DOS; however, it does not include messages that you can easily interpret on your own. For easy reference, messages are divided into categories according to when you are most likely to run into them.

When DOS issues some error messages, it displays choices for you, such as Abort, Retry, Fail? You type **A** for Abort if you want to cancel the request. You type **R** for Retry if you want to try again—for example, if you forgot to insert a disk in a drive before issuing a command that needs to access that disk. Finally, you press **F** for Fail if you want to skip just this one command and then continue with other commands or the program. If you choose Fail, some data may be lost.

Start-Up Errors

Bad or Missing Command Interpreter. DOS cannot find the COMMAND.COM file; you may have inadvertently deleted the file or the SHELL command may not correctly direct DOS to the COMMAND.COM.

Use a system disk and reboot your computer. Access the hard drive and search for COMMAND.COM. If you can't find it, copy the COMMAND.COM from your system

disk to your hard drive. If you do find the COMMAND.COM, review the Shell statement in your CONFIG.SYS to make sure it is correctly phrased.

Bad or missing filename. This message appears during start-up if DOS cannot find a device driver file name. Check your CONFIG.SYS for all DEVICE statements; make sure each statement is typed correctly and that the locations are correct. If everything in your CONFIG.SYS seems fine, the device driver may be bad; contact the vendor who sold you the driver.

Configuration too large for memory. You've assigned too many buffers or files in your CONFIG.SYS. Decrease the number of BUFFERS and FILES commands.

Disk boot failure. If you receive this message during start-up, it means DOS couldn't load into memory. Reboot; if the error appears again, use a system disk to reboot. If the error appears again, you may have a hardware problem; contact your computer dealer.

Error loading operating system. If DOS displays this error and then doesn't start, boot the computer from a floppy system disk. Try the DIR command to see if the hard disk responds. If it does respond, use the SYS command to copy DOS to the hard disk. Also copy the COMMAND.COM file to the hard disk. If it doesn't respond to the DIR command, you may have a hard disk problem; contact your computer dealer.

Non-System disk or disk error. Replace and strike any key when ready. A very common error that occurs when you inadvertently leave a disk in the floppy drive and try to start, or restart, DOS. Remove the disk and press Enter to continue.

Command Errors

Bad command or file name. DOS cannot recognize the command you entered; check your spelling and syntax, and make sure you didn't leave out a necessary parameter.

Cannot CHDIR to path - tree past this point not processed. The CHKDSK command could not go past a certain point in your directory structure. If you receive this message while you are checking your disk with CHKDSK, run the CHKDSK /F command to correct the error.

Cannot format an ASSIGNed or SUBSTed drive. You can't format any drive that the ASSIGN or SUBST commands have been applied to; remove the assigned or substituted designations and try formatting again.

Code page requested (xxx) is not valid for given keyboard code. The keyboard code and the code page code you entered are not compatible; check the documentation for the correct codes and try again.

Copy process ended. If you get this error when you're using DISKCOPY, test the floppy disk with the CHKDSK command. If the floppy disk is OK, complete copying with the XCOPY command.

Compare process ended. When comparing two disks, an irreversible error occurred. Format the floppy disk and try running DISKCOPY again.

File Errors

Access denied indicates that you or a program tried to change or delete a read-only file.

File not found. The file is not on the specified disk or in the specified directory. Check the path and command, then try again.

Program Errors

Cannot find file QBASIC.EXE. If you have deleted the QBASIC.EXE from your disk, you cannot run the DOS Editor. Use the original DOS disks to load QBASIC.EXE.

DOS memory-arena error. This message appears in DOS Editor when you have a serious memory problem. Save your work and reboot your computer.

Memory allocation error. Cannot load COMMAND, system halted. If you receive this error, a program has caused a problem in the area where DOS keeps track of memory. Reboot the computer. If the error message appears again while using the same program, a program file may be damaged. Reinstall the program to alleviate the problem.

Unable to load MS-DOS Shell, Retry? (y/n)? If DOS can't load DOS Shell, the program may be corrupted. First try rebooting your computer and loading DOS Shell again. If you receive the same message, copy DOS Shell from a backup disk and try again.

Configuration or Memory Errors

Internal stack overflow. System halted. Although this error doesn't occur often, it certainly is disconcerting when it does occur. It just means that your programs and DOS have used all temporary memory space. Reboot your computer and all should be well. If you receive this error often, try increasing the number of STACKS in your CONFIG.SYS file. You can adjust the first value to as much as 64 (although that uses a lot of system memory) and the second number to 512 (again using a lot of memory). Experiment with the numbers to find what best works for your system.

Insufficient memory or Not enough memory or Program too big to fit in memory. These errors mean a program or command needs more RAM to run. You can try unloading any memory-resident programs or optimizing your memory. Ultimately, you may have to install more memory in your computer.

Hard Disk Errors

A program was run that took memory that Backup requires. The program must be removed from memory before Backup can continue. A memory-resident (TSR) program is loaded and is taking up too much memory for Backup to run. Unload the TSR.

This appendix lists DOS commands with their purpose, syntax, notes, and examples. The commands are divided into four groups: batch commands, configuration commands, DOS commands, and DOS programs.

Some commands, switches, and special options for commands—such as those used for programming—are not listed here; this appendix is geared towards the more common uses for DOS commands.

For more help on any command, use DOS Fasthelp, which is explained in the article "Getting Help" in the "DOS Basics" section. For information about paths and commands, see the articles "Entering Commands" in the "DOS Basics" section, and "Using Paths" in the "Directories" section.

Batch Commands

Batch commands direct how a batch program runs; use these commands in batch files.

CALL

Use the CALL command in a batch file to tell DOS to carry out the commands in a second batch file and then return to the first.

Syntax
CALL <*drive:path*> <*batchfile*> <*parameters*>

<*drive:path*> is the drive and path to the batch file; use if the current directory does not hold the batch file.

<*batchfile*> is the name of the batch file you want to call; the batch file must use the BAT extension.

<*parameters*> include information such as switches, file names, and replaceable parameters (%1, %2, and so on).

Notes
Do not use the redirection symbols—such as the pipe (|) or the greater than sign (>)—with the CALL command.

Example
Suppose that you're writing a batch program to load some TSRs—memory-resident programs—you use during your work session. After loading several standing TSRs, you want to check the system memory. Include the CALL command with a batch program called MEMCHECK.BAT. After the memory is checked, the first batch file resumes. To add the CALL command, enter the following on a separate line in the batch file:

CALL MEMCHECK

CHOICE (MS-DOS 6 only)

The CHOICE command momentarily stops the batch file and prompts the user to make a choice before the batch file resumes.

Syntax

CHOICE /C:<keys> <text>

/C:<keys> tells DOS which keys are displayed in the prompt. For example, /C:yn means *y* for yes, *n* for no.

<text> is the question or prompt that the user sees on-screen, and must answer. Quotation marks (") can be used to enclose the text, but they do not have to be used unless *<text>* contains a forward slash (/), which is a switch character, or a trailing space.

Notes

The user answers the text prompt by pressing one of the suggested keys; if the user presses a key other than the ones suggested, the computer beeps.

Example

Suppose that you add a command to format a floppy disk in one of your batch files. The disk may not always need to be formatted; therefore, you use the CHOICE command. The line in the batch file looks like this:

CHOICE /C:YN "Format the disk?"

The screen prompt looks like this:

```
Format the disk? [Y,N]
```

ECHO

The ECHO command controls whether DOS displays a command in a batch file as it carries it out.

Syntax

ECHO <on/off> <message>

ECHO without a parameter, displays the current echo status.

<on/off> specifies the feature displays (on) or hides (off) commands as they are processed.

<message> text you can display on-screen.

Notes

The @ (at sign) placed in front of the ECHO command prevents the word "echo" from displaying.

Examples

ECHO.
Adding the period (.) creates a blank line on-screen; useful for adding space between menus, messages, and so on.

@ECHO OFF
Hides the command and turns echo off for the rest of the file, unless you turn echo on for each line.

ECHO Have a nice day!
Displays "Have a nice day!"

FOR

FOR carries out a command once for each member of a set—such as a set of file names.

Syntax

FOR %%<variable> IN (set) DO <command>

FOR...IN...DO all are part of the FOR command.

%%<variable> represents a replaceable variable. Use %%a, or %%b, and so on; you cannot use numbers or redirection characters.

(set) specifies one or more text strings or files, separated by spaces; the parentheses must be used.

<command> is the command to be carried out on each file in the set.

Notes

You can also use FOR at the system prompt; use % (one percentage symbol) as the variable instead of %% (two percentage symbols).

You can use wild-card characters and redirection characters (such as the pipe symbol) with the FOR command.

Example

Suppose that you want to delete all files in the current directory that have a REP, DOS, and 123 extension. In the following command, %%a represents each file ending in REP, DOC, and 123; thus "FOR" every file with a REP, DOC, and 123 extension, delete that file.

more ▶

```
FOR %%a IN (*.rep *.doc *.123) DO
    DEL %%a
```

GOTO

GOTO tells DOS to move to a line in the batch file that contains a label that you specify; DOS then continues the batch file from that line.

Syntax
GOTO *label*

label is a heading or tag that identifies where DOS is to go before continuing to carry out the batch commands. The label can only be eight characters long and must not contain semicolons, equal signs, backslashes, or other separators; the label can contain spaces.

Notes
Specify a label in the GOTO command; you must use that exact label elsewhere in the batch file. The label in the batch file must be preceded with a colon. DOS recognizes any line that begins with a colon as a label and not as a command, so don't place a command on the same line as a label.

GOTO is regularly used in conjunction with the IF command.

Example
Suppose that you've created multiple configuration CONFIG.SYS and AUTOEXEC.BAT files. The CONFIG.SYS contains two configurations, one called REPORT and the other called DOCUMENT. You can specify, in your AUTOEXEC.BAT file, that if the REPORT configuration is used, certain commands should load from the AUTOEXEC.BAT. If the DOCUMENT configuration is loaded, however, other commands should load. This is how you would type the command in your batch file:

```
GOTO %CONFIG%

:REPORT

PATH C:\DATABASE\REPORT

GOTO END

;DOCUMENT

PATH C:\WINDOWS\AMIPRO

GOTO END

:END
```

GOTO %CONFIG% directs DOS to check the CONFIG.SYS file; the two labels in the CONFIG.SYS file are REPORT and DOCUMENT.

:REPORT is a label.

PATH C:\DATABASE\REPORT is the command that is loaded if the REPORT con-figuration was chosen.

GOTO END skips the next section and moves to the label END.

:DOCUMENT is a label.

PATH C:\WINDOWS\AMIPRO is the command that is loaded if the DOCUMENT configuration was chosen.

GOTO END skips to the label END.

:END is the END label.

IF

The IF command tests to see if a specified condition exists. If the condition exists, DOS carries out the command; if the condition does not exist, DOS skips the command.

Syntax
IF *not <condition> <command>*

not tells DOS to carry out the command if the condition does not exist.

<condition> is what the IF command is testing for. The condition can be one of three situations:

ERRORLEVEL *x* checks the outcome of a command by the exit code—or error level. If the number is equal to or greater than the number—*x*—then the statement is true; thus DOS completes the command.

EXIST *<filename>* checks to see if a specific file exists in the current directory; if it exists, DOS carries out the command.

<string1>==*<string2>* tests the first and second strings to see if they are identical; you can use to compare file names, character strings, replaceable parameters, and so on.

<command> is any DOS command.

Notes

ERRORLEVEL	When DOS performs a command, it returns an exit code from 0 to 255, although most exit codes are single digits.
<string1>==*<string2>*	When DOS checks the two text strings, it compares character to character; uppercase and lowercase are not considered the same in this condition.

Example

Suppose that you're creating a batch file to restore your hard disk. You may want to specify an errorlevel of 3, because that is the exit code for the user stopping the restore process. You would type a line in your batch file like this:

IF ERRORLEVEL 3 GOTO END

Naturally, you would need the **end** label in the batch file, as well.

PAUSE

Delays the batch program and displays a message prompting the user to press a key before the batch program can continue.

Syntax
PAUSE

PAUSE used without a parameter displays the message `Press any key to continue...`

Example

Suppose that you're copying files to several different floppy disks and you want to pause the batch program to change disks. You could just add the PAUSE command. You could also add an extra message using the ECHO command with the PAUSE command. That section of the batch file would look like this:

```
@echo off
echo Please remove Disk #1 from drive A and
insert Disk #2.
pause
```

The screen prompt looks like this:

```
Please remove Disk #1 from drive A and
insert Disk #2.
Press any key to continue...
```

REM

REM—or remark—enables you to include comments, headings, and so on in a batch file. DOS ignores any line of text beginning with REM.

Syntax
REM *<remark, comment, heading>*

<remark, comment, heading> represents any text you want DOS to ignore, including commands.

Notes

If you want to display these comments, you must use the command ECHO ON.

You can't use redirection characters, such as the pipe symbol, on the same line as the REM command.

REM can also be used in the CONFIG.SYS file.

Example

Suppose that you want to enter a comment to remind you about the batch file. This is what the comment would look like in your AUTOEXEC.BAT file:

more

```
@echo off
rem This batch file formats 3 1/2-inch ED
4MB disk.
```

SHIFT

SHIFT moves each replaceable parameter in a file one space to the left. Thus, you can use SHIFT to trick DOS into using more than nine replaceable parameters.

Syntax
SHIFT

Notes
SHIFT works by copying each parameter into the previous one. For example, %1 is replaced by %2, %2 is replaced by %3, and so on. After you shift parameters, you cannot shift them back.

Configuration Commands
Configuration commands—used in the CONFIG.SYS file—are used to customize your system. Use configuration commands to optimize memory and disk space, to install device drivers and memory-resident programs, and to initiate commands during DOS start-up.

BREAK
The BREAK command sets to either on or off when DOS looks for the Ctrl+C or Ctrl+Break character to stop a program or activity.

Syntax
BREAK=*on/off*

BREAK by itself displays current break status.

on/off turns on or off extended break-checking.

Notes
The default of the BREAK situation is off, which means DOS checks for the break character only while it reads from the keyboard or writes to the screen or printer. Setting BREAK to *on* extends break-checking to other functions—such as reading and writing to disk.

BREAK on slows your system down.

You can also use the BREAK command at the system prompt.

Example
Say that you want to be able to stop in the middle of saving a file to disk; set the break as follows:

BREAK ON

BUFFERS
The BUFFERS command holds data during read or write operations; BUFFERS enables you to set the number of buffers your system can use.

Syntax (for MS-DOS only)
BUFFERS=*x<,y>*

x is the number of buffers from 1 to 99.

y is a secondary buffer cache from 1 to 8.

Notes
Set buffers for between 20 and 40 for most ordinary use—such as word processing and spreadsheet programs or when you're using a slow computer.

The more buffers you set the less memory you have; however, if you load DOS into the high-memory area, the buffers are also in the high memory area.

The secondary buffer cache can speed your work when you're using a word processing program; specify 8. Do not use a secondary buffer cache if you use SMARTDrive.

Example
To create 40 buffers for use with, for example, a desktop publishing program, enter the following in your CONFIG.SYS:

BUFFERS=40

COUNTRY
The COUNTRY command specifies a specific country code that tells DOS how to input the date, time, currency symbol, and other conventions for that particular country.

Syntax
COUNTRY=<*code*>,<*codepage*>,
 <*countryfilename*>

<*code*> is the three-digit code representing the country.

<*codepage*> is another three-digit code that specifies the code page DOS uses.

<*countryfilename*> is the name of the file that contains information about the country.

Notes
Following are a few of the country codes and code pages available in DOS 6:

Country	Country Code	Code Pages
Belgium	032	850, 437
Canada (French)	002	863, 850
Denmark	045	850, 865
Hungary	036	852, 850
Italy	039	850, 437
Netherlands	031	850, 437
Poland	048	852, 850
Serbia	038	852, 850
United States	001	437, 850

Example
To use the Italian date format, place the following in your CONFIG.SYS file:

COUNTRY=039

DEVICE
The DEVICE command tells DOS to load and use a device driver. A device driver is a file containing instructions that tell DOS how to control a particular device, such as a mouse.

Syntax
DEVICE=<*filename*>

<*filename*> is the name of the device driver file, usually having an SYS or EXE extension.

Notes
Devices may also be programs like those that come with DOS—HIMEM.SYS, SMARTDRV.EXE, DBLSPACE.SYS, ANSI.SYS, and so on.

Example
To load a mouse driver, type the following in your CONFIG.SYS file:

DEVICE=MOUSE.SYS

DEVICEHIGH
DEVICEHIGH does the same job as DEVICE, except DEVICEHIGH loads the device driver into the upper-memory area, thereby freeing conventional memory.

Syntax
DEVICEHIGH=<*filename*>

Notes
To use DEVICEHIGH, a computer must have extended memory. Additionally, HIMEM.SYS and a memory manager that enables UMBs must be loaded—EMM386.EXE for example.

Example
To load SMARTDrive into the upper-memory area, your CONFIG.SYS must also contain HIMEM.SYS and a memory manager such as EMM386.EXE. This part of your CONFIG.SYS looks like this:

```
device=c:\dos\himem.sys
dos=high,umb
device=c:\dos\emm386.exe
devicehigh=smartdrv.sys
```

DOS
The DOS command tells DOS to load itself into the high-memory area and/or manage the upper-memory area.

Syntax
DOS=*high*<,*umb*>

high loads DOS into high memory, thereby freeing conventional memory; the default is *low*, or conventional, memory.

<,*umb*> tells DOS to maintain a link to the upper-memory area, therefore enabling you to load device drivers and TSRs into the upper-memory blocks. The default is *noumb*.

more ▶

Notes

Before you can load the DOS command as either *high* or *umb*, you must first install HIMEM.SYS.

Example

To load part of DOS into high memory and to maintain a link with the upper-memory area, enter the following in your CONFIG.SYS file:

DOS=HIGH,UMB

DRIVPARM

DRIVPARM (drive parameters) refers to the operating characteristics of a disk drive or a tape drive. DOS assumes the standard characteristics for a particular drive, if you do not specify. If you need to change the drive characteristics, refer to the device's documentation and to your DOS Reference Manual.

FCBS

DOS uses FCBs (file control blocks) as one way of keeping track of file usage; the other way is with the FILES command. The FCBS command lets you set the number of file control blocks that can be open at one time. You only use the FCBS command if a program requires it, and most newer programs do not require it. If you have an older program that requires FCBS, refer to your DOS reference manual for more information.

FILES

The FILES command is a common way to have DOS keep track of file usage. The FILES command sets the maximum number of files that can be open at one time.

Syntax

FILES=x

x is the number of files that DOS can access at one time; use a number from 8 to 255.

Notes

Although 8 is the default number of files in the FILES statement; it is not usually enough for standard word processing programs. Set FILES somewhere between 20 and 40; any more than 40 or 50 uses too much memory to be efficient.

Example

If you use Windows 3.1, set your files to at least 30 as follows:

FILES=30

INCLUDE (MS-DOS 6 and 6.2 only)

In multiple configurations, INCLUDE enables you to use configuration blocks a second or third time without entering all the commands again. A configuration block begins with a label, or header, and continues to the next label.

Syntax

INCLUDE=<blockname>

<blockname> is the configuration block name or heading.

Notes

Avoid using the INCLUDE command with MemMaker.

Example

In a multiple configuration, you may create a configuration for working with DOS, one for working with WINDOWS, and one for working with BOTH, as follows:

```
[menu]
menuitem=DOS
menuitem=WINDOWS
menuitem=BOTH
[common]
device=c:\dos\himem.sys
device=c:\dos\emm386.exe
dos=high,umb
files=40
buffers=20
[DOS]
devicehigh=delta.sys
set path=c:\dos;c:\document
[WINDOWS]
set temp=c:\windows\temp
set path=c:\windows;c:\dos
[BOTH]
include=WINDOWS
Include=DOS
[common]
```

INSTALL

The INSTALL command loads a memory-resident program into memory when DOS runs the CONFIG.SYS. The program remains in memory until you turn off your computer. Examples of valid programs you can use with INSTALL are Doskey, Keyb, Nlsfunc, and Fastopen.

Syntax
INSTALL=*\<filename\>\<options\>*

\<filename\> is the name of the program, plus the extension.

\<options\> include any switches or parameters used by the program.

Example
To load the Fastopen program each time you start your computer, enter the following in your CONFIG.SYS file:

INSTALL=C:\DOS\FASTOPEN.EXE

LASTDRIVE
The LASTDRIVE command specifies the last valid drive that DOS recognizes. The default is A through E—or 5 drives—one higher than the last physical drive. You can set the last drive as high as Z.

Syntax
LASTDRIVE=*x*

x is the letter representing the last drive.

Notes
The more drives you set, the more memory you use.

Use LASTDRIVE for RAM disks, logical drives, and when you use the SUBST command.

Example
If you use the SUBST command to assign three subdirectories to the drive letters D, E, and F, enter the following in your CONFIG.SYS:

LASTDRIVE=G

MENUCOLOR (MS-DOS 6 and 6.2 only)
MENUCOLOR lets you specify the colors of a CONFIG.SYS startup menu; use only in a [menu] block in multiple configurations.

Syntax
MENUCOLOR=*\<textcolor\>,\<backcolor\>*

\<textcolor\> specifies the color of the menu text.

\<backcolor\> specifies the color of the screen.

Notes
The default background color is black (0). The following table provides the other color codes:

Color	Code
Black	0
Blue	1
Green	2
Cyan	3
Red	4
Magenta	5
Brown	6
White	7
Gray	8
Bright blue	9
Bright green	10
Bright cyan	11
Bright red	12
Bright magenta	13
Yellow	14
Bright white	15

Example
To specify a startup menu with black letters on a yellow background, enter the following in your CONFIG.SYS:

MENUCOLOR=0,14

MENUDEFAULT (MS-DOS 6 and 6.2 only)
In a multiple configuration, MENUDEFAULT sets a default choice for the CONFIG.SYS startup menu and the amount of time to wait before starting the default. Use this command only in a [menu] block.

Syntax
MENUDEFAULT=*\<block\>,\<timeout\>*

more ▶

Crystal Clear DOS 281

<block> represents the label or heading of the default configuration, which is the configuration DOS will use if you do not choose one in the specified amount of time.

<timeout> sets the amount of time—from 0 to 90 seconds—DOS will wait for a response from you on which configuration to use.

Notes
If you do not specify a menu default, DOS defaults to item 1.

If you do not specify a timeout, DOS waits until you press Enter.

If timeout is 0, DOS immediately loads the default.

Example
To set the menu default as WINDOWS and the timeout as 25 seconds, enter the following in your CONFIG.SYS:

MENUDEFAULT=WINDOWS,25

MENUITEM (MS-DOS 6 and 6.2 only)
In multiple configurations, MENUITEM is the name of an item on the menu and corresponds with a menu block. Use MENUITEM only in the [menu] block in multiple configurations.

Syntax
MENUITEM=<block>,<text>

<block> is the name or heading of the block.

<text> is any text you want to display on the startup menu.

Notes
You can use up to nine MENUITEM commands.

The block, or name, of a menu item can be up to 70 characters long; do not use backslashes, forward slashes, semicolons, commas, brackets, or the equal sign in the block.

Example
To define two items as menu items, enter these lines in your CONFIG.SYS file:

[MENU]

**MENUITEM=WINDOWS, WINDOWS
   APPLICATIONS**

MENUITEM=DOS, DOS APPLICATIONS

NUMLOCK (MS-DOS 6 and 6.2 only)
NUMLOCK turns on or off the Numlock feature on your keyboard; use only in a [menu] or [common] block in multiple configurations.

Syntax
NUMLOCK=*on/off*

on/off turns NumLock on or off.

Example
To tell DOS to turn off NumLock, enter the following in your CONFIG.SYS in a [menu] block:

NUMLOCK=OFF

SHELL
The SHELL command identifies the command processor, COMMAND.COM, as the program that receives and sends your instructions to the appropriate DOS program. In DOS 6, the command processor is the COMMAND.COM; thus you need no SHELL command unless you want to use a different command processor, such as one from a third-party vendor. If you need to change the SHELL command, refer to the program requiring you to change it for instructions.

STACKS
The STACKS command tells DOS how much memory to set aside for temporary use.

Syntax
STACKS=*x,y*

x is the number of stacks—0, or from 8 to 64. The default for 286 processors and higher is 9.

y is the size of each stack in bytes—0, or from 32 to 512. The default for 286 processors or higher is 128.

Notes

Many modern software programs don't require stacks. You can try STACKS=0,0 if you need a little extra memory. If DOS indicates stack errors while you're running a software program, change the stacks to STACKS=9,128 and reboot your computer. The memory you save by changing stacks to 0 is, at best, minimal.

Windows 3.1 recommends 9 stacks of 256 bytes each.

Example

Add the following to your CONFIG.SYS if you use Windows 3.1:

STACKS=9,256

SUBMENU (MS-DOS 6 and 6.2 only)

In multiple configurations, SUBMENU lets you add another level of menus to the startup menu; use only in the [menu] block.

Syntax
SUBMENU=<block>,<text>

<block> is the name of the submenu block.

<text> is any text you want to display.

Notes

Use the same conventions for block and text as you would with the MENUITEM command.

Example

Say that you have two configurations: one for a stand-alone computer and one for a network. You have two networks installed; the submenu displays the two different network choices. You would type the following lines in your CONFIG.SYS file:

[MENU]

MENUITEM=STANDALONE

MENUITEM=NETWORKS

SUBMENU=TWONETS

[TWONETS]

MENUITEM=PEERTOPEER

MENUITEM=DEDICATED

SWITCHES (MS-DOS 6 and 6.2 only)

Use the SWITCHES command to set options in DOS for Startup.

Syntax
SWITCHES=/K /F /N /W

/K tells DOS to treat the enhanced keyboard like a conventional keyboard; use this switch if you have an application that requires a conventional keyboard.

/F tells DOS not to delay two seconds after the Starting MS-DOS message.

/N tells DOS not to recognize the F5 or F8 keys during Startup.

/W tells DOS that the WINA20.386 file, required by Windows 3.0 to run in enhanced mode, is no longer in the root directory.

Notes

F5 and F8 are valuable diagnostic tools if you're having problems with your configuration files; it's best not to use the /N switch unless you have a specific reason for doing so.

Example

To tell DOS to treat your enhanced keyboard as a conventional one, enter the following in your CONFIG.SYS file:

SWITCHES=/K

DOS Commands

The DOS commands are those that you enter at the system prompt. In addition, you can use DOS commands in batch files. If you need more help on any command, use DOS Fasthelp.

APPEND

The APPEND command tricks programs into thinking a data file is in the current directory. APPEND enables you to specify one or more directories for DOS to search. DOS and your programs then consider each searched directory as the current directory when they are searching for files.

more ▶

Syntax
APPEND *<path1>;<path2>;<path3>;...*
 /X

APPEND by itself displays the search path.

<path1>; <path2>; <path3> are paths to the directories you want DOS to search, in the order that you enter them. Include drive, directory, and subdirectories. Paths are separated by semicolons. APPEND tricks the program into thinking that each path is the current directory.

/X tells DOS to search the directories for program files as well as data files.

append ; disconnects the search path.

Notes
APPEND is a program that installs and stays resident until you turn off your computer.

Use the /X switch only when you first use the APPEND command during each session; you cannot use the PATH statement at the same time you use the /X switch. Disable the /X switch by using /X:OFF.

When you save a file that was located with APPEND, a copy of the file saves to the current directory; the original file is left intact. For example, say you are in the DBASE directory and you use the APPEND command to access your files from the MAILING directory. When you save a file, it saves to the DBASE directory leaving the original file intact in the MAILING directory.

Do not use APPEND when you're running Windows or Windows Setup.

Example
To enable the APPEND command to look for executable files and search through two paths, enter the following at the system prompt:

APPEND /X

APPEND C:\DOCUMENT;C:\BUSINESS

To disconnect the appended paths, enter the following:

APPEND;

ASSIGN (through MS-DOS 5.0 only)
ASSIGN directs DOS to look on a drive other than the one a program specifies. For example, if a program searches drive A for files but the disk is in your drive B, you can tell DOS drive B is drive A.

Syntax
ASSIGN *<drive1>=<drive2>* **/STATUS**

ASSIGN by itself returns the drive designations to normal.

<drive1> is the letter representing the original drive.

<drive2> is the letter representing the assigned drive.

/STATUS displays the status of assigned drives.

Notes
Do not use the BACKUP, RESTORE, LABEL, JOIN, SUBSTITUTE, or PRINT commands with an assigned drive.

Alternatively, you can use the SUBSTITUTE command in place of the ASSIGN command.

Example
To assign drive A as B and drive B as A, enter the following at the system prompt:

ASSIGN A=B B=A

ATTRIB
The ATTRIB command sets attributes for files and directories, including read-only, archive, system, and hidden.

Syntax
ATTRIB +R -R +A -A +S -S +H -H *<file>*
 /S

ATTRIB followed by the name of a file or directory displays the attributes assigned to that file or directory.

+R -R   +r assigns the read-only attribute
           -r removes the read-only attribute

+A -A   +a assigns the archive attribute
           -a removes the archive attribute

+S -S   +s assigns the system attribute
           -s removes the system attribute

+H -H   +h assigns the hidden attribute
-h removes the hidden attribute

<file> is the name of the file, plus the extension, that you want to assign the attribute to; alternatively, you can assign a hidden attribute to a directory.

/S applies the ATTRIBUTE command to specified files in a specified directory, and all subdirectories in that directory.

Notes
Wild-card characters are acceptable to the ATTRIBUTE command when assigning attributes to a file. For a directory, however, you must use the specific directory name.

If you do not provide a file name, the attribute is assigned to *.*.

Example
To assign a read-only and hidden attribute to a file, enter the following:

**ATTRIB +R +H
C:\BUSINESS\REPORT01.DOC**

BREAK
BREAK tells DOS when to look for the Ctrl+C or Ctrl+Break key sequence. Normally, DOS checks for a break character only when it reads or writes to devices—such as the display, printer, or keyboard. Using the BREAK on command tells DOS to check for the break character when it's reading or writing to disk, as well.

Syntax
BREAK *on/off*

BREAK displays the current break status.

on tells DOS to check for the Ctrl+C or Ctrl+Break character when it's reading or writing to devices and to disk.

off tells DOS to check for the break character only when it's reading or writing to standard devices.

Notes
You can also include the BREAK command in your CONFIG.SYS.

Example
To turn BREAK on, enter the following:

BREAK ON

CHCP
THE CHCP command tells DOS which code page to use when you want to change the language or character set that DOS uses. The code page is a character set (ASCII characters) that identifies certain languages to DOS; your computer has a built-in hardware code page that is built in to your keyboard, screen, and printer. DOS supplies five additional prepared code pages you can use that contain characters for other languages.

Syntax
CHCP *<codepagenumber>*

CHCP by itself displays the current code page.

<codepagenumber> is a three-digit number that represents the code page for a country.

Notes
You must use the COUNTRY command and load the Nlsfunc program before you can use the CHCP command.

Your printer may not be able to print all characters in the prepared code pages.

The following table lists the code page numbers used in DOS:

Code Page Number	Language
437	English
850	Multilingual (Latin I)
852	Slavic (Latin II)
860	Portuguese
863	Canadian-French
865	Nordic

Example
To change the code page to Canadian, enter the following at the system prompt:

CHCP 863

CD
The CD command changes or displays the current directory.

more ▶

Syntax
CD <*path*>

CD followed by a backslash changes the directory to the root.

CD.. followed by two periods changes the directory to the parent.

<*path*> represents the drive, if not the current drive, and the path to the directory.

Notes
You can move through several directories at a time with the CD command if you separate each directory name with a backslash (\).

You can display the current directory of a drive by entering **CD <*drive*>.**

Example
To change from C:\BUSINESS to C:\REPORT, enter the following at the system prompt:

CD\REPORT

To change from the current directory on the C drive to a subdirectory on the A drive, enter the following:

CD A:\BUDGET\QUARTER

CHKDSK
The CHKDSK command checks the File Allocation Table of the disk and issues a report of the total amount of disk space, available disk space, disk space used by directories and files, and total and available memory. CHKDSK also reports if any allocation units are lost; if you choose, CHKDSK can correct those errors.

Syntax
CHKDSK <*drive*> <*filename*> /F /V

<*drive*> represents the drive to be checked.

<*filename*> specifies a file to be checked for fragmentation; if you do not specify a file name, CHKDSK checks the entire drive.

/F tells CHKDSK to fix any errors or problems it finds.

/V (verbose) displays each file and directory as CHKDSK checks them.

Notes
Do not use CHKDSK /F while you are in Windows.

If you use CHKDSK without the /F switch, it checks for errors but does not fix them>. If you want the errors fixed, you must issue the command again with the /F switch.

If your disk is compressed with the DoubleSpace program, you must check the disk through the DoubleSpace program (Tools, Check Disk). Alternatively, you can enter the command at the prompt like this:

DBLSPACE CHKDSK /F

Example
To check drive C and fix any errors found, enter the following at the system prompt:

CHKDSK /F

To check and fix drive A when the current drive is C, enter the following:

CHKDSK A: /F

CLS
The CLS (Clear Screen) command cleans the screen and displays the system prompt in the upper-left corner.

Syntax
CLS

Notes
CLS is often added to batch files to keep the display clean between executed commands.

Example
To clear the screen, enter the following at the system prompt:

CLS

COMMAND

COMMAND loads another copy of the COMMAND.COM—the command processor—until you type **EXIT**.

Syntax
COMMAND

Notes
When you load a new copy of the command processor, DOS displays the sign-on message and the system prompt, and then waits for a command.

Example
To load another copy of the command processor, enter the following at the system prompt:

COMMAND

To exit the copy of the command processor, enter the following:

EXIT

COMP (through MS-DOS 5.0 only)

COMPARE compares two files or sets of files; if COMPARE finds any differences—up to 10—it displays the differences and locations of each.

Syntax
COMP *<file1>* *<file2>*

<file1> is the file name of the first file to compare, including the drive and path, if necessary.

<file2> is the file name of the second file to compare, including the drive and path.

Notes
Wild-card characters are acceptable.

After 10 mismatches, COMPARE aborts the process.

Example
To compare two files in the current directory, enter the following at the system prompt:

COMP DATA01.TXT DATA02.TXT

To compare two files from different directories but on the same drive, enter the following:

**COMP \BUSINESS\DATA01.TXT
\REPORT\BUDGET01.TXT**

COPY

The COPY command enables you to copy, combine, and print files. You can copy files from one directory to another and from one drive to another. In addition, you can combine two or more files to a destination file. You can even copy a file to a device, such as the printer, thereby printing the file.

Syntax
To copy a file to another directory or disk:

COPY *<file1>* *<file2>* **/V**

<file1> is the file to be copied, including drive and path, if necessary.

<file2> is a new name for the file, including drive and path. If you omit a new name, COPY copies the file using the same name as the original.

/V verifies that the file was correctly copied.

To combine two files:

COPY *<source1>*+*<source2>*+... *<target>*
/V

<source1> is the first file to be combined, including drive and path.

<source2> is the second file to be combined, including drive and path.

+... represents the third, fourth, and so on files to be combined.

<target> represents the name of the combined file, including drive and path.

/V verifies that the files were correctly copied.

To copy a file to a device:

COPY *<file>* *<device>*

<file> is the file or files to copy, including drive and path.

<device> is the device name—CON for display or PRN for printer.

more ▶

Notes

Wild-card characters are allowed. Beginning with MS-DOS 6.2, if the operation will overwrite an existing file, you'll be prompted for confirmation.

Example

To copy the file NEWSLET1.DOC to NEWSLET2.DOC in the same directory, enter the following at the system prompt:

**COPY NEWSLET1.DOC
   NEWSLET2.DOC**

To combine two files into a third file, enter the following:

**COPY FORM08.TXT+FORM10.TXT
   DFORM01.TXT**

To print a file using the Copy command:

COPY REPORT.DOC PRN

CTTY

CTTY specifies the standard input and output device—such as a communications port.

Syntax
CTTY <*device*>

<*device*> is the device—capable of both input and output—that is to be used for the standard input and output.

Notes

The device must be a valid DOS device name, such as CON, AUX, PRN, LPT*x*, or COM*x*.

Example

To assign standard input and output to a serial port, enter the following:

CTTY COM1

DATE

The DATE command displays or changes the system date.

Syntax
DATE <*mm-dd-yy*>

DATE by itself displays the system date and prompts for a new date.

<*mm-dd-yy*> sets the new date: *mm* is for the month (01 through 12); *dd* is for the date (01 through 31); *yy* is for the year (1980 through 1999).

Notes

If you type all four digits for the year, you can move into the next century—2000 up to 2099.

Example

To enter a new system date, type the following at the system prompt and press Enter:

DATE 11-21-93

Now type **DATE** at the system prompt and DOS responds with:

```
Current date is Sun 11-21-93

Enter a new date (mm-dd-yy):
```

Press Enter to accept the new date.

DEL

The DEL command deletes a file or set of files.

Syntax
DEL <*filename*>

Notes

DEL accepts wild-card characters—but be careful. You could delete more than you want to by using wild cards.

Example

This is the one to be careful of: To delete everything in the current directory, type:

DEL *.*

DELTREE (MS-DOS 6 and 6.2 only)

DELTREE (Delete Tree) lets you delete a directory and all of its subdirectories, plus all files in the directory and subdirectories.

Syntax
DELTREE <*path*>

<*path*> is the drive and path to the directory, including the directory name you want to delete.

Notes

You can use wild-card characters, but be careful you don't delete too much.

Example

To delete the BUDGET directory, all of its subdirectories and files, enter the following at the system prompt:

DELTREE C:\BUDGET

DIR

The DIR command lists the files and subdirectories included in a directory. In addition to the file and subdirectory names, DIR lists the disk's volume label and number, each file's size and date stamp, the number of files in the directory, the total bytes listed, and the number of available bytes on disk.

Syntax
**DIR *<filename>* /W /P /A:*<attrib>*
  /O:*<sortorder>***

<filename> is the name of a file or set of files using wild cards.

/W lists the directory in wide format; the file size and date stamp are not listed.

/P pauses the directory listing so you can view one screen at a time; a message is displayed telling you to press a key to continue.

/A:*<attrib>* displays only files with specific attributes where *<attrib>* is the attribute. For example /A:h displays hidden files only.

/O:*<sortorder>* displays files in a specific order using the following options:

s   sorts by size from the smallest to the largest; -*s* sorts from largest to smallest

n   sorts names alphabetically from A to Z; -*n* sorts from Z to A

e   sorts by extension alphabetically from A to Z; -*e* sorts from Z to A

Notes

Additional switches can be found in DOS Fasthelp.

Example

To list the current directory of files and subdirectories in wide format, one screen at a time, enter the following:

DIR /W /P

To list a directory sorted by extension in alphabetical order, enter the following:

DIR /O:E

DISKCOMP

The DISKCOMP (Disk Compare) command compares two floppy disks of the same size and capacity and issues a report of its findings. DISKCOMP can only be used on floppy disks.

Syntax
DISKCOMP *<drive1>* *<drive2>*

<drive1> is the drive—followed by a colon—containing the first disk to be compared.

<drive2> is the drive—followed by a colon—containing the disk to compare to the first.

Notes

Both drive 1 and 2 can be the same drive; DISKCOMP prompts you to insert first one disk and then the other.

Example

To compare the disk in drive A to the disk in drive B, enter the following:

DISKCOMP A: B:

DISKCOPY

DISKCOPY copies a source floppy disk to the target floppy, sector by sector, thus making an exact copy. DISKCOPY can only be used on floppy disks.

Syntax
DISKCOPY *<source>* *<target>* /V

<source> is the drive letter—followed by a colon—containing the disk to be copied.

<target> is the drive letter—followed by a colon—containing the disk to which the first disk will be copied.

more ▶

/V verifies that the data was copied correctly.

Notes
If the source and target are the same drive, DISKCOPY prompts you to insert first one disk and then another.

Example
To create a copy of a disk in drive A on a second disk in drive A, enter the following:

DISKCOPY A: A:

ERASE
Erases a file. See DEL.

Exit
The EXIT command quits the COMMAND.COM loaded by COMMAND. See COMMAND for more information.

FC
The FC command compares two files and displays a report. You can use FC to compare either text files or executable files. If several lines in the file do not match, FC stops the comparison and issues a message saying that the files are too different to continue.

Syntax
FC /A /B /C /L *<filename1>*
   <filename2>

/A abbreviates the report so that only the first and last lines of each group of matched/mismatched lines are displayed.

/B compares files byte by byte; /B must be used with no other parameters except the file names.

/C ignores differences within the file of uppercase and lowercase.

/L compares text files as ASCII text.

<filename1> is one file to be compared; use drive and path, if necessary.

<filename2> is the second file to be compared, including drive and path.

Notes
Additional switches are available; consult DOS help for more information.

Example
To compare two text files byte by byte, enter the following:

**FC /B C:\BUSINESS\SALESREP.TXT
A:\SALESREP.TXT**

To compare every file in the current directory with a file of the same name in drive A, enter the following:

FC *.TXT A:*.TXT

FDISK
FDISK prepares your hard disk for use by an operating system—such as MS-DOS. When you FDISK your hard disk, everything—data and program files—will be lost. Use FDISK only if you want to completely delete everything from your hard disk, reformat the disk, and load an operating system back onto your disk. If you need to FDISK your hard drive, refer to DOS Help for more information.

FIND
FIND searches one or more files for specific text and displays each matching line.

Syntax
FIND /V /C /N /I "*<text>*" *<filename>*

/V searches for lines of text that do *not* contain the text specified.

/C displays the number of lines that match instead of the lines themselves.

/N displays the line number with the line of text.

/I ignores uppercase and lowercase.

"*<text>*" is the text you're searching for and must be in quotation marks.

<filename> the name of the file or files to be searched; can include a path. Separate files with a space.

Notes

You cannot use wild-card characters in the file name.

Example

To find the text "1993" in the files ANNUAL01.DOC, ANNUAL02.DOC, and ANNUAL03.DOC, enter the following:

FIND "1993" ANNUAL01.DOC
ANNUAL02.DOC ANNUAL03.DOC

FORMAT

FORMAT prepares a disk for use by DOS. You can format a hard disk or a floppy disk; formatting a disk causes all information on the disk to be erased.

Syntax

FORMAT *\<drive\>* /4 /F:*\<size\>* /S /Q /U

\<drive\> indicates the letter of the drive containing the disk to be formatted.

/4 formats a 5 1/4-inch, 360K floppy disk in a 1.2M drive.

/F:*\<size\>* specifies the capacity of the disk; valid values are 160, 180, 320, 360, 720, 1.2, 1.44, and 2.88.

/S formats the disk plus adds the system files, making the disk a system disk.

/Q quick formats an already formatted disk.

/U performs an unconditional format that is irreversible with the UNFORMAT command.

Notes

For more information about formatting floppy disks, see the article "Formatting a Floppy Disk" in the section "Floppy Disks."

Example

To format a 3 1/2-inch double-density disk in a high-density drive, enter the following:

FORMAT A: /F:720

HELP

HELP, as a command, gives you quick access to the Help program.

Syntax

HELP *\<command\>*

Notes

After entering the HELP command and the name of the command you need more information about, the DOS Help program starts.

Example

To get help on the FORMAT command, enter the following at the system prompt:

HELP FORMAT

JOIN

JOIN connects one drive to an empty subdirectory on another drive; DOS then treats the joined drive as if it were a directory on the other drive.

Syntax

JOIN *\<drive\>* *\<path\>* /D

\<drive\> is the drive to be joined; once joined, DOS does not recognize the drive letter as valid.

\<path\> is the drive and path of the directory to which *\<drive\>* is to be joined.

/D disconnects the join when used with the normal name for *\<drive\>*.

Notes

The *\<path\>* cannot be the root directory of a drive; and the *\<path\>* must be empty.

If the directory doesn't exist, JOIN creates it.

Do not use JOIN with these commands: ASSIGN, BACKUP, CHKDSK, DISKCOMP, DISKCOPY, FDISK, FORMAT, LABEL, MIRROR, RECOVER, RESTORE, or SYS.

Example

To join drive A to C:\BUSINESS, enter the following:

JOIN A: C:\BUSINESS

more ▶

To disconnect the join, enter the following:

JOIN A: /D

LABEL

The LABEL command enables you to display, create, change, or delete a disk's volume label.

Syntax
LABEL *<drive><label>*

<drive> refers to the drive containing the disk.

<label> is the name you want to assign to the disk.

Notes
Volume labels can be up to 11 characters long, including spaces. You cannot use these characters in a volume label:

* ? & ^ < > \ / ! . , ; : + = [ ] ( )

Do not use LABEL with any drives affected by the JOIN, ASSIGN, or SUBSTITUTE command.

Example
To assign a volume label to a disk in drive A, enter the following:

LABEL A:DOS SYSTEM

LOADFIX

LOADFIX loads and runs a program above the first 64K of conventional memory.

Syntax
LOADFIX *<program> <parameters>*

<program> is the name of the program, plus drive and path.

<parameters> are any options used for the program.

Notes
Use LOADFIX when DOS returns the error message Packed file corrupt, which happens when only a few programs are loaded into the first 64K of conventional memory.

Example
To load a program above the first 64K of memory, enter the following:

LOADFIX DEALT.EXE /T

LOADHIGH

LOADHIGH loads devices and memory-resident programs into the upper-memory area, thus freeing conventional memory.

Syntax
LOADHIGH *<program> <parameters>*

<program> is the name of the program you want to load into upper memory.

<parameters> are any options used with the program.

Notes
To use LOADHIGH, you must have an upper-memory manager such as EMM386.EXE, have HIMEM.SYS loaded, plus have the DOS=UMB statement in your CONFIG.SYS file.

Example
To load a program into upper memory, enter the following:

LOADHIGH DOSKEY

MD

The MD command creates a new directory or subdirectory.

Syntax
MD *<dirname>*

<dirname> is the name of the new directory, plus the drive and path.

Notes
If you do not establish a path, DOS creates the directory in the current directory.

Do not use MD with the ASSIGN, JOIN, or SUBSTITUTE commands.

Example
To create the subdirectory LETTERS in the C:\BUSINESS directory, enter the following:

MD C:\BUSINESS\LETTERS

MEM

The MEM (Memory) command displays the amount of memory used and available—including conventional, expanded, and extended. In addition, MEM displays the programs in memory and how much memory they are using.

Syntax
MEM /C /P

/C classifies the memory by displaying the programs in conventional and upper memory and showing how much memory they use. Also displays total free conventional and upper memory.

/P pauses after the first full screen; press any key to continue.

Notes
Use /C and /P together because the MEM command classified is two screens long.

Example
To display the memory on your computer, classify it, pause after the first screen, and enter the following:

MEM /C /P

MODE

The MODE command configures system devices—including display characteristics, keyboard repeat rate, serial communications parameters, line width and spacing for a parallel printer, and preparation of code pages for language support. Each function

of the command is varied and complex; therefore the MODE command is not included in this command reference. For more information about the MODE command, refer to your DOS reference manual or DOS help.

MORE

MORE displays one screen of output at a time, pauses, and waits for you to press a key to continue the display.

Syntax
<command> ¦MORE

Notes
Use MORE with the pipe redirection symbol.

Example
To display a directory one screen at a time, enter the following:

DIR ¦MORE

MOVE (MS-DOS 6 and 6.2 only)

The MOVE command moves one or more files to a new location or renames a directory.

Syntax
To move files:

MOVE <filename> <target>

<filename> is the name of the file, plus drive and path; wild card characters can be used.

<target> is the drive and directory the file is moved to. If no file name is specified, DOS uses the original name; if you want to change the name of the file, specify the new name after the path.

To rename a directory:

MOVE <olddirname> <newdirname>

<olddirname> is the old directory name.

<newdirname> is the new directory name.

Notes
If a destination directory for the move does not exist, DOS prompts you and then creates the directory.

You can rename the file when you move it.

If you move several files, separate them with commas.

Example
To move a file from one directory to another, enter the following:

MOVE C:\BUSINESS\LETTER01.DOC C:\DOCUMENT

To move a file and rename it:

MOVE C:\BUSINESS\LETTER01.DOC C:\DOCUMENT\NEWLET01.DOC

more ▶

To rename a directory:

MOVE C:\BUSINESS C:\NEWBUS

MSCDX
The MSCDX (MS CD Extension) command gives DOS access to a CD-ROM drive and assigns the drive a letter. If you need more information about this command, refer to the DOS manual and DOS help.

NLSFUNC
The NLSFUNC command activates the CHCP command and supports extended country information. Enter the NLSFUNC command before you enter the CHCP command.

Syntax
NLSFUNC *<filename>*

<filename> is the name of the country-information file; usually COUNTRY.SYS. Include drive and path.

Notes
NLSFUNC is loaded into memory; therefore it remains effective until you restart your computer.

Example
To load NLSFUNC, enter the following:

NLSFUNC C:\DOS\COUNTRY.SYS

PATH
The PATH command specifies the directories DOS is to search through for a command file—EXE, COM, or BAT extension—if the file is not in the current directory.

Syntax
PATH *<path1>;<path2>;...*

PATH by itself displays the current path.

<path1> includes the drive and directory.

... refers to *path3*, *path4*, and so on.

PATH ; clears the current path.

Notes
Separate multiple paths with semicolons.

DOS searches the paths in the order you enter them in the PATH statement.

Example
To tell DOS to search through the root directory, followed by the DOS and BATCH directories, enter the following:

PATH C:\;C:\DOS;C:\BATCH

PRINT
The PRINT command enables the printer to print one or more files while you and the computer do other things.

Syntax
PRINT */d:<device>* */q:maxfiles* */b:bufsiz* */s:timeslice* */u:busytick*

/d:device is the name of the printer; the name must be a valid DOS device, such as LPT1, LPT2, LPT3, COM1, COM2, AUX, or PRN.

/q:maxfiles is the number of files that can be in the print queue—from 4 to 32. The default is 10.

/b:bufsiz is the size of the memory buffer used while files are printing—from 512 to 16,384. The default is 512.

/s:timeslice is the time that PRINT is allowed to control the computer—measured in ticks of the computer's internal timer—from 1 to 255; the default is 8.

/u:busytick is the maximum clock ticks PRINT should wait, if the printer is busy, before giving up its time slice—from 1 to 255; the default is 1.

Notes
In addition to managing the device, the PRINT command can manage the queue with the following switches:

/C   cancels printing of the current file and all files up to the /p parameter

/P   lines up the files in the queue for printing

/T   terminates printing

Example
To print to the LPT3 and specify a buffer size of 1,024, enter the following:

PRINT /D:LPT3 /B:1024

To print all TXT files in the REPORT directory, enter the following:

PRINT C:\REPORT*.TXT

To cancel the print job enter:

PRINT /T

PROMPT

The PROMPT command defines the system prompt. C:\> is the usual prompt, but you can define other characters and even use text for the prompt.

Syntax
PROMPT *<string>*

<string> is the text or prompt code.

Notes
You can use any of the codes in the following table, or your own text, for the prompt:

Prompt Codes	Displayed
$t	Time
$p	Current drive and directory
$n	Current drive
$g	Greater-than sign (>)
$b	Vertical bar (¦)
$_	Starts a new line
$d	Day of week and date
$v	DOS version number
$l	Less-than sign (<)
$q	Equal sign (=)
$$	Dollar sign ($)

Example
To make the prompt C:\>, enter the following:

PROMPT PG

RECOVER
RECOVER salvages damaged files or files from damaged directories.

Syntax
To recover a file:

RECOVER *<filename>*

<filename> is the name of the file, including drive and path.

To recover a damaged directory:

RECOVER *<drive>*

<drive> is the drive containing a damaged directory.

Notes
RECOVER cannot work with the JOIN or SUBSTITUTE command.

If RECOVER can salvage a data file, you'll probably lose some of the data.

Example
To recover a damaged directory on the A drive, enter the following:

RECOVER A:

To recover a damaged file:

RECOVER LETTER.DOC

RD
The RD (Remove Directory) command deletes a directory.

Syntax
RD *<path>*

<path> is the drive and directory.

Notes
The directory must be empty of files and subdirectories; you cannot remove the current directory or the root directory.

Example
To remove the DOCUMENT directory, enter the following:

RD C:\DOCUMENT

REN
The REN (Rename) command changes the name of a file or set of files.

Syntax
REN *<oldname>* *<newname>*

<oldname> is the present file name, including extension.

more ▶

<newname> is the new file name, including extension.

Notes

The renamed file must remain in the same directory; the new name cannot already exist in that directory.

Wild-card characters are acceptable.

You can't rename a directory; use the MOVE command instead.

Example

To change the name of NEWSLET.DOC to NEWS12.DOC, enter the following:

REN NEWSLET.DOC NEWS12.DOC

To change the extensions of a set of files:

REN *.DOC *.OLD

REPLACE

The REPLACE command replaces files on the target disk or adds files to the target.

Syntax

REPLACE *<source>* *<target>* /A /S /U /P /R /W

<source> is the file to be copied, including the drive and path.

<target> is where the source is to be copied—the drive and path but not the file name.

/A adds files from the source that are not on the target; don't use with the /S and /U switches.

/S replaces all files with names that match in all subdirectories on the target; don't use with the /A.

/U replaces only older files on the target drive; don't use with /A.

/P prompts for confirmation before replacing each file.

/R includes read-only files in replacement.

/W prompts you and waits for the source disk to be inserted.

Notes

If you do not specify paths, DOS replaces and adds files in the current directory to the current directory on the target.

Example

To replace the older files on drive A with files from C:\BUSINESS, enter the following:

REPLACE C:\BUSINESS*.* A: /U

SCANDISK (MS-DOS 6.2 only)

SCANDISK diagnoses and repairs both DoubleSpace and uncompressed drives. Unlike CHKDSK, this command can perform an analysis of the disk's surface.

Syntax

SCANDISK *<drive>* /ALL /AUTOFIX /CHECKONLY /CUSTOM /MONO /NOSAVE /NOSUMMARY /SURFACE

<drive> represents the drive to be checked.

/ALL diagnoses and repairs all local drives.

/AUTOFIX diagnoses and repairs errors without prompts. Uses the settings in the SCANDISK.INI file.

/CHECKONLY diagnoses a drive without repairing errors.

/CUSTOM runs SCANDISK using the settings in the SCANDISK.INI file.

/MONO forces a monochrome display.

/NOSAVE frees lost clusters instead of converting them to files. Use with /AUTOFIX.

/NOSUMMARY prevents display of summary screens during operation. Use with /AUTOFIX or /CHECKONLY.

/SURFACE performs a surface scan after other diagnostics.

Notes

Only SCANDISK /CHECKONLY should be used while you are in Windows. If Scandisk indicates the presence of errors, exit Windows and run SCANDISK.

SET

SET changes, shows, or removes an environment variable—the system prompt or temporary directory, for example.

Syntax

To set a variable:

SET <*variable*>=<*element*>

SET by itself displays current variables.

<*variable*> is the environment variable—PROMPT, TEMP, DIRCMD, and so on.

<*element*> is the information assigned to the variable.

To delete a variable:

SET <*variable*>=

Notes

Other contents of the environment are the Comspec—location of the COMMAND.COM and the Path.

Example

To set a prompt that displays: Congratulations! enter the following at the system prompt:

SET PROMPT=CONGRATULATIONS!

SETVER

SETVER can be used either as a device or a command. When SETVER is loaded as a device driver, it loads into memory the DOS version table. The version table contains various applications and drivers and the DOS version they require—for instance, DOS's Edlin program requires version 5 to run. If the program asks DOS what version it is, DOS reports the version number the program wants.

SETVER used as a command, adds, deletes, or displays the entries of the version table.

Syntax

To use SETVER as a device, place the following in your CONFIG.SYS file:

DEVICE=C:\DOS\SETVER.EXE

C:\DOS is the path to the file; alter the path if necessary.

Alternatively, you can use the DEVICEHIGH statement.

To add, delete, or display entries:

SETVER <*filename*> *n.nn* /DELETE /QUIET

setver by itself displays the version table; use the pipe and MORE command to see one screen at a time.

<*filename*> the name and extension of the program or driver that you want to add or delete from the version table.

n.nn the DOS version—such as 3.3 or 5.0.

/DELETE deletes the program or driver in <*filename*>.

/QUIET can be used with /DELETE to prevent messages from being displayed

Notes

Be careful when you use SETVER. You must make sure your data will not be lost or corrupted if you change your DOS version with SETVER; consult the application's documentation or contact the software vendor for more information.

Example

Before you can carry out either of the following examples, SETVER must be loaded as a device in your CONFIG.SYS.

To display the version table, enter:

SETVER

To remove WIN100.BIN from the version table, enter the following:

SETVER WIN100.BIN /DELETE /QUIET

SMARTDRV

When used as a device driver, SMARTDrive is a disk cache. For more information about SMARTDrive as a device driver, see the article "Using SMARTDrive" in the "Hard Disks" section.

more ▶

When used at the system prompt, the SMARTDRV command can clear the cache, change cached drives, and change the type of caching.

Syntax (for MS-DOS 6 and 6.2 only)
SMARTDRV *<drive+/->* *<typecache>*
 /C /R /S

Note: SMARTDRV doesn't operate from the command line in earlier versions of DOS.

<drive> is the drive to be cached; *drive* by itself enables read-caching but disables write-caching.

<+/-> + (plus sign) enables both read- and write-caching; – (minus sign) disables caching.

/C tells SMARTDrive to write the contents of the cache to disk.

/R clears the cache.

/S displays the status of the cache.

/X disables write-caching on all drives (MS-DOS 6.2 only).

Notes
If you don't specify read- or write-caching, the default is read-caching only on a floppy drive and read- and write-caching on a hard drive.

Example
To display SMARTDrive's status, enter:

SMARTDRV /S

To enable read- and write-caching to drive A, enter:

SMARTDRV A+

To write data from the cache before turning off your computer, enter:

SMARTDRV /C

SORT
SORT reads lines from standard input—the keyboard— and sorts the lines alphabetically or numerically. SORT then writes the lines to standard output—the display.

Syntax
SORT /R /+C *<filename>*

/R sorts in reverse order—Z to A for example.

/+C specifies the column number to start sorting; the default is column number 1.

<filename> is the file to sort.

Notes
You can use the redirection characters to send output to the printer or even another file.

Example
To sort a file in alphabetical order and view the results on-screen, enter the following:

SORT <MYDOC.TXT

To sort a file and place the results in a new file, enter the following:

SORT <MYDOC.TXT >SORTDOC.TXT

SUBST
The SUBST command creates a drive name (letter) and assigns it to a subdirectory for some applications that don't recognize path names. For more information about the SUBST command, see the article "Substituting Drives for Paths" in the "Customizing" section.

Syntax
SUBST *<drivename:>* *<path>* **/D**

<drivename:> is the letter that represents the alias drive you are creating; the drive cannot be one that is already in use and cannot be the current drive.

<path> is the path to the subdirectory to be substituted; you must begin the path at the root directory.

/D deletes the substitution.

Notes
The *<drivename>* must be equal to or less than the drive specified in LASTDRIVE in your CONFIG.SYS file.

Do not use these commands with SUBST: ASSIGN, BACKUP, CHKDSK, DEFRAG, DISKCOPY, DISKCOMP, FORMAT, JOIN, LABEL, RESTORE, or SYS.

Example
To substitute the alias *E* for the subdirectory LETTERS, enter the following:

SUBST E:
\BUSINESS\DOCUMENT\LETTERS

SYS
SYS transfers the system files to a floppy disk. Since the system files are hidden and require special storage on the disk, you must transfer them with this command.

Syntax
SYS *<source> <target:>*

<source> is the drive and directory where the system files are stored.

<target:> is the drive the files transfer to.

Notes
The transferred system files include: IO.SYS, MSDOS.SYS, and COMMAND.COM.

Example
To transfer the system files from your hard disk (C:) to a floppy, enter the following:

SYS A:

TIME
Time displays the system time and enables you to change the time.

Syntax
TIME *<hh:mm:ss.xx> a/p*

TIME by itself displays the current time and enables you to enter a new time.

<hh:mm:ss.xx>
hh is the hour (1 to 12) and *mm* is the minute (0 to 60). *hh* and *mm* are separated by a colon.

ss are seconds, separated from the minutes by a colon.

.xx is hundredths of a second and preceded by a decimal point. To set the time, you do not have to include the seconds and hundredths of a second.

a/p represents a.m. or p.m. You must specify *a* or *p* if you specify hours in 1 to 12. If you use military time 1 to 24, you don't have to specify a or p.

Notes
When you want to change the time, just enter the time, for example, 3:30p or 4:45a. Make it easy on yourself and let DOS figure out the seconds.

Example
To view the system time, enter:

TIME

DOS displays the current time and prompts you to enter a new time. To accept the current time, press Enter. To change the current time, enter a new time.

To enter a new time without first viewing the system time, enter the following:

TIME 1:36P

TREE
TREE displays all directories and subdirectories on a disk; and can also display all files.

Syntax
TREE *<drivepath>* /F

TREE by itself displays the tree of the current directory.

<drivepath> specifies a drive and/or a path to view in tree form.

/F displays all files within the specified tree.

Notes
This is an especially handy command to use with the DELTREE command. View your directory structure and decide which subdirectories you can delete; then use DELTREE to delete them all at once.

Example
To view the directory tree of C:\BUSINESS\BUDGET, enter the following:

TREE \BUSINESS\BUDGET

more ▶

Crystal Clear DOS **299**

To view the directory tree of drive A plus all the files in the tree, enter the following:

TREE A: /F

TYPE
Type displays a file's contents on-screen.

Syntax
TYPE <*filename*>

Notes
Use the pipe and the MORE command to view one screen at a time.

The TYPE command displays files in ASCII; therefore some files may appear as garbage or have strange graphic characters. In addition, some files may cause the computer to beep a lot; if this happens, press Ctrl+C to interrupt the command.

Example
To display the contents of MYDOC.TXT one screen at a time, enter the following:

TYPE MYDOC.TXT ¦MORE

UNDELETE
UNDELETE recovers files that were deleted with the DEL command. Files cannot always be recovered. Successful undeletion depends on recent disk activity; if you've saved files, opened and edited files, or added new programs or files to your disk since the deletion, UNDELETE may not be able to recover the deleted files.

Syntax
UNDELETE <*filename*> /ALL /DOS /LIST

UNDELETE by itself begins the undelete process on the current drive and directory.

<*filename*> is the file name you want to undelete, including drive and path. You can use wild-card characters to specify a set of files.

/ALL undeletes all files without prompting.

/DOS undeletes files that DOS lists as deleted; prompts before restoring each file.

/LIST lists deleted files but does not undelete them.

Notes
UNDELETE cannot restore a file if you deleted the subdirectory that contained the file.

Example
To undelete all recoverable files with a DOC extension in the current directory without prompting, enter the following:

UNDELETE *.DOC /ALL

UNFORMAT
UNFORMAT recovers data on a disk that was accidently formatted. UNFORMAT may or may not be able to recover your files successfully.

Syntax
UNFORMAT <*drive:*> /TEST /P

<*drive:*> is the drive letter to be unformatted; if the formatted drive is your hard drive, you must boot from a floppy system disk and use the UNFORMAT command on the floppy.

/TEST examines the state of the drive and the chances of unformatting the disk; /TEST does not unformat the disk.

/P directs Unformat's messages to the printer—LPT1.

Notes
If you formatted a disk with the /U (unconditional) switch, UNFORMAT cannot unformat the disk.

Example
To unformat the disk in drive A, enter the following:

UNFORMAT A:

VER
The VER command displays the version of DOS on-screen.

Syntax
VER

Example
To display the version of your operating system, enter the following at the system prompt:

VER

VERIFY

VERIFY confirms whether the data written to disk was written correctly.

Syntax
VERIFY *on/off*

VERIFY by itself displays the status of VERIFY.

on/off turns VERIFY on or off.

Notes
VERIFY slightly slows the process of storing data.

Example
To turn VERIFY on, enter the following:

VERIFY ON

To view the status of VERIFY, enter the following:

VERIFY

VOL

The VOL command displays a disk's volume number and serial number.

Syntax
VOL *<drive:>*

VOL by itself displays the volume label and serial number of the current drive.

<drive:> displays the volume label and serial number of the specified drive.

Example
To display the volume label and serial number of the hard disk, enter the following:

VOL

XCOPY

XCOPY efficiently copies groups of files. XCOPY can copy all directories and subdirectories that contain files without you specifying each directory. In addition, XCOPY can backup files whose archive attribute is on, or files that have changed since a specific date.

Syntax
XCOPY *<source>* *<target>* **/A /M /E /P /S /V**

<source> is the name of the drive or file to be copied; wild-card characters are acceptable.

<target> is where the files copy to; include drive and path.

/A copies only files whose archive attribute is on, leaving the attribute on.

/M copies only files who archive attribute is on, turning the attribute off.

/E creates subdirectories on the target if they do not exist; must use the /S with this switch.

/P prompts for confirmation before copying each file.

/S copies all specified directories, subdirectories, and files; will not copy empty directories.

/V verifies that the copy was correctly stored.

Notes
Do not use XCOPY with the APPEND command. Beginning with MS-DOS 6.2, if the operation will overwrite an existing file, you'll be prompted for confirmation.

Example
To XCOPY all subdirectories and files in the directory C:\BUSINESS, enter the following command:

XCOPY \BUSINESS A:

To XCOPY all files that have been updated to drive A from C:\BUSINESS and to turn off the archive bit, enter the following command:

XCOPY \BUSINESS A: /M

more ▶

DOS Programs

Following are programs that can be started at the system prompt by entering the program name. For more information about each program, see related articles in this book.

DoubleSpace (MS-DOS 6 and 6.2 only)

DoubleSpace is a disk-compression program. If you type **DBLSPACE** at the system prompt, you invoke the DoubleSpace program. The program contains information about the compressed disk, plus commands for checking the disk, defragmenting the disk, and changing the size of the disk.

You can use the commands in the DoubleSpace program, or you can enter the following commands at the system prompt:

DBLSPACE CHKDSK *<drive>*

DBLSPACE DEFRAGMENT *<drive>*

<drive> is the compressed drive.

For more information about DoubleSpace, see the article "Using DoubleSpace" in the "Hard Disks" section.

Defrag (MS-DOS 6 and 6.2 only)

Defrag is the defragmenting program in DOS that optimizes your disk contents. Defrag consolidates the free space on your disk and rearranges files so each is located in one contiguous portion of the disk. Entering **DEFRAG** at the system prompt starts the program. For more information about Defrag, see the article "Defragmenting Your Hard Disk" in the "Hard Disks" section.

Doskey (MS-DOS 5.0, 6.0, and 6.2 only)

The Doskey program enables you to record and recall recent commands. In addition, Doskey enables you to create macros—or mini-programs—of often used commands. To start the Doskey program, type **DOSKEY** at the system prompt and press Enter. For more information about Doskey, see the article "Using Doskey" in the "Customizing" section.

DOS Shell (MS-DOS 4.0, 5.0, and 6.0 only)

DOS Shell is a graphical environment you can use in place of or in addition to the system prompt. To start DOS Shell, you enter **DOSSHELL** at the system prompt. For more information about DOS Shell, see the section "DOS Shell."

Editor (MS-DOS 5.0, 6.0, and 6.2 only)

The MS-DOS Editor is a text editor that enables you to create, open, and save text files. Use Editor to create and edit batch files, edit configuration files, and even create memos. To start MS-DOS Editor, enter **EDIT** at the system prompt. For more information about Editor, see the section "MS-DOS Editor."

Expand

With the Expand program, you can copy a compressed file from the original DOS floppy disk to your hard drive and uncompress the files so that you can use them. Compressed files have an underscore as the last letter of their extension.

To use Expand, enter the command, the drive, path, and file name of the compressed file (source), and the drive and path of the destination (target), like this:
EXPAND *<source> <target>*

Fasthelp (MS-DOS 6 and 6.2 only)

The Fasthelp program enables you to access command information at the system prompt. To get information on any DOS command, enter the following at the system prompt: *<command>* **/?**. For more information about Fasthelp, see the article "Getting Help" in the "DOS Basics" section.

Fastopen

The Fastopen program stores file locations—directory and subdirectory information—in memory. When you or one of your programs accesses a file, DOS first checks the memory for the location. If the file's location is in the memory, DOS can access it faster than reading the disk for the information. For more about the Fastopen program, see the article "Using Fastopen" in the "Customizing" section.

Graphics

DOS keeps the Graphics program in memory so you can capture a picture of your screen and send it to the printer. At the system prompt, enter **GRAPHICS** and then press Shift+Print Screen. The display contents print if your printer can reproduce the graphic image. You can specify printer model plus many switches with the Graphics program. For more information about the Graphics program, see DOS help.

Help

Help is an on-line system of information about commands. Help displays command syntax, examples, and notes about each command. To get help, enter **HELP**. For more information about Help, see the article "Getting Help" in the "DOS Basics" section.

Keyboard

You can use the Keyboard program to change the keyboard layout to that of another country. For more information about Keyboard, see the article "Changing the Keyboard" in the "Customizing" section.

MemMaker (MS-DOS 6 only)

The MemMaker program optimizes your memory by moving as many device drivers and memory-resident programs to upper memory as possible. For more information about MemMaker, see the article "Optimize with MemMaker" in the "Memory" section.

Msav (MS-DOS 6 and 6.2 only)

Msav is the name of the anti-virus program that comes with DOS. MS Anti-Virus can scan and remove viruses from your disks—hard and floppy. For more information about the anti-virus program, see the section "Viruses."

MS Backup (MS-DOS 6 and 6.2 only)

The MS Backup program enables you to create full, incremental, and differential backups of your hard disk. DOS includes a backup program for DOS and one for Windows. For more information about MS Backup for DOS, see the articles

"Configuring for Backup," "Planning Your Backup," Performing a Full Backup," and "Performing Partial Backups" in the "Hard Disks" section. For more information about MS Backup for Windows, see the article "Backing Up Your Disk" in the "Windows" section.

MSD (MS-DOS 6 and 6.2 only)

The MS Diagnostics program can display technical information about your system: the manufacturer, bus type, video display, mouse, adapters, and so on. You may need this information when you install new hardware. To run the program, type **MSD** at the system prompt and press Enter. For more information about this program, refer to DOS Help.

QBasic (MS-DOS 5.0, 6.0, and 6.2 only)

QBasic is a menu-based program for creating QBasic programs. For more information about QBasic, use the Help menu in QBasic. To start QBasic, enter **QBASIC** at the system prompt.

VSafe (MS-DOS 6 and 6.2 only)

VSafe is a memory-resident program that detects possible virus activity. If VSafe detects activity that indicates a virus, it displays a warning message. For more information about VSafe, see the article "Using VSafe" in the "Viruses" section.

Index

Symbols

@ (at sign) command, 188
@ECHO OFF command, 192-193
3 1/2-inch floppy disks, 119
5 1/4 -inch floppy disks, 119

A

Activate menu bar (F10) shortcut key, 205
All Files command (View menu), 208-209
American Standard Code for Information Interchange, *see* ASCII
ANSI.SYS program, 182-184
Anti-Virus (Microsoft), 244-245, 247-251
APPEND command, 166-167, 235-236, 283-284
Archive attribute, 74-75, 88
ASCII (American Standard Code for Information Interchange) files, 64, 212
ASSIGN command, 236, 284
asterisk (*) wild card, 48
ATTRIB command, 42-43, 284-285
attributes, 42-43
AUTOEXEC.BAT file, 10
    DATE and TIME command, 160
    disabling TSRs, 236
    editing, 152-159
    starting DOS, 256-257

B

backslash (\), 33
Backup
    Compare, 89, 93
    compatibility testing, 80-85
    full backups, 87-91
    partial backups, 89, 92
    Restore, 94-95
backups
    comparing with originals, 89, 93
    configuring for, 80-85
    files
        restoring, 239-241
        selecting choosing, 86
    full, 87-91
    partial, 87-92
    planning, 86
    restoring, 94-95
    Windows, 238
        comparing, 240-241
        types, 239
BAK file name extension, 46
BAS file name extension, 46
BAT file name extension, 46
batch commands, 188-189, 274-278
batch files, 186-187, 191
    menus, 192-195
    parameters, 190
bits, 133
boot viruses, 250
bootable system disks, 76
booting computers, 10-11, 77
branches (Directory Tree), 208-209
BREAK command, 146, 278, 285
BUFFERS command, 147, 278

buttons, 80
Bypass CONFIG.SYS and AUTOEXEC.BAT (F5) shortcut key, 257
bytes, 133

C

CALL command, 188, 274
Cancel (Ctrl+C) shortcut key, 31
Cancel Help (Esc) shortcut key, 207
Cancel menu selection (Esc) shortcut key, 205
canceling
    LABEL command, 101
    processes or dialog boxes, 91
CD command, 14, 32-34, 37-38, 41, 154, 193, 285-286
CD-ROM drives, 111
CHCP command, 285
check boxes, 204
chips, 132
CHKDSK command,106-109, 113, 255, 261, 286
CHKDSK/F command, 235
CHOICE command, 275
CKDSK command, 116
Clear (Del) shortcut key, 231
CLS command, 154, 188
clusters, 106-107
Collapse Branch command (Tree menu), 209
command buttons, 204
COMMAND command, 287
command files, 44

INDEX